Thinking Theory Thoroughly

D0209292

Thinking Theory Thoroughly

Coherent Approaches to an Incoherent World

Second Edition

James N. Rosenau
The George Washington University

Mary Durfee
Michigan Technological University

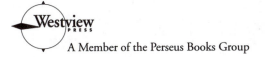
Westview
PRESS
A Member of the Perseus Books Group

All rights reserved. Printed in the United States of America. No part of this publication may be reproduced or transmitted in any form or by any means, electronic or mechanical, including photocopy, recording, or any information storage and retrieval system, without permission in writing from the publisher.

Copyright © 2000 by Westview Press, A Member of the Perseus Books Group

Published in 2000 in the United States of America by Westview Press, 5500 Central Avenue, Boulder, Colorado 80301-2877, and in the United Kingdom by Westview Press, 12 Hid's Copse Road, Cumnor Hill, Oxford OX2 9JJ

Visit us on the World Wide Web at www.westviewpress.com

Library of Congress Cataloging-in-Publication Data
Rosenau, James N.
    Thinking theory thoroughly : coherent approaches to an incoherent world / James N. Rosenau, Mary Durfee.—2nd ed.
        p.   cm.
    Includes bibliographical references and index.
    ISBN 0-8133-6676-3 (pb.)
    1. International relations—Philosophy.   2. World politics—1945-   I. Durfee, Mary.
II. Title.

JZ1242 .R665   1999
327.1'01—dc21   99-051431

The paper used in this publication meets the requirements of the American National Standard for Permanence of Paper for Printed Library Materials Z39.48-1984.

10   9   8   7   6   5   4   3   2

For all those who are willing to
acknowledge and probe the
complexities of world affairs

Contents

Tables and Figures

Preface

Since our concern here is to elaborate on the uses and virtues of abstract theorizing that can be applied at any time, it might be wondered why we have revised the original version. The answer is twofold. First, a limitation of the first edition was that it presented only two theories. At the time a comparison of two major theories seemed sufficient to demonstrate our central reason for writing the book, namely, that how one understands world affairs is crucially dependent on the theoretical lenses through which one interprets the course of events. But several colleagues expressed regret that we had limited our theoretical scope, and so the addition of a third theory, liberalism, seemed worthy of a revised edition. Second, persuaded that in a fast-moving, dynamic world seemingly significant developments quickly become obsolete, we believe it made sense to replace the crisis cases that were included in the original edition to illustrate how situations are subject to varying interpretations if assessed from different theoretical perspectives. Accordingly, Chapter 6 is now composed of new cases based on crises that marked the late 1990s.

Yet, four of the chapters in the first edition are presented here essentially unchanged, thus preserving our initial intent to stress the desirability of thinking theoretically. At the same time, we remain as proud of the origins of the first edition as we were at the time we wrote it. Indeed, the origins are a story worth telling. The idea of writing the book was inspired by undergraduates who were taking an introductory international relations (IR) course taught by Mary Durfee at the University of Dayton in fall 1991. Their insights in coping with the challenges of abstract theorizing about world politics motivated us to refine our thinking about IR theory.

The story began when Durfee offered the students an option of no term paper in exchange for separate weekly meetings and short papers devoted to a systematic, chapter-by-chapter reading of Rosenau's *Turbulence in World Politics: A Theory of Change and Continuity.*

Seven students chose the option and then, week after week, sustained a surprising level of remarkably insightful and broad discussions of world affairs. Put off at first by the abstract formulations early in the book, they soon began to interpret the diverse dimensions of the subject in complex ways and became unusually adept at being playful with the ideas underlying the turbulence model, often advancing their own theories even as they found flaws in Rosenau's formulations. At the last meeting of the group, on December 1, 1991, Rosenau was present and had the exhilarating experience of participating in a sophisticated discussion of the book's complex propositions with seven sophomores who were just completing their first IR course.

Over dinner that evening the two of us firmed up our plans to co-author this book. The day's invigorating discussion reinforced our respective experiences in teaching the turbulence model. It seemed clear to us that, despite its length and new ways of probing the basic parameters of international affairs, *Turbulence in World Politics* made a difference for undergraduates, even for those starting from scratch in the field. At the same time, we agreed that the encounter with the turbulence model would be enriched by an alternative framework against which to compare its premises, that comparing coherent approaches to an incoherent world was the quickest way to deepen one's understanding of the course of events. Accordingly, we decided to develop a volume organized around comparisons of the turbulence model and the theory, realism, that has long dominated the field. The original edition of this book offered an overview of both theories and a chapter that compared them along key dimensions.

In addition, our respective teaching experiences had taught us that theories are more fully grasped when applied to specific issues. Thus we have included three "case" chapters to bring out the differences between the theories and thereby demonstrate how the raw materials of IR take on different meanings when interpreted from different theoretical perspectives. Through it all we have sought to highlight the joys and rewards of theorizing. That, in the end, is the central purpose of the book.

The project seemed straightforward enough at the start: Lay out the main dimensions of the three theories, then use them to interpret some standard IR phenomena, and conclude with a few suggestions as to how one might undertake theorizing on one's own. Wanting to be fair to all three approaches, we pressed each other in the case chapters to revise any wording that appeared to favor one theory over the other. In fact, we sought to develop the theories with enough detachment that the reader would find it difficult to discern our own theoretical preferences. We hope the debates we had over the phone, through letters, in face-to-face meetings, and via e-mail, have had that result.

The collaboration, however, proved more invigorating and certainly less straightforward than we had anticipated. In a test of the original manuscript with a class of beginning IR students at Michigan Technological University, students challenged us to show how the theories explained international crises. In effect, they argued that we had failed to put the theories to a fair trial because not a word on crises appeared in the original draft even though the world seems beset by an endless series of tense and critical situations. So we undertook to add a chapter on the subject and found ourselves continuously challenged by the task of applying such all-encompassing schemes as the realism, liberalism, and turbulence models to the specifics of those abbreviated moments in history when events are overtaken by climactic conflicts. Since most inquiries into crises focus on foreign policy decisional processes, the literature of the field provided little guidance, compelling us to forge the links between crises and systemic theories on our own. Two of Durfee's students, Matthew Hoffmann and Peter Ouillette, were particularly helpful in this regard, and we are indebted to them for their incisive observations. Throughout this effort to extend the scope of the book in the crisis chapter, we tried to live by our advice on how to think theoretically. Whether we did so thoroughly is for the reader to judge.

*   *   *

Parts of Chapter 4 originally appeared in James N. Rosenau, *Turbulence in World Politics: A Theory of Change and Continuity* (Princeton: Princeton University Press, 1990), and James N. Rosenau, *The United Nations in a Turbulent World* (Boulder: Lynne Rienner, 1992), and we are grateful to the Princeton University Press and the International Peace Academy for permission to reprint revised versions of these materials. Chapter 9 is a revision of James N. Rosenau, "Thinking Theory Thoroughly," originally published in K. P. Misra and Richard Smith Beal, eds., *International Relations Theory: Western and Non-*

Western Perspectives (New Delhi: Vikas Publishing House, 1980), pp. 14–28, and again we are grateful to the Vikas Publishing House for permission to reprint this revision.

Many students and colleagues contributed to the evolution of the manuscript. We extend special thanks to the "Rosenau Group" of students at the University of Dayton who provided the impetus for the book: Tory Callaghan, Michelle D. Crone, Rico Falsone, Lizanne Martin, Amy McGough, Dan Okenfuss, and Suzanne Schlak. In the summer of 1994, students at Michigan Tech read the entire first draft of the manuscript and did exercises based on it, thus helping us to identify problems that required further thought and revision. We are happy to acknowledge our gratitude to these students: Natalie Dimitruck, Scot Eichorst, Peter Ouillette, Chris Porter, Diana Richardson, Kashif Siddiqui, Ognjen Similjanic, Mike Stachnik, Douglas Stark, and Karie Toronjo. We also appreciate the comments on early drafts of the Antarctica chapter by students in an introductory IR course at Wittenberg University and by those at Michigan Tech who took Durfee's course in environmental problems, especially Misi Boge.

We are also grateful to several colleagues for their criticisms and suggestions relative to the original edition, especially Christopher Joyner, who commented on the Antarctica chapter; Martha Finnemore, Richard Friman, David Johnson, and Hongying Wang, who read early versions of the realism chapter; Joseph Lepgold, who made suggestions on the first four chapters; and Margaret P. Karns, who read much of the manuscript and was also helpful in preparing this revised edition. Indeed, it was Margaret who brought us together for the 1991 end-of-the-semester meeting with the students and who was a supportive colleague to both of us throughout the subsequent writing of the book. A good friend makes a huge difference and Peg is all of that! In preparing the original edition we were also especially fortunate to have had the assistance of Jennifer Knerr, Brenda Hadenfeldt, Jane Raese, and Eric Wright at Westview Press. A good editor makes a huge difference and Jennifer is all of that! In preparing this revised edition we are grateful to Michael Doyle and Andrew Moravscik for their e-mailed assistance in writing the new chapter on liberalism. The support of Leo Wiegman, our present editor at Westview, is also acknowledged with pleasure.

Needless to say, we owe much to the support of our spouses—to Don, who managed the turbulence a book produces in family life so very well, and to Hongying, who did the same in her own inimitable way.

Valuable as was the help of all those we have named, however, they are not responsible for the final product. For that we alone are answerable.

James N. Rosenau
Mary Durfee

1
The Need for Theory

It is sheer craziness to dare to understand world affairs. There are so many collective actors—states, international organizations, transnational associations, social movements, and subnational groups—and billions of individuals, each with different histories, capabilities, and goals, interacting to create historical patterns that are at all times susceptible to change. Put more simply, world affairs are pervaded with endless details—far more than one can hope to comprehend in their entirety.

And if these myriad details seem overwhelming during relatively stable periods, they seem that much more confounding at those times when dynamism and change become predominant. Such is the case as a new century dawns. In all parts of the world, long-established traditions, institutions, and relationships are undergoing profound and bewildering transformations. Indeed, the pace of change has been so rapid, with the collapse of the Soviet Union, the war of a coalition of thirty-two nations against Iraq, the end of apartheid in South Africa, the Asian financial crisis, and the North Atlantic Treaty Organization's (NATO) bombing of Yugoslavia following so soon after the end of the Cold War—to mention only the most dramatic of the changes that have cascaded across the global landscape—that it becomes reasonable to assert that change is the only constant in world affairs.

And we dare to think we can make sense of this complex, swift-moving world, with its welter of details, intricate relationships, mushrooming conflicts, and moments of cooperation! How nervy! How utterly absurd! What sheer craziness!

But the alternatives to seeking comprehension are too noxious to contemplate, ranging as they do from resorting to simplistic and ide-

ological interpretations to being propelled by forces we can neither
discern nor influence. So dare we must! However far-fetched and arrogant it may seem, we have no choice as concerned persons but to
seek to fathom the meaning and implications of the events and stunning changes that bombard us from every corner of the world.

Happily, there are at least two handy mechanisms available for eas-
ing the task. One involves a sense of humility. If we can remain in awe
of the complexities and changes at work in the world, ever ready to
concede confusion and always reminding ourselves that our conclusions must perforce be tentative, then it should be possible to avoid
excessive simplicity and intellectual paralysis. Second, and much
more important, we can self-consciously rely on the core practices of
theory to assist us in bringing a measure of order out of the seeming
chaos that confronts us. For it is through theorizing that we can hope
to tease meaningful patterns out of the endless details and inordinate
complexities that sustain world politics.

Moving Up the Ladder of Abstraction

Being self-consciously theoretical is not nearly as difficult as it may
seem at first glance. For inevitably we engage in a form of theorizing
whenever we observe world affairs. It is impossible to perceive and
describe all that has occurred (or is occurring), and there is just too
much detail to depict every aspect of any situation, much less numerous overlapping situations. Put more forcefully, asking a student
of world affairs to account for all the dimensions of an event is like
asking geographers to draw a life-sized map of the world. Clearly,
such a map could not be drawn (where would they store it?); thus,
one is compelled to make choices among all the possible details that
could be described, to select some as important and dismiss others as
trivial for the purposes at hand (much as geographers might select
mountains and rivers as salient and treat hills and streams as irrelevant). And it is at the very point when one starts selecting the relevant details that one begins to theorize. For we do not make the se-
lections at random, for no reason, capriciously. Rather, crude and
imprecise as they may be, our observations derive from some notion
of what is significant and what is not—distinctions that amount to a
form of theory, a sorting mechanism that enables us to move on to the
next observation.

To acknowledge that the selection process always accompanies effort to develop understanding is not, however, to ensure a self-consciousness about theory. It is all too tempting to lapse into thinking that the aspects of a situation selected form an objective reality that any observer would perceive. From the perspective of our unrecognized theories, everything can seem so self-evident that we may be inclined to equate our understanding of events with the "truth" about them, a practice that can lead to all kinds of problems once we try to share our understandings with others. Even worse, we may be inclined to see the "facts" of a situation as telling us what the "truth" is. But the facts do not—and never—speak for themselves. To repeat, they only take on meaning as we select some of them as important and dismiss others as trivial.

To avoid or overcome these difficulties, and thereby heighten our theoretical sensitivities, it is useful to conceive of raw observations—the endless details noted above—as located at the lowest rung on a huge ladder of abstraction. One then ascends the ladder each time one clusters details at a given level into a more encompassing pattern. The broader the generalizations one makes, of course, the higher one goes on the ladder, stopping the ascent at that rung where one is satisfied that the kind of understanding one seeks has been achieved. In a like manner, one descends the ladder when one perceives that more detail is needed to clarify the understanding developed at higher rungs.

The notion of understanding arrayed at different levels of abstraction promotes theoretical self-consciousness because it constantly reminds us that we are inescapably involved in a process of selecting some details as important and dismissing others as trivial. Aware that, perforce, we must teeter precariously on a rung of delicately balanced interpretations whenever we move beyond raw facts, we are continuously impelled to treat any observation we make as partly a product of our premises about the way things work in world politics.

Another way of developing a keen sensitivity to the imperatives of theorizing is to evolve a habit of always asking about any phenomenon we observe, "Of what is this an instance?" Though brief, the question is powerful because it forces us to move up the ladder of abstraction in order to identify a more encompassing class of phenomena of which the observed event is an instance. Suppose, for example, one is investigating the former Soviet Union and observes that in 1991 it underwent a coup d'état that failed, and further suppose that one then asks of what is this failure an instance. Immediately one comes upon a number of possible answers at different rungs on the ladder. At the next highest rung the coup attempt may loom as a botched power grab by a small clique of politicians frustrated by their progressive loss of influence. At a higher rung it can be seen as an instance of factional and ideological tension among an elite accustomed to unquestioned leadership. At a still higher rung it might be interpreted as an instance of the kind of political tensions that follow when an economy enters a period of steep decline. Near the top rung the failed coup can readily be viewed as an instance of profound change in a long-stagnant society. At the very top it might be seen as the final stage in a long process of systemic collapse.

In the sense that they are broadly explanatory, each of these interpretations is profoundly theoretical. None of them is more correct than any other—since they offer explanations at different levels of aggregation—but all of them select certain aspects of the failed coup as relevant and impute meaning to them. And, in so doing, they nicely demonstrate how the of-what-is-this-an-instance question impels us to use theory as a means of enlarging our understanding. More than that, the several interpretations of the coup highlight the satisfactions inherent in the theoretical enterprise. For there is little to get excited about at the lowest rungs on the ladder of abstraction. To be sure, the raw facts and historical details are important—one could hardly theorize without them—but it is only as one moves up the ladder that the interesting questions begin to arise and allow one's mind to come alive, to probe and ponder, to delve and discard, to roam and revise. Taken by itself, the failed coup in August 1991 was no more than nine men imprisoning a president and issuing orders; but as an instance of more encompassing processes, it was one of the most dynamic moments of recent history.

The Refinements of Theory

It follows that at least crude forms of theorizing are at work whenever we undertake observation. The facts of history or current events do not speak to us. They do not cry out for attention and impose themselves upon us. Rather, it is we who make the facts speak, accord them salience, give them meaning, and in so doing endlessly engage in the theoretical enterprise. Since this is the case irrespective of whether we are aware of ourselves as theoreticians, it is obviously preferable to move consciously up and down the ladder of abstraction. Indeed, since theorizing is the surest and most expeditious route to understanding, there is much to be said for making a habit out of the of-what-is-this-an-instance question, of training oneself to ask it constantly in order to ensure that one proceeds explicitly from observation to inference to explanation. By being habitual about the question, that is, one assures always seeing larger meanings even as one focuses on particular events. And by being explicit, one can identify where one may have erred if it turns out that an interpretation proves unwarranted in the light of subsequent developments.

Explicitness, in other words, is a crucial refinement of the theoretical enterprise. It is what allows us to test and revise our theories. By being explicit we can not only check our reasoning against further observations but also submit our theories to the scrutiny of those who doubt the soundness of our theorizing. In this way knowledge cumulates and both specific events and broad trends come into focus and pave the way for ever more enriched understanding. Thus is a task that may seem like sheer craziness transformed by the theorist into a challenging and rewarding endeavor.

There are, of course, many other rules and procedures that underlie the theoretical enterprise. Theory is not a means of giving vent to one's intuitions, of randomly asserting whatever pops to mind as a response to the of-what-is-this-an-instance question. A hunch or impression may serve as an initial stimulus to theory building, but no observation acquires a theoretical context until such time as it is integrated into a coherent and more encompassing framework and then subjected to the rigors of systematic analysis. Like any other intellectual enterprise, in other words, theorizing is founded on rules—in this case, rules for transforming raw observations into refined hypotheses and meaningful understandings. In themselves, the rules are neutral; they allow for weak theory as well as powerful theory, for narrow theory that explains a limited set of observations as well as broad theory that purports to account for a wide array of phenomena. Whatever the strength and scope of any theory, however, it is unlikely to advance understanding if it strays far from the core rules that underlie the enterprise.

Toward the Higher Rungs

Although this is not the place to elaborate the rules to which theoreticians adhere, it is useful to note that the higher one moves up the ladder of abstraction, the less one worries about anomalous situations and the more one focuses on patterns that reflect central tendencies. Located at the top of the ladder are comprehensive perspectives that organize our overall understanding of cause and effect. We all have such theories, even if we are not consciously aware of them. Pluralists, for example, understand social life to be moved by a variety of groups with differing agendas that may nevertheless intersect. Any such broad perspective is consistent with several more specific theories; pluralism implies interest-group liberalism or "world society" approaches. Even though such theories require somewhat different testable hypotheses, they are fundamentally related in that they share basic axioms about social and political life.

Consequently, as one approaches the rungs at the top of the ladder, one's theories subsume diverse details and become all-encompassing, ranging across the full gamut of human affairs. At the highest rung, a theory may also be called a paradigm or a model, terms that refer to an integrated set of propositions that account for any development within the purview of the theory.[1] Virtually by definition, therefore, paradigmatic formulations rest on simple propositions that subsume many diverse forms of activity and thus cannot be readily overturned or embarrassed by exceptions to the central tendencies they depict. Put differently, paradigms tend to be closed systems of thought that cannot be broken by the recitation of specific examples that run counter to their premises. A thoroughgoing paradigm closes off the anomalies by resort to deeper explanations that bring the exceptions within the scope of its central tendencies. Marxists, for example, were long able to preserve their paradigm by treating any challenge to their theoretical perspective as conditioned by class consciousness and thus as explicable within the context of their core premises. It follows that the only way one can break free of an entrapping paradigm is by rejecting its core premises and framing new ones that account in a different way for both the central tendencies and the anomalies. Once one develops a new formulation out of the new premises, of course, one acquires a new paradigm that, in turn, is both all-encompassing and all-entrapping.

In short, we inevitably bring to world politics a broad paradigmatic perspective that enables us to infuse meaning into the latest development. And inescapably, too, we are bound to feel quarrelsome with respect to those who rely on different paradigms to explain the same events.

Notwithstanding the combative impulses induced by paradigmatic commitments and the occasional moments of insecurity over being entrapped in a conceptual jail of one's own making, the higher rungs of the ladder serve the valuable purpose of infusing coherence into all that we observe in global politics. The paradigm of our choice may be excessively simple and it may be closed to all challenges, but it does guide us through the complexities of an ever more interdependent world. Our perch high on the ladder of abstraction enables us to identify key questions and develop a perspective on how to answer them. Without a self-conscious paradigmatic commitment, one is destined for endless confusion, for seeing everything as relevant and thus being unable to tease meaning out of the welter of events, situations, trends, and circumstances that make up international affairs at any and every moment in time. Without a readiness to rely on the interlocking premises of a particular paradigm, our efforts at understanding would be, at best, transitory, and at worst they would be arbitrary, filled with gaping holes and glaring contradictions.

To demonstrate the virtues of climbing to the highest rungs on the ladder of abstraction, as well as to show how thoroughly the substance of the field is a product of the broad theories we employ, in the following chapters we present three very different paradigms and then contrast them through a series of case studies. There are, of course, more than three well-developed theories available for use by students of the subject. Rather than attempting to be exhaustive, however, we have chosen to be intensive, to show how a theory founded on the continuity and stability of the anarchic state system (the realism paradigm) yields a very different picture of global politics than one organized around transformations initiated by open markets, individual freedoms, or international cooperation (the liberalism paradigm) or one based on changes generated by an expansion of individual skills and a greater readiness of individuals and groups to challenge authority (the turbulence or postinternational paradigm). In the next three chapters we present, respectively, these three paradigmatic perspectives in broad outline, and in Chapter 5 we compare the points at which they overlap and diverge. Chapters 6, 7, and 8 carry the comparisons into the empirical realm with several very different case studies—one on major crises that mark recent history, a second on the United Nations, and a third on the Antarctic Treaty. The final chapter offers some suggestions for readers who would like to improve their capacities as theorists.

It will be noted that we have identified more than one central dimension of each paradigm. As will be seen in Chapters 2, 3, and 4, in some instances these dimensions are reflective of paradigmatic contradictions, of paradoxes indicative of the fact that all three paradigms are undergoing alteration in response to the growing complexity of world affairs. This is especially the case for the liberal paradigm. Although the "liberal" label once referred almost exclusively to the virtues of open markets and free economic competition, subsequently it also came to be applied to individual freedoms in a domestic context and to international cooperation in a worldwide context. Thus, some liberals—Franklin D. Roosevelt comes to mind—believed that markets were capable of excesses and imbalances that governments should seek to prevent on behalf of individual well-being, even as others— say, the economist Milton Friedman—argued that people would be better off in the long run if governments stayed out of the economy. To cope with this problem, in each of the case studies presented in Chapters 6, 7, and 8 we do not undertake to contrast all the dimensions of each paradigm; rather, we confine the analysis to the most relevant dimension. In applying the liberal paradigm to the Asian financial crisis, for example, we focus mainly on economic liberalism and only at the end suggest how liberals who stress the cooperation-enhancing virtues of international institutions have offered solutions that might prevent recurrence of such crises.

To elaborate these paradigms and their several dimensions, which may on occasion be contradictory, is to raise the important question of whether one can shift back and forth among paradigms or their dimensions depending on the issue one seeks to comprehend. The answer is complex: No, ordinarily one is locked into the paradigm comprising those underlying presumptions with which one is most comfortable; but, yes, one may have to shift out of one's preferred paradigm on those rare occasions when an issue that seems salient lies outside its scope. Such occasions are rare because as already indicated, paradigms are so thoroughly integrated that they tend to define the saliency of issues on the global agenda and to dismiss as unimportant those that fall outside its scope. Yet, some observers have a sufficiently wide-ranging curiosity to be engaged on occasion by an issue that they regard as important even as they acknowledge that their preferred paradigm cannot handle it, with the result that they may either revise and extend their own paradigm or turn to another for guidance. For example, if postinternationalists ascribe salience to the formation of an alliance, they may turn to realist premises about when and why states sign treaties with each other, whereas realists might turn to postinternationalism in the unlikely event they become interested in when and why nongovernmental groups press for greater attention to environmental issues. Why? Because the premises of postinternationalism are short on values pertaining to territorial security, whereas realism tends not to focus on environmental issues.

This is in no way to imply that facts speak for themselves, that what develops in the world arena precedes and points to the paradigm we should employ to interpret developments. To repeat, our preferred paradigm normally serves to define the saliency of what transpires on the global stage. But there may be occasions when an unfamiliar issue provokes our curiosity and leads us to shift paradigms to grasp its meaning, a shift that involves a temporary adoption of another perspective and does not represent the facts speaking for themselves. To be sure, at some extraordinarily high level of abstraction—such as the values we attach to human dignity or the degree to which we ascribe causation to human agency or to economic, social, or political structures—we may apply a common set of values to any situation irrespective of the issues involved. But this commonality is, so to speak, above and beyond the ladder—a few organizing assumptions (rather than an integrated paradigm) that are much too general to sort out the phenomena in world politics we wish to explain. Our choice of paradigms may be informed by the degree of our concern for human dignity, but our understanding of the meaning of our observations will nonetheless derive from the paradigm with which we are most comfortable.

Understandably, some students are resistant to self-consciously employing one or another paradigm, on the grounds that they cannot be readily applied to specific policy problems or situations and thus have no practical value. After all, some would argue, policymakers rely on their experience, even their "gut feelings," about what is at work in a situation, especially as they do not have time to climb the ladder of abstraction in search of theoretical guidance. This line of reasoning is deeply flawed. Policymakers also proceed from abstract premises as to what is important and trivial in situations. They may not be conscious of these premises and they may think their experiences and gut feelings underlie their recommendations and decisions, but such self-perceptions do not negate their unrecognized reliance on broad paradigms through which to view the world. It follows that students need not fear that developing sensitivity to moving up the ladder of abstraction takes them further and further away from the "real" world of international affairs. On the contrary, such sensitivities better enable them to evaluate critically any immediate policy issues with which they may be faced as citizens or as young policymakers seeking to enhance the work of their superiors.

Nor need readers fear that our own paradigmatic commitments underlie the ensuing chapters. On the contrary, it must be emphasized that in both the presentations and the comparisons we have sought to be fair and to avoid loading the analysis in the direction of our own preferences. Paradigms are not superior or inferior to each other, and we do not wish to imply that they are. Their purpose is to clarify and explain phenomena in the context of underlying premises. Hence they are neither right nor wrong; rather, they are either useful or not useful depending on what one wishes to emphasize and accomplish through systematic inquiry. We hope that the ensuing pages will help readers to develop paradigmatic commitments appropriate to their substantive interests and philosophic orientations.

2
The Realist Paradigm

In 1948 Hans Morgenthau published a remarkable book, *Power Among Nations*. His aim was nothing less than to expound a theory of international relations designed to explain past and current events and suggest the likely direction and shape of future relations. He explicitly attached a label—"political realism"—to his theory. Some of the ideas he offered bore a resemblance to earlier writings on world politics and represented continuity with the past; others have been radically changed by newer members of the realism school and served to prompt new theoretical research.[1] The older writers did not share Morgenthau's belief in the value of theory. In contrast, the new writers on realism most certainly do. In this chapter we offer an overview of the major claims that modern realists make about the nature of world politics.

Realism hopes to explain why states behave the way they do. Since states engage in a number of behaviors with considerable regularity, something must underlie that regularity. What, for instance, accounts for war and peace? Why do states survive or fail? These are the questions central to realist theory.

Realism, Neorealism, and Idealism

The realist approach to world politics can be traced back as far as Thucydides, the chronicler of the ancient Peloponnesian War, who wrote, "The strong do what they have the power to do, the weak accept what they have to accept."[2] During this great ancient war, which dragged on for more than a quarter century, Athens and Sparta fought each other on land and sea. They tried to make peace, but their agreements failed to hold. They sought, lost, coerced, and destroyed allies; allies and neutrals made their own calculations of power and chose sides.

Thucydides made it clear that a first-class navy and the wealth of empire gave an edge to Athens. Indeed, it was "the growth of Athenian power and the fear this caused in Sparta" that, in Thucydides' opinion, caused the war.[3] The fact of Athenian power and the fact, known to his readers, that Athens ultimately lost the war creates a terrible tension in his book.[4] Why, if Athens was so powerful, did it lose? The answer, according to Thucydides, was that the city-state overextended itself and fell victim to its own sense of grandeur. Its citizens forgot the necessity for moderation and denigrated the virtues of taking justice as well as advantage into their political calculations. Both raw power, as expressed in ships and money, and the moral character of the warring cities accounted for the final outcome of the war.

The concept of power also underlies the two strands of realism that have evolved in the modern era. The first, which we will call traditional realism, evolved in the 1930s and in the immediate post–World War II period as a reaction, among scholars as well as policymakers, to an excessive reliance on idealism during the interwar period. This form of realism is grounded in a view of human nature. It argues that humans are self-interested, rational, and seek power; qualities that lead to the consistent, regular behavior of states. Traditional realism holds that we live in "a world of opposing interests and of conflict among them, moral principles can never be fully realized, but must at best be approximated through the ever temporary balancing of interest and the very precarious settlement of disputes."[5] What matters in the realm of politics, in short, is interest defined in terms of power.

In contrast, the idealism that produced the realist reaction assumed that humans are reasonable, good, and moral. Idealism, wrote Hans Morgenthau, "assumes the essential goodness and infinite malleability of human nature, and blames the failure of the social order to measure up to the rational standards on lack of knowledge and understanding, obsolescent social institutions, or the depravity of certain isolated individuals or groups. It trusts in education, reform, and the sporadic use of force to remedy these defects."[6]

When idealists of the 1920s and 1930s sought to bring an end to war in the conduct of international relations, they relied on law and morality. This reliance, according to realist writers like E. H. Carr[7] and Morgenthau, led to an inadequate response to the aggressions of Germany, Italy, Japan, and the Soviet Union. Had the leaders of Britain, France, and the United States paid more attention to power and not imagined that good will and accommodation would be adopted by all, then actions to counter the aggressions of the 1930s might have prevented the outbreak of World War II.

The second strand of realism, neorealism (also called structural realism), emphasizes the structure of the international system rather than human nature to account for the behavior of states.[8] What individuals might prefer does not particularly matter, because individuals themselves do not matter a great deal in explaining the behavior of states. It is the lack of central authority in the international system that causes states to behave the way they do.[9] The structure of the international system forces states to attend not just to their own interests but to any changes in the power of other states. Thus, according to one theorist, "The fundamental goal of states in any relationship is to prevent others from achieving advances in their relative capabilities."[10]

The Main Assumptions of Realist Theory

Both schools of modern realist thought would agree that the use of war and diplomacy by states is as important to the international system today as they were to the Greek city-state world 2,500 years ago. For realists of any stripe, the nature of interstate politics has not changed significantly over the millennia, nor is it likely to do so any time soon. Then, as now, the search for power motivated state behavior. Compared to neorealism, however, traditional realism more readily admits the possibility of restraint, choice, and even some moral foundations, such as prudence, as sources of state behavior. We can catch a glimpse of this difference by considering how traditional and neorealists would explain the Peloponnesian War. Neorealists would focus on "the rise of Athenian power" in a system where no authority was greater than that of the city-states themselves. Sparta had to respond to the growth in Athenian power because no matter how powerful Sparta was in absolute terms, Athens was gaining (or growing) in power relative to Sparta and the other cities. For neorealism, conflict is the natural condition for members of the international community (or for members of the Greek city-state system). In contrast, although traditional realists would not ignore the search for power in their evaluation of the causes of the war, they would also focus on the quality of diplomacy and the rational incentives for cooperation that prudential calculations of interest might suggest.

Thucydides offers a complex realism, as Michael Doyle explains. Thus the structure of the system intersects with the nature of individual states and with human nature. The choices individuals can make are strongly constrained by larger forces, but structure is not enough to account for the decisions actually made. Structures, for Thucydides, "are *too narrow* and *too shallow.*"[11] The choices facing decisionmakers are often in conflict, and any explanation of the Peloponnesian War had to take into account all the different forces pulling on the leaders and peoples of the city-states caught up into the conflict. The only unavoidable feature was that the polities could not escape the state of war. Within that constraint, however, different mixes of "fear, self-interest and prestige" produce different choices.[12]

Neither school of modern realism concerns itself with the internal structures, histories, and cultures of states. It does not matter whether a state is organized along authoritarian, nonmarket or democratic, capitalist lines. Given the same external stimuli, all states will behave in a similar manner. Faced with attack, they will defend themselves. If one state seems to be growing in power, the other states will either match that growth or find allies. If some states agree to regulate a problem by law, then other states may seize the opportunity of—temporarily—solving the problem by also signing the agreement.

Realism assumes that states are unitary actors, that is, that a state does not speak to the rest of the world through multiple voices. If a conflict arises between a state's foreign and defense departments, realists say it will be resolved authoritatively: Only one policy will be directed toward the world.[13] Since realists assume that states are able to rely on a single position in their foreign policy, they need not take domestic politics into account when explaining a state's international behavior.

Both realist schools conceive of states as rational. For traditional realism, a wide range of behaviors are available to states that are rationally consistent with their perceived interests. "Rationality," says George Tsebelis, "is nothing more than an optimal correspondence between ends and means."[14] For neorealists, however, choices are strongly constrained by the international system, which has no cen-

tralized authority presiding over states.[15] Rational decision derives
from calculations in which states link means and ends in a logical
fashion. Presumably, states do not act in any way that might injure
their own self-interests. Rationality also means that state preferences
are consistent, not just purposeful.[16] Given a number of ends and
means, the rational-actor state will order them from the least to the
most optimal. In sum, the premises of modern realism posit that
states "behave in ways that are, by and large, rational, and therefore
comprehensible to outsiders in rational terms."[17]

States must meet a number of requirements to make their claim to
rationality. "To say that governments act rationally . . . means that
they have consistent, ordered preferences, and that they calculate the
costs and benefits of all alternative policies in order to maximize their
utility in light both of those preferences and of their perceptions of the
nature of reality."[18] This observation suggests that states do not hold
contradictory beliefs at a particular point in time because then any
option might be viewed as logically acceptable. If a state believed that
peace and war were equally important goals, it could choose either
course and be consistent with its preferences. That approach would
not be rational, and other states would have considerable difficulty
coping with a state that behaved in this way. The reader may wonder
whether states *are* rational in the way described. Although it would
not be correct to say that, in actual practice, states always act in per-
fectly rational ways, it would be generally correct to say that states
presume that other states act to maximize their preferences.

Similarly, states tend to assume that the preferences of other states
are always transitive. Realist theory claims that security is more important than economics and economics is more important than, say,
human rights. According to realist theory, then, states faced with a
choice between their security interests and their human rights concerns will choose security. Likewise, they will choose economics over
human rights, but security over economic goals.[19] In trying to maximize their preferences, states will take the value of what they expect
to get from some action and multiply it by the likelihood they can actually get it (producing what is known as an "expected utility"). A
state might highly value getting industrialized tomorrow, but this
value will be sharply reduced for the state because there is little reason to expect that it can get rich so quickly. Of course, sometimes

states misjudge the probability of a desired outcome and take actions that seem "crazy." Nevertheless, both realists and policymakers presume that states behave rationally most of the time.

For scholars who adhere to this perspective, the assumption of rationality makes theoretical analysis possible. When realist scholars want to understand some action, they engage in what is called "rational reconstruction."[20] This process entails imagining that one is a rational decisionmaker for a state and then explaining international behavior from that perspective. The decisionmaker or political analyst tries to imagine the goals and means of achieving those goals that other states have. This may help the individual engaged in rational reconstruction to understand the other side and to respond appropriately.

The Modern International System

Most theorists regard 1648 as the date when the modern international system was founded. That year, the states of Europe signed the Treaty of Westphalia, which ended the Thirty Years War over the religion to be practiced in different territories. Until this treaty it was not clear whether leaders "owned" their territories and the people in them or whether other authorities, like the Catholic Church, claimed some rights over citizens. The Thirty Years War ended the dispute: The religion of the ruler would be the religion of the region. Westphalia, in effect, clarified questions of property and authority.

Thus it is that the modern international system is based on the building blocks of sovereign states. There are many theories about the nature of sovereignty.[21] For realists, though, only a few main ideas need be stressed. First, states occupy a given bit of territory and control what happens inside that territory. Second, no "superstate" or "world government" can tell that state what to do. Sovereignty entails "the lack of any links which place the state concerned in a subordinate constitutional position in relation to another state. . . . Sovereignty may be seen as a moat, cutting the state off from constitutional subordination to other states and thus expressing the fact of its own constitutional independence."[22] Sovereignty does not mean that states have some kind of impenetrable barrier. States open their borders in more ways than one, often leaving the "drawbridge" down to others; thus, the moat metaphor is apt.

The Westphalian system put states at the center of the world stage, unconstrained by any higher political authority. If all states are masters of their own fates, if no government exists above them, then the system lacks hierarchy. The absence of a higher authority is termed anarchy. Anarchy in this sense, it should be emphasized, does not mean chaos.[23] Rather, anarchy means that states have to protect and look out for themselves—that they must rely on themselves to insure order and obtain needed resources. Self-help is the basis for enforcing rules and protecting interests. Thus, according to neorealists, all states tend to perform the same functions for their people and in the international system (which is why there is no need to inquire into their domestic politics). Most notably, they seek to enhance their security from military threat. Without security they cannot maintain sovereignty.

Since security is the highest goal of states and since the anarchic nature of the international system prevents enforcement of contracts, self-help may lead to unfortunate—but quite comprehensible—behaviors on the part of states. Conspicuous among these unfortunate, but understandable, behaviors is the constant preparation for war. As realists see it, all states face what is called the security dilemma: An effort by one state to increase its security decreases the security of other states. The other states respond by building arms of their own. The initiating state may feel even more insecure and build more arms, and therein lies a major source of arms races and possibly wars. The dilemma is that increasing one's own security decreases everyone else's; yet not working to improve one's security may prove disastrous.[24] The only way it can be resolved is for states to find ways, through law and diplomacy, to keep an eye on each other. Arms control agreements are one approach. Each state, however, will want to be sure that all the parties to an arms agreement are actually doing what they agreed to do to. Failure to comply or outright efforts to cheat could decrease the security of others while, at least in the short term, increasing that of the noncomplying state. Thus, states seek to verify that obligations are being met.[25] If all parties carefully comply with the agreement, the dilemma itself (should I trust that I'm secure) can at least temporarily be eased. For neorealists, such situations of assurance are few and far between and do not last very long.

For traditional realists, sovereignty also encourages states to keep each other in business. That is, states much prefer keeping their international system in operation over contributing to its demise. Thus, although states resort to war if that is the only means through which they can maintain their sovereignty, ordinarily they opt for the less risky paths of diplomacy, negotiation, and such tactics as economic sanctions when dealing with other states.

For some analysts, the recognition of mutual as well as conflicting interests means that the system of states is actually a society: an anarchical society.[26] According to this line of reasoning, the anarchical society attempts to achieve four goals. The goals reflect the transitivity requirement of rationality. That is, the first goal is the most important, followed by the second, and so on.

According to Hedley Bull, "First there is the goal of the preservation of the system and society of states itself."[27] Any challenges to the healthy existence of states will be met decisively by the states. One power will not be allowed to dominate, and entities that are not states will be consigned roles secondary to those of states. This means that when nonstate entities (such as multinational corporations or the U.N.) attempt to act independently, they will be stopped or regulated by states. In effect, this was the very point of the Treaty of Westphalia—religion, an alternative form of authority—was made subordinate to the political authority of the territorial state.

"Second," according to Bull, "there is the goal of maintaining the independence or external sovereignty of individual states."[28] Although the first goal takes precedence and may result in some small states being destroyed or occupied by great powers (e.g., Tibet), most of the rules of international law and the informal behaviors of states aim at preserving the independence of states.[29] This rule explains why states accept and obey international law: To get one's own independence recognized, one must extend the same courtesy to everyone else. Neorealists would tend to downplay this point, but it has a prominent place in traditional realism.

"Third, there is the goal of peace."[30] Most nations are at peace with most other nations most of the time. War is not the day-to-day experience of states, although it lurks constantly in the background. If threats to the first two goals arise, states may indeed prefer war to peace. For the most part, however, states go about their daily business in a peaceful fashion and have developed a large array of methods for the peaceful settlement of disputes.

"Fourth are . . . the common goals of all social life: limitations of violence resulting in death or bodily harm, the keeping of promises, and the stabilization of possession by rules of property."[31] Evidence that states value this goal can be found across a wide range of issues. For example, there are rules aimed at protecting the lives of soldiers and civilians during war; the most recent Law of the Sea treaty outlines how states can claim mining and fishing areas in an effort to stabilize property rights; the international agreement to protect the ozone layer by banning chlorofluorocarbons has provisions aimed at ensuring the performance of promises made; and the World Trade Organization was recently created to cope with emerging problems of global commerce.

Interests and Power

Since realism posits all politics as deriving from interests defined in terms of power, it is important to take note of the power concept as it is understood by realists.[32] Although all sovereign states are legal equals, not all states are equal in terms of either absolute or relative capabilities. Thus, the United States and the former Soviet Union were called superpowers, just as in an earlier age Britain, France, Russia, and Prussia were called great powers.[33]

Neorealist Kenneth Waltz and traditional realist Hans Morgenthau agree that a great power must excel in virtually all elements of physical power. A state's power status depends on how it scores on *all* of the following items: size of population and territory, resource endowment, economic capability, military strength, political stability, and competence in diplomacy.[34] Table 2.1 suggests the kinds of analyses to which this conception of international status leads.

Large land territory provides protection from attack. The Soviets traded space for time in World War II as they built up power to defeat the Nazi invaders. Without modern roads and railways, however, even a state occupying a large territory will find it difficult to go to war or to trade with others and gain wealth. Coastlines make one vulnerable to other sea powers but also provide ready access to the rest of the world during both peace and war. Britain, the United States, and Japan are all sea powers (the United States is unusual in that it is also a land power). The Soviet Union could be a sea power, but its location makes good, year-round ports difficult to maintain.[35]

Population fills armies and industries. Canada has the virtue of large space but has few people. Japan has many people but not much

TABLE 2.1 Power Comparisons

	U.S.	Japan	Canada	Mexico	Iraq
GNP/GDP US$ (a) 1997 constant 1995$	7200 bn.	5100 bn.	542 bn.	237 bn.	18.2 bn. (b)
Population (a), (d)	21.7 mil.	274.9 mil.	125.9 mil.	30.6 mil.	102 mil.
Territory (c)	9,373 km^2	378 km^2	9,976 km^2	1,958 km^2	435 km^2
Defense Budget (a) (current $, 1995)	277.8 bn.	50.2 bn.	9 bn.	2.3 bn.	2.7 bn.?
Defense as % GNP (a)	3.8	1.0	1.7	1.0	15(?)
Active Military	1.62 mil.	240,000	70,000	175,000	382,500
Military per 1,000 pop. (a)	6.2	1.9	2.5	1.9	52.2
Literacy (d)	97%	99%	99%	89%	58%
Per capita energy consumption, mil. Btu, 1996	352	170	407	58	58

	UK	Germany	China	Russia	India
GNP/GDP	1,100 bn.	2,100 bn.	2,750 bn.	676 bn.	326 bn.
Population	59.2 mil.	82 mil.	1,200 mil.	145.9 mil.	1,000 mil.
Territory	244 km^2	357 km^2	9,597 km^2	17,075 km^2	8,512 km^2
Defense Budget	33.4 bn.	41.1 bn.	63.5 bn. (?)	76.8 bn.	7.8 bn.
Defense as % GNP	3.0	1.9	2.3 (?)	11.4	2.4
Active Military	233,000	352,000	2.93 mil.	1.4 mil.	1.2 mil.
Military per 1,000 pop.	4.0	4.2	2.4	9.4	1.4
Literacy	99%	99%	80%	99%	50%
Per capita energy consumption, mil. Btu, 1996	171	176	30	176	12

Sources: a) US Statistical Abstract 1998; b) Anthony H. Cordesman, Military Balance in the Middle East Vol. IV, The Gulf. Center for Strategic and International Studies (Washington, DC, 1998); c) Oxford Atlas of the World (Oxford, 1992); d) CIA, World Fact Book, 1998 Online edition.

land. Mexico is in between. Other factors, such as literacy, also play a role in determining the population's contribution to a nation's strength. Mexico, for example, is closer in literacy rates to Iraq than it is to the industrial societies, but both Iraq and Mexico are fast closing in on the near-universal literacy of industrial countries.

Natural resources provide a measure of independence from economic control by others. They provide raw materials for economic development and for the engines of war. Japan's overall economic performance takes on a remarkable appearance seen in the light of its virtual lack of mineral and gas resources.

Iraq at one point had a military manpower strength that would have put it in the top ten of the world. At first glance this seems like an impressive achievement, but it was won only by putting nearly 25 percent of all military-aged men in service and requiring enormous expenditures of hard-earned money in an economy of modest size. Even after the Gulf War, Iraq's military manpower levels are higher than Japan, Canada, or Mexico, despite its small population. Iraq spends a greater percentage of its gross national product (GNP) on the military than any of the other states in Table 2.1. Indeed, it spends far more as a percentage of its economy than either India or China. In contrast, the United States has the third largest military in the world (after China and Russia), but only a small proportion of its population serves in the armed forces. Moreover, its economy is by far the largest in the world.

When the war between the U.S.-led coalition and Iraq broke out, even critics of the United States were amazed at how quickly the United States delivered a large number of fully equipped forces to the scene. Without drawing down the numbers of units and ships stationed elsewhere, the United States put 230,000 troops in Saudi Arabia in a matter of three months; the number was ultimately increased to half a million. No other nation in the world could have done this. Thus, with respect to military power, the United States appears preeminent; certainly the challenger state of Iraq could not hope to match the overall capacity and ability of the United States to project force abroad.

In terms of sheer economic size, too, no other state rivals the United States. Consider gross national product (GNP). Japan's is about two-thirds the size of that of the United States, and that proportion precedes Asia's 1997 financial crisis. Mexico looks like a great economic power compared to Iraq; it has more in common economically with medium-sized powers like Canada than with weaker developing nations like Iraq.

The consumption per capita of energy as measured in millions of British thermal units (Btus) offers another way to consider power. Industrialized countries use more energy than less industrialized ones. Thus, Btus indirectly tell us something about the industrial capacity of a country; it may even suggest the capacity of the high energy user to extract resources from places all around the globe. Very low numbers may mean uneven economic development in which a few industrial centers take the bulk of the nation's energy and rural areas with low energy use dominate the national scene. The downside to such numbers is that they also represent environmental destruction. Moreover, the significantly lower Btu level for Japan relative to the United States may signify higher energy efficiency and thus more economically rational use of resources, a point borne out if one looks at energy use by industrial sectors.

In terms of absolute capability, the United States is by far the strongest nation. Indeed, with the collapse of the Soviet Union it may well be the only great power. Still, many assert that the United States is in decline. What accounts for this concern with U.S. power? The answer lies in the concept of relative power. Waltz, a neorealist, says states care about *relative* position.[36] This is where doubts about U.S. power arise. The United States is weaker relative to other states than it was in 1947. In 1947 the United States accounted for 50 percent of all world manufacturing and had 70 percent of all the gold in the world. It had atomic weapons (and the USSR did not). It was virtually unscathed by the recently fought (and won) World War II. Yes, compared to 1947 the relative position of the United States has declined. Even so, according to historian Paul Kennedy, the United States has the relative strength today that Britain had at the height of its power in the 1870s.[37]

Susan Strange also maintains that the United States remains very powerful. Not only is it extremely capable in military affairs, but it still has important clout in other areas. First, virtually all international prices are determined and denominated in U.S. dollars. Although it is certainly true that until the financial crisis Japanese yen greased international financial wheels, the centrality of the dollar remains. Second, the United States alone accounts for almost 20 percent of all world trade. It is the world's largest exporter and the world's largest importer.[38] Third, when European and Japanese firms have research and development (R&D) dollars to spend, they generally spend it in U.S. universities. That means the United States dominates in knowledge production.[39] It should be added, moreover, that the English language has become the world's lingua franca; indeed, most of the world's knowledge has been stored in English.

System Polarity

One might ask how the distribution of capabilities between the interacting units in a situation of anarchy affects the structure of the international system. "Behavior and outcomes," according to neorealists, "change as interactions among a system's units become sparser or denser, as alliances shift, as nations adapt their policies to one another. These are changes within the system and often system dynamics are identified with and limited to such changes."[40] In other words, the anarchical international system can change as the number of powerful states increases or decreases, but in so doing it does not lose its essential characteristic of anarchy.

Over the 350 years of the modern system, the number of great powers has varied between two and five. When there are two dominant powers, the international system is said to be bipolar. When there are four or more, it is viewed as multipolar. A system with three powers could be called multipolar but is usually called tripolar. A structure with only one great power is called unipolar.

Some writers say the current international scene is multipolar, with the United States, the People's Republic of China (PRC), Russia, Japan, and the European Union (EU) operating as the poles. Others say neither Japan nor the EU count as poles. The EU is rejected because its individual members still retain considerable independence in security affairs, and Japan is not viewed as meeting great-power standards because it is too weak militarily and lacks natural resources. According to this interpretation, the world is tripolar (United States, Russia, PRC). Still others say the world remains bipolar (United States and Russia), but recent changes in the former Soviet Union undermine this perspective.

Soon after the Cold War ended, one hardy soul claimed that the collapse of the USSR put the world in a "unipolar moment," with the

United States first among equals.[41] Samuel Huntington says this moment has passed and that "U.S. policymaking should reflect rational calculations of power rather than a wish list of arrogant, unilateralist demands."[42] Historian Paul Kennedy does not think the world has quite become unipolar, but he does regard the power of the United States as exceptional. "Because it has so much power for good or evil, because it is the linchpin of the western alliance system and the center of the existing global economy, what it does, *or does not do,* is so much more important than what any of the other Powers decides to do" (emphasis in original).[43] Perhaps the best term for today's world, drawn from realists primarily interested in economic relations, is hegemonic. The United States (the hegemon) has the capacity and sometimes the desire to lead the world in a variety of contexts, but other states can resist U.S. preferences.

Attributes of the Balance of Power

Deciding who is a great power may seem like an exercise in bragging rights, but for realists the number of major powers matters considerably. There is reason to think that states alter their behaviors depending on the polarity of the international system. This changed behavior is expressed through the operation of the balance of power. The balance may operate differently depending on the polarity of the system.[44] Moreover, overall systemic stability and the propensity for war or peace may be affected by polarity.

The balance of power, according to one observer, serves three purposes:

1. to ensure the continued existence of the state system by preventing a universal empire through conquest. In other words, "let no one power predominate";
2. to assist, at the regional level, in maintaining the independence of states; and
3. to facilitate the growth of law and organization by providing a kind of enforcement by great powers.[45]

In this view, it follows that the balance of power is essential to maintaining order in international politics. The balance is one of the methods, along with law, war, and diplomacy, that states use to serve the goal of maintaining the state system. Sometimes the powers may be unable to balance; in other cases, they may see no reason to do so. For example, China maintained a suzerainty over East Asia for centuries. That is, it dominated all other regions so thoroughly that no actor could gain power internally or make enough allies to balance the power of China. A somewhat similar picture emerges in the Western hemisphere, where the United States dominates most countries in the region. At the same time, none of the Latin American states has built enough power or successfully allied with others to counterbalance the United States.[46]

Traditional realists and neorealists differ in their views on how much choice states have in balancing. Traditionalists see considerable leeway for states. Neorealists assume balances arise naturally from the anarchy of the system.[47] In either case, failure to balance is rather rare. Traditional realists take some pains to explain these rare occasions; neorealists do not. Balances may fail to arise, according to traditional realists, when states have low perceptions of threat or have no other options.

Sentiments favoring the threat perception view can be found in the writings of early writers on international relations. For example, Emerich von Vattel, who wrote about the law of nations in the eighteenth century, observed, "Power alone does not constitute a threat of injury; the will to injure must accompany the power. . . . As soon as a State has given evidence of injustice, greed, pride, ambition, or a desire of domineering over its neighbours, it becomes an object of suspicion which they must guard against."[48]

Stephen Walt says proximity, growth in arms, and obvious hostile activities contribute to making a state seem threatening.[49] A state next door that adds a hundred aircraft to its military inventory is more threatening than a state 2,000 miles away that adds a similar number to its ledger. If the nearby state also tries to coerce other states to do things they otherwise would prefer not to do, then it becomes even more menacing. Very powerful states can take their time to react to such threats, but smaller ones cannot.

Walt also offers an explanation for the failure to balance based on the availability of allies. If a state lacks good external options and has only a limited capacity to build power domestically, it bandwagons with the threat. That explanation accounts for the lack of balancing against U.S. aggressive behavior in Latin America; these states have few options. If the states of Latin America build up power (and the United States dominates many of their economies, so this scenario is unlikely), then they may achieve greater success in balancing against the United States.

Although the functions of the balance of power remain constant irrespective of the polarity of the international system, polarity does affect the actual implementation of the balance. A set of categories for analyzing the means by which states keep a balance in bipolar and multipolar systems is shown in Table 2.2. Here, "alliance" refers to mutual agreements to assist (or not to get involved with) another state in military situations; "coalition" involves four or more states working together against a threat; "moderation" means preservation of essential players and includes allowances for those vanquished in war to have a say in postwar decisions; "vigilance" denotes sensitivity to changes in power; "intervention" entails intrusion into the affairs of another state; "holding the balance" refers to a third party that sits "outside" a major conflict and shifts its weight depending on who has the upper hand; and "compensation" involves agreements giving a state that lost land or people in one area equivalent land or people elsewhere.[50] The last row, war, is self-explanatory.

The operation of the balance of power was quite evident in 1990 in the Persian Gulf. President Saddam Hussein built up the military power of Iraq to the point where it became a regional power. This course of action was a response to both Iranian and Israeli power. He also evidently hoped to gain more economic resources via force of arms. Earlier he had warred with Iran; the world mostly ignored that war. But his grab for Kuwait was different: It sought the outright conquest of an independent state. As we have seen, one of the most important goals of the international society, and one of the major reasons for any balance of power, is to protect the independence of states. Beyond that, Kuwait had oil, a factor critical to the industrial lifeblood of many states. If Iraq had gained access to Kuwaiti oil, it would have controlled a large share of world petroleum resources. That would be too much power, in the view of many states who import large quantities of oil and gas from the gulf. Consequently, a thirty-two-nation coalition fought a quick and successful war to redress the balance by ousting Iraq from Kuwait.

Based on Table 2.2, this response to Iraq's aggression fits a multipolar operation of the balance better than a bipolar one. The coalition

TABLE 2.2 Operation of the Balance of Power in Two Types of Polarity

	Bipolar	Multipolar
Alliance	Permanent	Flexible
Coalition	Alliances become permanent coalitions	Rare; only formed in times of military crisis
Moderation	No; only with respect to nuclear weapons	Only toward great powers
Vigilance	Globalized	Other great powers only
Intervention	Endemic	Only when there is sudden shift in power of another great power
Holding the Balance	No; requires third party	Yes; Britain said this was its policy toward Europe
Compensation	No; closest analog is that main power sometimes transfers resources to allies	Yes
War	Yes, but not against the other power; may be a function of nuclear weapons	Yes, as last resort against other powers

Source: Categories and multipolar characteristics derived from Edward Vose Gulick, Europe's Classical Balance of Power (Ithaca, N.Y.: Cornell University Press, 1955), Chap. 3.

formed to solve the problem was temporary. Iraq had perhaps gotten away with the invasion in the first place because it was not important enough to watch vigilantly. Once the war ended, considerable moderation was employed by the other states with respect to Iraq's independence. Iraq was not destroyed, and it still participates in decisions over its future, as the ongoing difficulties with U.N. weapons inspections attests. War was certainly the last resort; months of negotiations occurred before the U.S.-led coalition took military action. Only the entries for the holding-the-balance and the compensation rows in Table 2.2 do not conform to the facts of the Iraq conflict.

Cooperation and Realism

Given the large number of incentives to protect one's state against the possible military actions of other states, there would seem to be few reasons to cooperate. Is cooperation ever rational? For neorealists, the answer is a qualified no. For more traditional realists, the answer is yes. There are two related ways of approaching the problem. One approach uses the balance-of-power idea and the other takes us back to rationality. Traditional realists will argue that prudence can sometimes yield cooperation. Neorealists say that, in view of the attention to relative power that the anarchical system tends to force on states, it is very difficult for states to achieve cooperation.

To grasp this distinction, let us return to the war between Athens and Sparta. Early in the war, Athens threatened Sicily. Thucydides recounts the speech Hermocrates of Syracuse gave to convince all the peoples of Sicily to unite against the impending Athenian aggression. Hermocrates begins with a line of reasoning that realists would find familiar: "If it is natural to want to dominate, it is also natural to want to resist domination."[51] Indeed, actors ought to take active preparation to resist domination.

Although this observation explains why states maintain the balance, it does not explain why states cooperate. Hermocrates' reasoning, however, takes a surprising turn as he makes an allowance for the fact that actions occur under conditions of uncertainty about the future. Realism's assumption of rationality, strictly speaking, means that states act with perfect information; in the absence of such perfection, caution may be warranted. Uncertainty is likely to be quite high about the distant future[52] because it becomes difficult to calculate how one's moves will interact with countermoves by other states. The more variables that must be factored into the calculation, the harder the choice. This uncertainty ought to constrain any thought of aggrandizement. Wrote classicist Robert Connor, "The surest means of security is not ingenuity and speed in plotting nor a rational means of prediction, but a recognition of the limits of knowledge in a world that cannot totally be predicted or controlled. . . . [Hermocrates] urges settlement, accommodation, and common action based on restraint."[53] In other words, because it is natural both to dominate and to resist domination, and also because uncertainty is a feature of political life, the best course for the powerful is to accommodate the weaker so that they will be less inclined to balance with others against the powerful.

The very prospect of retaliation is one reason why, as Bull has claimed, the balance of power may produce cooperation.[54] But since one cannot be sure whether retaliation will occur or what the effects of retaliation might be if executed, caution and preference for non-military solutions may be the best course of action. It is easy to see why small states might be cautious—they have less power and hence fewer choices. Less clear are the reasons why the powerful should be cautious and attempt cooperative approaches to gain their desired ends. Prudence for great powers means avoiding unnecessary injury to others that might goad the weaker powers into defensive action. Hans Morgenthau explained the enormous success of Great Britain, which was a great power well into the twentieth century, as follows:

> The only nation that in modern times could maintain a continuous position of preponderance owed that position to a rare combination of potential superior power, a reputation for superior power, and the infrequent use of that superior power. Thus Great Britain was able, on the one hand, to overcome all serious challenges to its superiority because its self-restraint gained powerful allies and, hence, made it actually superior. On the other hand, it could minimize the incentive to challenge it because its superiority did not threaten the existence of other nations.[55]

Similarly, U.S. restraint in the war with Iraq more readily generated cooperation on the part of other states. President Bush's use of the United Nations to "restrain" and legitimate U.S. power in the Persian Gulf was yet another instance of this sort of leadership. Did he demand more than the U.N. asked? No. Did he demand the removal of Hussein—an action that would probably have been in contravention of international law? Not officially. Thus moderation and restraint by the dominant power probably increased international collaboration. Despite the astonishing power of the United States, its actions did not directly threaten other states.[56]

Neorealists and traditional realists diverge in their thinking about this kind of hegemonic leadership. Neorealists argue that if cooperation emerges at all it is because a powerful state sets the rules and helps implement them. Once that leadership declines, so will the cooperation. Traditional realists, as suggested by Morgenthau, can imagine leadership where other states believe the powerful state is acting legitimately.[57] In contrast, a power that forces other states to do things is exercising coercive leadership; other states do not believe the powerful state is acting legitimately. Legitimate leadership by a hegemon produces cooperative outcomes at a lower cost than does sheer coercion even as it is also less likely to engender counterbalances. Coercive leadership is expensive and may motivate those states being coerced to withdraw support for the powerful state and coalesce against it.

Thus, hegemonic leadership can be viewed as the powerful's use of "accommodation and common action based on restraint." Coercive leadership fails to accommodate others and lacks restraint. Any common action in a setting of coercive leadership comes, essentially, at the point of a gun. Walt's research into alliances touches on this point in describing the ever-increasing difficulties the former Soviet Union had in maintaining its leadership in its bloc compared to the United States.[58] David Forsythe puts the idea of hegemonic leadership like this: "Because the hegemon's policy position is seen as good and because the hegemon is seen as having the power to compel implementation of policy if necessary, or at least the power to induce compliance through payments, there is 'voluntary' deference from others."[59]

Hegemonic leadership may be critical to the creation of international regimes. Regimes are collections of rules, obligations, and decisionmaking procedures in specific issue areas.[60] There are, for instance, regimes for money, trade, human rights, and the Antarctic. In economic matters the United States was not just important, it was dominant in the decades following World War II. Its policies also made sense to others. Through negotiation the United States and its allies agreed to treaties and international organizations to facilitate international policy coordination. When the United States would not lead, however, inaction occurred: An international trade organization failed to form after World War II because the United States changed its mind about the value of the proposed organization.

Smaller powers can maneuver widely in the space created by the hegemon, especially if they can organize themselves—for example, as the Organization of Petroleum Exporting Countries (OPEC) did during its early years—or if they can make a bargain that advances their economic interests and the hegemon's security interests. By threatening not to cooperate—which would increase the costs of leadership to the hegemon—smaller states can gain more resources than they might otherwise be permitted. The hegemonic leader, moreover, understands the utility of cooperation and the danger that would be posed by states "resisting domination"; thus, hegemons may give way when—in sheer power terms—they need not.

For instance, the purpose of the General Agreement on Tariffs and Trade (GATT) is to reduce tariffs and promote free trade. During the

Cold War, however, the developing countries objected to free trade because their economies were so weak that they needed preferential arrangements. Preferential treatment meant that Third World goods could go more readily to the North than the other way around. This the United States in concert with other important powers agreed to do. The wealthier states made a short-term concession for long-term gain. Power considerations were not absent: Former colonial powers like Britain and France did it as a means of assisting—and retaining some control over—former colonies, whereas the United States accepted the idea as a means of keeping the countries out of Soviet hands. In short, U.S. power kept things in bounds and also moderated disputes between the rich countries.

Change in International Politics

One of the most difficult questions for an adherent of realism is accounting for change. More correctly, except for increases or decreases in the capabilities of states, the question of change is not an important one to realists. To be sure, states come and go, but the behavior of the system and the remaining states in the system stays quite constant. Because realism assumes all states perform similar functions and therefore does not inquire into their internal characteristics, it is not especially interested in the question of why any particular state drops out of the picture.

Realism is concerned, however, about the impact of system polarity on the behavior of states. Thus some realists speculate on what causes the polarity of the system to undergo change. Two approaches, the effects of war and the role of hegemons, offer potential avenues for realists who want to explain polarity changes.

Major wars seem to ratify underlying power changes. The Napoleonic Wars marked the beginnings of Britain's dominance in world affairs; World War II marked the rise of the United States and the USSR to preeminence. Jack S. Levy observes, "In spite of the traditional importance of 'balance of power' and related . . . hypotheses in the study of international conflict, there is no explicitly 'realist' theory of general war and no compilation of wars based on realist assumptions."[61] Since realism does not explain war very well, it is hard to say how war as a cause of change would work within realist theory.

Possibly it is hegemonic leadership that causes change. Britain, after the Napoleonic Wars, launched a virtual peace offensive toward the United States and let it become dominant in the Western hemisphere. Britain attempted a similar operation in the early twentieth century with respect to Japan. More recently, the United States rebuilt former enemies, Japan and Germany, in order to counter Soviet power. But the evidence on hegemonic leadership as a source of rule change and facilitator of power transitions remains unclear. After all, if all states still act approximately the same way due to the anarchical nature of the system, a hegemon's efforts to order the world along its preferred lines is hardly surprising or indicative of change.

A key question about change was raised by a critic of realism, John Ruggie, who believes that major systemic changes have occurred and thinks realists ought to account for them: How can we account for changes in the system as a whole?[62] Waltz considers one component of a system to be the differentiation of its units, in this case sovereign states; at the same time he allows this component to drop out when he explains the operation of the international system. For Waltz, the medieval and the modern state systems are essentially similar. But, notes Ruggie, during the medieval period anarchy existed, but sovereignty did not. Accordingly, one problem with Waltz's neorealism is that "it provides no means by which to account for, or even to describe, the most important contextual change in international politics in this millennium: the shift from the medieval to the modern international system."[63] One could respond to this point by observing that realism is a theory that explains behaviors when there is anarchy in the system and sovereignty for its units.

How realism handles the dynamics of change is nicely summarized by the following observation:

> If history is "just one damn thing after another," then for realists international politics is the same damn things over and over again: war, great power security and economic competitions, the rise and fall of great powers, and the formation and dissolution of alliances. International political behavior is characterized by continuity, regularity, and repetition because states are constrained by the international system's unchanging (and probably unchangeable) structure.[64]

Conclusion

By assuming states matter more than any other global entity, the realist paradigm simplifies the world. The parsimony (few elements explain many things) of the theory stands as its greatest achievement. Some say its simplicity greatly impoverishes realism's capacity for explanation and for rich description. And yet, the main components of the theory do seem to account for much of world politics, so perhaps the loss is unimportant.

In addition, in assuming that states are rational and unitary, realism offers a simplification that assists one in imagining how any nation— in general or in particular—is likely to act. Vast amounts of subnational politicking can be collapsed into the utility-maximizing entity known as a state.

Realism helps us see how the lack of hierarchy in authority at the systemic level creates rules that confine the choices available to states. At the same time, the emphasis on power helps to explain why some states are more successful in achieving their goals than are others.

In summary, the theoretical approach to world politics called realism has a long, distinguished history and offers a coherent, parsimonious explanation for much of what goes on across the globe. It does not purport to explain every global phenomenon, but its simplicity and utility commends it to policymakers and theorists alike.

3
The Liberal Paradigm

Freedom to pursue economic gain, liberty to participate in the affairs of public life, respect for political human rights, and minimal government are the hallmarks of liberal theory. It was a radical ideology in the 1700s and remains a threat today to traditional and authoritarian political systems. It has been spectacularly successful as a political ideology. Over the past 250 years, liberalism has shaped modern democratic governments within states, provided justification for respect for basic human rights, founded a coherent justification for international law and organization, and constituted the ideational underpinning for the astonishing expansion of global markets. It is not too much to claim that the liberal paradigm has done much to give us our present world politics, especially the politics of globalization and democratization.

Liberalism has operated primarily within countries. This is an important point to remember when liberalism is applied to the realm of world politics, because liberal theory treats the domestic circumstances of states as crucial variables in explaining their international behaviors. Through commerce and industrialization, liberal states soon find that war is wasteful and injurious to the operation of the market, thus reinforcing the desire to resolve disputes peacefully. Through their commitment to human political rights, liberal states find that cooperation is easier to achieve with democracies than with nondemocracies, thus producing a spreading sphere of peace. Michael Doyle, drawing on classical liberal theorists Emmanuel Kant, John Locke, Jeremy Bentham, Adam Smith, and Joseph Schumpeter, outlines the general claims liberalism makes about world politics:

1. Although states live under international anarchy, meaning
    the absence of a global government, they do not experience a
    general state of war.
2. States are inherently different "units," differentiated by how
    they relate to individual human rights. So liberals distinguish
    Liberal from non-Liberal societies, republican from autocratic
    or totalitarian states, capitalist from communist, fascist, and
    corporatist economies. Differences in international behavior
    then reflect these differences.
3. The aims of the state, as do the aims of the individual, go be-
    yond security to the protection and promotion of individual
    rights.[1]

Let us briefly consider these three propositions before moving on to
the ways contemporary IR theorists use liberal principles to explain
world politics.

*Although states live under international anarchy, meaning the absence of
a global government, they do not experience a general state of war.* Classical
liberal theorists imagined that states were in a "state of nature" and
this meant they were free and rational. The state of nature for most
liberals is not naturally one of violence and war. States recognize that
other states are due respect and independence simply by their existence, just as are individuals within a country. If others willfully violate the independence of states, self-defense and even collective defense are permissible activities. This produces a "troubled state of
peace"[2] for countries. Errors in information, communication, and
other impediments to reason may make peace more troubling than it
need be. Consequently, states are led to set rules (international law)
and to find ways of clarifying intentions through international organizations or regimes. In this way, the troubled peace becomes more
settled and certain.

*States are inherently different "units," differentiated by how they relate to
individual human rights. . . . Differences in international behavior then reflect these differences.* Not all states respond similarly to the system in
which they find themselves. The domestic structures and circumstances of states matter as explanations for their external behaviors.
States that routinely use force to abuse the rights of their own citizens
behave differently in world affairs than states that strive to protect

human rights. Similarly, states willing to engage in trade and to open their markets[3] behave differently from those who attempt to close their economies to outsiders.

The aims of the state, as do the aims of the individual, go beyond security to the protection and promotion of individual rights. Liberal theorists of the eighteenth and nineteenth centuries imagined that individuals left the state of nature voluntarily to form governments. By trading full individual freedom for some government, individuals gain the capacity to do more with others and to engage in a wider array of economic activities simply through the elimination of misperceptions and inefficient communications. In exchange, governments are supposed to protect human rights and liberty. As a consequence, states represent the many interests of the people, but with the additional obligation of providing them security from attack. Thus states have as many interests as their inhabitants. They are not just focused on military affairs, although this is a function they have a particular obligation to perform.

To varying degrees post–World War II international relations theorists use these principles outlined by classical liberal theorists to interpret what they observe in world politics. Liberal theory emerged first to explain parts of world politics, such as phenomena of international political economy and the rise of cooperation. Liberal theory has since been extended to more phenomena. Now it offers a coherent, systematic way to think about contemporary world politics. In the next section, we illustrate these uses through a discussion of "pluralistic security communities," the democratic peace, interdependence, and the societal basis of state preferences in world politics.

Security Communities and the End of the Cold War

Consistent with liberal notions of peace through a league of democracies,[4] some analysts focused on how cooperation might arise among liberal democratic states. This scholarly effort yielded one of the field's most important claims, one that is still being explored by scholars and demonstrated by countries. In 1957 Karl Deutsch and his colleagues claimed that increased trade, democracy, and participation in international organizations (integration) reduced the chances of war,[5] a claim that is presently supported by the facts. Democracies do not fight other democracies. Democracies do fight with nondemocracies. Deutsch's group distinguished two kinds of peace and cooperation processes based on this observation. One process leads to *amalgamated security communities* wherein once-independent political entities actually combine to form a single political unit. This, for example, happened with the thirteen states of the United States between 1776 and 1787. The other process leads to a *pluralistic security community*. In this case, the independent political entities retain their sovereign independence but have a vanishingly small chance of warring with one another.

The United States and Canada have created a pluralistic security community. Both are independent countries, yet it seems preposterous to expect them to go to war against each other. Similarly, New Zealand, Japan, and Australia have built such a community, as have the countries that now form the European Union. In fact, it can well be argued that all these liberal democracies today have constructed a pluralistic security community among themselves. They participate in military security arrangements, trade, economic organization, and a host of other cooperative arrangements. Here and there, then, countries have apparently escaped war with each other even though they may have many conflicts over important issues. Wars with states outside these islands of security still remain within the realm of possibility.[6]

The NATO bombing of Serbia and Kosovo in 1999 indicates how war with a nation outside a security community might arise. This conflict was, in many respects, a liberal war. Led by Serbian Slobodan Milosevic, Yugoslavia had warred in Bosnia and committed many atrocities. When Milosevic then launched campaigns against ethnic Albanians in Kosovo, NATO hammered out a diplomatic deal in late 1998. Milosevic refused to sign it and stepped up pressure on the Kosovar Albanians and eventually had his troops resort to ethnic cleansing. A long history of human rights abuse had caused NATO nations to become fed up with his behavior. In a remarkable decision—one where NATO held firm for over two months of difficult political activity—NATO began bombing Belgrade and other towns in Yugoslavia. The security community that is NATO and the vigorous human rights standards found in Western Europe made Serbia's policies of ethnic cleansing internationally unacceptable. The actions of the allied force showed that a war between democracies and authoritarian regimes was still possible—indeed, the action may set a new standard for human rights in Europe. It also illustrated the point that liberals distinguish between kinds of states. States that kill their own citizens are also states that may destabilize international affairs.

Late Cold War Arguments for the Ease of Cooperation: Interdependence

The phenomenal growth of governmental and nongovernmental international organizations[7] and the absence of war between the United States and its allies slowly provoked a more general interest among liberal theorists of world politics in explaining why cooperation was so common among states. These theorists produced propositions highly similar to those of the classical liberal theorists. Their line of theorizing proposed that states were the dominant actors (but not the only ones); anarchy characterized the international system (but could be mitigated); states were rational actors (but they had multiple interests); and international organization made cooperation easier. Taken together, these claims suggested that cooperation might be achievable, especially when security was not at stake.

A crucial contribution to this line of reasoning came with a book by Robert Keohane and Joseph Nye.[8] They offered an explanation for a wider range of cooperative (meaning no use of force) outcomes between states. They called their approach *complex interdependence.* They assumed that "the *structure* of a system refers to the distribution of capabilities among similar units"[9] and that these units were states, or, more properly, the governments of states. Bargaining processes connect the units. Interdependence between states requires that two states experience mutual costs from their relationship. "Where there are reciprocal (although not necessarily symmetrical) costly effects of transactions there is interdependence. Where interactions do not have significant costly effects, there is simply interconnectedness."[10] The United States and the USSR were interdependent in nuclear affairs, due to mutual costly effects, but were not interdependent in much else. Cooperation grew primarily, therefore, only in the realm of arms control. In contrast, complex interdependence has been extensive between the United States, Canada, Japan, and Europe.

Complex interdependence has three main characteristics: First, "Multiple channels connect societies"[11]—that is, actors other than states, such as firms, the U.N., or environmental groups, can influence how states behave relative to issues and each other. Second, there are multiple issues, but *no hierarchy* of issues. Military issues do not necessarily outweigh economic or environmental issues. The lack of issue hierarchy is a precondition to a third characteristic: "Military force is not used between the governments to solve any disputes between them."[12] In other words, full-scale interdependence can really only appear within the confines of a pluralistic security community.

Interdependent countries face distinct problems and opportunities in their relationships. In the first place, trade-offs between issues—what has been called "linkage politics"[13]—can be problematic because the influence of nongovernmental actors makes it difficult to anticipate how states might tie economic issues to those involving the environment or any of a number of other problems. Second, agenda setting—what to talk about as countries resolve conflicts—becomes more important. Because nongovernmental actors influence domestic agendas, it is hard to distinguish between the domestic and international realms. Last, international organizations become more important because they provide a context in which states can undertake to resolve conflicts.[14]

After the Cold War: Structural Liberalism

Daniel Deudney and John Ikenberry have further elaborated the insights of Deutsch and his colleagues and of Keohane and Nye. They argue that the countries of the West, with their internal democratic structures, shared capitalist markets, peaceful relations supported by mutual membership in security organizations, and acceptance of U.S. leadership, have produced a coherent political subsystem within the international system. They call this system "structural liberalism." It suggests a "deep" security community with many sources of support for the continuity of peace. In structural liberalism, states do not balance each other; instead they tie each other down through "mutually constraining institutions" which "co-bind" the states.[15] Here we see the concept of mutual cost suggested by Keohane and Nye: States cannot do anything they like, and that constraint is the cost of doing things they could not do without each other.[16] Yet, each state retains its individuality and its international juridical equality. Co-binding in a setting of juridical equality softens the effects of anarchy but does not eliminate it.

Hegemonic leadership by the United States does not impose hierarchy or even pose a great threat to the autonomy of other states because the domestic institutions of the United States permit other countries to influence its policies. The very openness of U.S. liberal, democratic, and society-dominated institutions permits other countries to coformulate U.S. foreign policy. Deudney and Ikenberry call this "penetrated hegemony." For example, firms and environmental groups talk with like actors in and between other countries, which allows other nations to influence U.S. policies. Thus, communication about interests is continuous and the gap between the official policies of governments is small.

Moreover, two potential great powers—Germany and Japan—have apparently accepted an international status as "semi-sovereign, partial great powers."[17] Through their constitutions, which were imposed and structured by the United States after World War II, these countries have given up the goal of large militaries. Nevertheless, they do have "activist"[18] foreign policies, especially in the realms of economics, peacekeeping, environment, and (for Germany) European integration.

These sociopolitical features are further buttressed by a mutual commitment to the market. The vast absolute gains to be had through peace and cooperation outweigh any temporary (or even actual) loss in relative gains. Thus, the constant fear of relative loss of power that underlies the security dilemma for the realists simply does not come into play among those who subscribe to structural liberalism. More correctly, the prospect of absolute gains encourages states to moderate the anarchy of the international system. "Advanced capitalism creates such high prospects for absolute gains that states attempt to mitigate anarchy between themselves so as to avoid the need to pursue relative gains."[19] The prospect of economic gain, then, helps drive the strategy of co-binding through international institutions.

Concern over relative gains is also weakened by the very operation of the market. "In highly dynamic markets with large numbers of sophisticated and fast moving and autonomous corporate actors, it is very difficult to anticipate the consequences of policies and thus the relative distribution of gains and losses."[20] Even the "civic identities" of the citizens of liberal states contribute to this reduction in the importance of relative gains. Deudney and Ikenberry believe that individual identities in the West are all oriented around capitalism and its "business and commodity culture."[21]

In sum, and for many of the reasons adduced long ago by Deutsch and his collaborators, the West has multiple and reinforcing patterns that lead to a realm of peaceful resolution of conflicts. Even though conflicts abound between liberal states, there are limits within which conflicts are handled. The result is a subsystem of the international system that is deeply committed to peace among its members. It is this pattern, say Deudney and Ikenberry, that explains the real end of the Cold War. Wealth, cooperation, and genuine independence of the allies proved an overwhelming combination compared to what the Soviet bloc possessed. It also explains the fact that NATO is alive and well despite the loss of its "enemy," the Soviet Union—that is, the cooperation was meaningful and not superficial. It is also a pattern that helps explain why international regimes designed to coordinate planning and work on global problems have not fallen apart, despite the relative decline of U.S. power. Enough states expect peaceful resolution of disputes and cooperation that they can keep cooperation going and growing.

State-Society Liberalism

We end this discussion of IR liberal theories with Andrew Moravcsik's conception of liberalism, called "state-society liberalism." It eliminates any necessary role for systemic anarchy, can apply in many settings, and elaborates on how societal actors produce change in world politics. Moravcsik's approach has three core assumptions. First, societal actors have primacy over the international system and its states. "The fundamental actors in international politics are individuals and private groups, who are on the average rational and risk-averse and who organize exchange and collective action to promote differentiated interests under constraints imposed by material scarcity, conflicting values, and variations in societal influence."[22] Second, these societal actors are sources of a state's preferences in foreign affairs. "States (or other political institutions) represent some subset of domestic society, on the basis of whose interests state officials define state preferences and act purposively in world politics."[23] Last, the overall pattern of each state's preferences that originates within

the state creates the constraints of the international system. Moravcsik puts it this way: "The configuration of interdependent state preferences determines state behavior."[24]

Let us consider this approach to liberalism through a brief example.
If we want to understand why the United States opposes including
deep reductions in greenhouse gases in a climate change convention,
we need to know which industry, labor, subnational governments,
and environmental groups favor the proposal and which do not. We
need to understand how much access they have to Congress, the
president, and the federal government bureaucracy. The same would
be true in explaining the preferences of countries that favor vigorous
reductions in these gases. The explanation for the actual outcome in
the treaty comes from finding where the interests of societal groups in
states overlap or conflict with those in other states. Thus, the U.S.
government may be listening to the most powerful economic actors
or to the governors of the states who fear a slowing of economic
growth. Meanwhile, in the Netherlands, there may be widespread
agreement among industry and local officials and environmental organizations that reductions are needed. The treaty will reflect less
than either of these countries might want. The future evolution of the
treaty as a part of an international regime on global warming will depend on changes in preferences by the societal groups. If firms in Europe convince firms in the United States that reductions are necessary
(economically less wasteful), then eventually the U.S. government
will change its preferences.

State-society liberalism both intersects with and diverges from the
other versions of liberal international theories. It claims to be applica-
ble regardless of whether there is a security community in place.
Rather than saying states can mitigate anarchy, as Deudney and Ikenberry do, it drops the concept. Indeed, one might even make the case
that sovereignty itself matters little, so central are patterns of state-society relations.

State-society liberalism concedes that individuals are moderately
rational and that they organize themselves for a variety of purposes,
good and bad. As de Tocqueville, the nineteenth-century French com-
mentator on American life wrote, Americans organize themselves for
purposes "religious, moral, serious, futile, extensive or restricted,
enormous or diminutive"[25] to advance their preferences. State-society
liberalism also acknowledges that social actors are not equally strong

and do not have equal access to government. As a result, it accords no special role to democratic institutions. The central insight of state-society liberalism is that domestic groupings and interests exist whether a country is based on democracy, monarchy, or some sort of despotism. Democracies may well have special relations, but the theoretical point of state-society liberalism is that international politics emerge from domestic pressures no matter what kind of government a country may have.

The Pleasures and Paradoxes of Liberalism

Liberal theory's appeal, at least for those already living in democracies, is its familiarity. The emphasis it places on the importance of human rights, cooperation, and the operation of markets as rational ways of managing daily life makes sense in terms of personal experience. It has a manageable number of propositions, so its complexity as a paradigm is also low. Yet, relatively simple as they may be, the principles of liberalism produce a distinctive explanation for world politics. Liberal theorists see anarchy as strongly moderated—or even irrelevant—due to the gradual appearance and development of international law, international organizations, and the global market. Given these diverse modifiers of anarchy, the sovereignty of states is seen to have eroded.

The erosion of sovereignty is not a negative outcome for liberals but a natural and reasonable consequence of the internal structures of countries being governed by diverse governmental, corporate, and societal institutions. Individuals matter in this setting, because governments are set up to protect the citizenry from external threats while preserving liberty at home. The liberty of individuals to do precisely as they please, however, is limited by the opposing duty to respect others and the rule of law, including representative democratic procedures. Similar duties apply to states. Although citizens tend to accept what leaders negotiate with other states, citizens can strongly influence policymaking through participation in pressure groups. Societal groups use issues to influence others, both at home and abroad. They can work within their country and with counterparts in other countries and even provide information to international organizations. In such a setting, it is knowledge and access (often obtained with money) that provide crucial levers of power.

Thus, force is not that useful to citizens or to their governments in re-solving problems.

Liberalism contains within it, however, two important paradoxes, especially when applied to world politics. These are the authority dilemma and the representation dilemma, both of which have their roots in the principle of individual liberty. Liberalism as domestic ideology and practice elevates individual liberty to a place among the highest goods. To protect liberty and to govern well, liberal democra-cies represent citizen interests through elected legislatures and other techniques of popular sovereignty. Popular sovereignty expressed through representatives both provides government with enough au-thority to get things done on the public's behalf and checks arbitrary behavior by government. It is not clear, however, if these principles are being used effectively in today's world of complex transboundary environmental and economic issues. If states cannot make authorita-tive decisions for the citizens of their country, then where does au-thority come from? If many important decisions are made at such a distance from a citizen's representational government, is not liberty hedged in on all sides?

The authority dilemma arises from this ongoing problem: How can the freedom of individuals to achieve satisfaction with their lives mesh with the necessity for some elementary level of social order, an order that governments are designed to provide? The answer within countries is representative government and the protection of human rights. If markets go truly global and if consumers begin to notice the abuse of power by those best able to get favorable terms—corpora-tions—do we not need more authority rather than less to protect human rights? Similar difficulties may emerge as the world copes with other issues on its agenda.

Liberalism taken to its limits, however, might hold that sovereignty resides only in the people and not in territorial states. If so, how can any kind of authority be maintained to achieve public ends? As we have seen, many liberals imagine the foreign behaviors of states as emerging from bargaining between social and other interest groups. Governance at home and abroad is essentially a struggle over the preferences of groups. These groups are strongest within a given country, but they also operate transnationally across sovereign bor-ders. States may possess sovereignty, but the concept is not particu-larly important. Society dominates the state and thus societal actors define the politics between states as well. At most, states are seen as useful organizational devices for organizing, articulating, and expressing group preferences.

Some liberals might argue that the strong influence of societal groups is the prime source of authority in world affairs, and thus an effective substitute for territorial state authority and the principle of representative government. All "actors" have potential access to the technology and communications needed to influence policy at all levels. Yet, this potential will not be realized effectively by all states or all groups seeking to influence outcomes. The poor and, in some cases, the disenfranchised will have little chance of getting their views heard in corporate boardrooms, national legislatures, or international councils. Lack of access to communications media, in particular, will limit the effectiveness of poor groups and states in influencing global policy. It will be difficult for social groups with limited resources to form transnational coalitions with like-minded counterparts, with the result that their preferences will be incompletely expressed. All of these factors will be further exacerbated because liberal states will find it difficult to dislodge socioeconomic privilege from the halls of government or to protect individuals from the powerful in *society*. Consequently, the fundamental principle of liberalism, human political rights, may be violated.

The representation dilemma is the mirror image of the authority dilemma. Let us begin with what some liberals see as the engine of liberty: the market and free trade. The market is supposed to be created among equals (rather than on a representational principle) with nearly perfect information. Yet, this is hardly the case in practice. Market failures arise for numerous reasons—such as cartel power or erroneous information—and sometimes the best response to failures is government intervention.[26] For example, contracts for goods and services are supposed to be based on equal power between buyer and seller. Today, however, consumers are locked out of communications and making inputs. Contracts routinely provide that one party (the corporation) can change the terms of the contract at will, its only duty being to inform the consumer of the change. Or, in an effort to improve their internal efficiencies, firms may draw on resources and capital from any place in the globe but in the process cause job losses, public health problems, and environmental destruction. To solve these problems, national governments could set international rules (at considerable distance from popular sovereignty) or they could arrange for more representation in boardrooms or other international forums that assist in building free markets.

In sum, one problem caused by the success of liberal economics is the loss of political and economic power for large numbers of people. Relative to the increasingly globalized market, there is no citizenship, only consumership, and thus merely agreeing to unequal terms in order to buy a good reduces liberty.[27] How can individual rights to freedom and liberty be squared with their loss to private corporations and distant economic decisions?

Even the growth of international cooperation among governments impinges on the representation dilemma. If countries make international rules that strongly limit self-rule at more local levels, has the principle of representation been violated? One answer is that democratic countries have rules for accepting treaties that are based on constitutions or at least on long-standing customs, thus providing people with representation by the elected officials who approve these agreements. In a related vein, governments turn international rules into domestic law using national legislative procedures. This issue has raised the specter of the "democratic deficit"[28] in the European Union (EU), as citizens discover their elected leaders moving decisions to the EU level when local parliaments and voters oppose the policy. Even the creation of the representative European Parliament has not quelled this concern. Similar difficulties may emerge as other international agreements that require individual change take shape.

Liberalism may be a relatively "young" set of political ideas, dating back only to the eighteenth century, but it gives every sign of continuing to be robust. It opens avenues to testable propositions about world politics. No matter how policy issues eventually turn out, the several kinds of liberal theory give us ways to link the internal and external circumstances of states. This theoretical paradigm reminds us that domestic and international political processes bear similarities to each other and also shape options at home and abroad.

4

Postinternationalism in a Turbulent World

Although the realism, liberalism, and postinternational politics paradigms have some common elements, in most important respects they rest on very different, even contradictory, premises. Both the similarities and the differences are discussed in Chapter 5. Here the task is to set out the underlying rationale for viewing world politics as having undergone turbulent transformations that are so profound as to warrant the framing of a new, postinternational paradigm.[1]

As the label implies, the structures and processes depicted by the new paradigm are still in the process of taking shape. Its outlines are not so clear-cut as to be easily summarized by a distinctive phrase. Yet, "postinternational politics" is an appropriate label because it highlights the decline of long-standing patterns without at the same time indicating where the changes may be leading. It suggests flux and transition even as it implies the presence and functioning of some stable structures. It reminds us that "international" matters may no longer be the dominant dimension of global life, or at least that other dimensions have emerged to challenge or offset the interactions of nation-states. And, not least, it permits us to avoid premature judgment as to whether present-day turbulence is an enduring or a transitional condition.

Unlike the realist and liberal paradigms, in other words, the postinternational paradigm is not founded on a few basic premises about the universal tendencies at work among individuals, organizations, and states. Quite to the contrary, postinternationalism springs from the presumption that accelerating change and deepening complexity are the major tendencies at work in the world, with the result that a multiplicity of contradictory dynamics—eleven are identified here—account for varying forms of behavior and degrees of conflict and cooperation among diverse actors. Postinternationalists wish they could reduce global affairs to a few organizing propositions, but they fear that in doing so much of the complexity that marks the current world would be ignored, rendering their explanations at best partial and at worst misleading. They accept the contradictions and ambiguities that result when the world is viewed as sustaining both dynamic changes and static continuities, with some countries and regions experiencing integration while others are marked by fragmentation.

Toward a New Paradigm

There is no dearth of indicators—such as the launching of wars by states and their efforts to negotiate postwar arrangements—to highlight the many ways in which world politics are marked by continuity. Nevertheless, it is also clear that huge transformations have been unfolding in the global system, transformations that are of sufficient magnitude to suggest the emergence of new global structures, processes, and patterns. Daily occurrences of complex and uncertain developments in every region, if not every country, of the world are so pervasive as to cast doubt on the viability of the long-established ways in which international affairs have been conducted and analyzed. It almost seems as if anomalous events—those developments that are unique and surprising because they deviate from history's normal paths—have replaced recurrent patterns as the central tendencies in world politics.

This is not the place to enumerate the many anomalous developments that point to profound and rapid change, but it is useful to recall the utter surprise that greeted the abrupt end of the Cold War. Pundits, professors, politicians, and others conversant with world politics were literally stunned, with not one claiming to have anticipated it and with all admitting to ad hoc explanations. Since the sudden collapse of the Communist world was the culmination of dynamics that had been subtly at work for a long time, the intensity and breadth of the surprise it evoked can only be viewed as a measure of the extent to which our understandings of world politics have lagged behind the deep transformations that are altering the global landscape. Anomalies indicative of profound change began to flow well before the end of the Cold War,[2] but the series of events that transformed Eastern Europe late in 1989 surely arrested attention on the presence of powerful change agents.

Equally important, in the years since 1989 the world has not settled back into the familiar patterns of international politics. The interactions of states have not again become the exclusive, or at least the predominant, form of transaction across national boundaries. States have not recovered strict control over the flow of people, goods, and money in and out of their countries. Publics have not subsided into quiescent acceptance of governmental policies. The United Nations and other international organizations are no longer merely convenient stages for the power plays of states. The boundaries between domestic and international politics have continued to erode as the principles of sovereignty are no longer barriers to external interventions into situations where famine, civil war, and violations of human rights are out of control. In short, there is no lack of incentives to frame a new paradigm with which to comprehend the course of events.

Most notable perhaps, the removal of the Cold War from the equations of world affairs did not result in a return to earlier patterns. Rather than simply being an extreme variant of great-power competition, the rivalry between the United States and the Soviet Union that lasted some forty years proved to be a lid that contained underlying transformations in the way people sustained their daily lives and societies conducted their public affairs. The Cold War, in other words, did not stimulate change so much as it masked it, thereby adding to the impulse to treat the swelling flow of anomalies as requiring a new paradigmatic formulation. As one analyst put it:

> Not only the configuration of great powers and their alliances but the very structure of political history has changed. . . . The very sovereignty and cohesion of states, the authority and efficacy of the governments are not what they were.
>
> Are we going to see ever larger and larger political units? . . . Or are we more likely going to see the break-up of several states into smaller ones? Are we going to see a large-scale migration of millions of peoples, something that has not happened since the last century of the Roman Empire? This is at least possible. The very texture of history is changing before our very eyes.[3]

Assuming that the quickening flow of anomalies preceded the end of the Cold War, what gave rise to them? What underlying dynamics were eroding the long-standing patterns of world politics and fostering the evolution of new, postinternational structures and processes? How can we begin to understand the emergence of a new global order at a level of deep and turbulent change that is more fundamental than the advent of a NATO bombing campaign against Yugoslavia, the fashioning of a thirty-two-nation coalition against Iraq, and the reunification of Germany? How do we account, in short, for an acceleration of the pace of change in international affairs that has altered "the very texture of history"?

The Turbulence Paradigm

Postinternational politics are perhaps most conspicuously marked by turbulence, by dynamics that foster intense conflicts, unexpected developments, pervasive uncertainties, and swift changes. Indeed, the turbulence is so global in scope that we shall use the term "turbulence model" interchangeably with "postinternational politics" as a label for the new paradigm. Lest there be any terminological confusion, however, it must be stressed at the outset that the notion of turbulence is used here as more than a metaphor for great commotion and uncertainty. The purpose is not to wax eloquent about change, but rather to probe its underlying dynamics in a systematic way.

Put most succinctly, the precise meaning ascribed to the turbulence concept focuses on changes in three prime parameters of world politics. When these fundamental patterns that normally bind and sustain the continuities of international life are overcome by high degrees of complexity and dynamism—that is, when the number, density, interdependencies, and volatility of the actors occupying the global stage undergo substantial expansion—world politics are viewed as having entered into a period of turbulence.

The three parameters conceived to be primary include the overall structure of global politics (a macro parameter), the authority structures that link macro collectivities to citizens (a macro-micro parameter), and the skills of citizens (a micro parameter). According to this perspective, all three parameters are presently undergoing extensive complexity and dynamism and the world is experiencing its first period of turbulence since the era that culminated with the Treaty of

Westphalia some 350 years ago.[4] Perhaps more to the point, the relative simultaneity that marks the impact of much greater complexity and dynamism on all three parameters has given rise to what might well be the central characteristic of world politics today, namely, the presence of persistent tensions between tendencies toward integration, globalization, and centralization on the one hand and those that foster fragmentation, localization, and decentralization on the other.[5] Viewed in this way, for instance, it is hardly anomalous that even as the former components of Yugoslavia aspired to admission to the European Community they engaged in violent conflict with each other. Or consider the example of Indonesia, where reforms imposed by International Monetary Fund (IMF) in exchange for loans contributed to a mass upheaval that toppled the Suharto government. As will be seen, these interactive integrating-fragmenting tensions are especially evident in the transformation of each of the three prime parameters.

Table 4.1 summarizes the changes in the three parameters, but the order of their listing should not be interpreted as implying causal sequences in which the actions of individuals are conceived to precede the behavior of collectivities. On the contrary, incisive insights into the turbulence of world politics are crucially dependent on an appreciation of the profoundly interactive nature of the three parameters—on recognizing that even as individuals shape the actions and orientations of the collectivities to which they belong, so do the goals, policies, and laws of the latter shape the actions and orientations of individuals. Indeed, much of the rapidity of the transformations at work in world politics can be traced to the ways in which the changes in each parameter stimulate and reinforce the changes in the other two.

The Micro Parameter: A Skill Revolution

The transformation of the micro parameter is to be found in the shifting capabilities of citizens everywhere. Individuals have undergone what can properly be termed a skill revolution. For a variety of reasons ranging from the advance of communications technology to the greater intricacies of life in an ever more interdependent world, people have become increasingly more competent in assessing where they fit in international affairs and how their behavior can be aggregated into significant collective outcomes. Included among these newly refined skills, moreover, is an expanded capacity to focus emotion and imag-

TABLE 4.1   Transformation of Three Global Parameters

	From	*To*
Micro parameter	Individuals less analytically, emotionally, and imaginatively skillful	Individuals more analytically, emotionally, and imaginatively skillful
Macro-micro parameter	Authority structures in place as people rely on traditional and/or constitutional sources of legitimacy to comply with directives emanating from appropriate macro institutions	Authority structures in crisis as people evolve performance criteria for legitimacy and compliance with the directives issued by macro officials
Macro parameter	Anarchic system of nation-states	Bifurcation of anarchic system into state- and multi-centric subsystems

ine alternative lifestyles as well as to analyze the causal sequences that sustain the course of events. These skills permit individuals to think through the steps needed to gain a better lifestyle or to understand how distant events in the larger world might affect them.

Put differently, it is a grievous error to assume that citizenries are a constant in politics. Indeed, it is hard to imagine that such rapid changes and increasing complexity could not have consequences for the individuals who make up the collectivities that interact on the global stage. As long as people were uninvolved in and apathetic about world affairs, it made sense to treat them as a constant parameter and to look to variabilities at the macro level for explanations of what happens in world politics. Today, however, the skill revolution has expanded the learning capacity of individuals, extended the detail and concepts of the cognitive maps through which they perceive the world, and elaborated their scenarios of how states, leaders, and publics will interact in the future. Among the many skills that populations have refined, perhaps the most important is an enlarged capacity to know when and how to participate in collective action.[6] It is no accident that in recent years the squares of the world's cities have been filled with large crowds demanding change.

It is tempting to view the impact of the skill revolution as leading to positive outcomes. Certainly the many restless publics that have protested authoritarian rule suggest a worldwide thrust toward an expansion of political liberties and a diminution of the governments' central control of economies. But there is nothing inherent in the skill revolution that leads people in more democratic directions. The change in the micro parameter is not so much one of new orientations as it is an evolution of new capacities for cogent and imaginative analysis. The world's peoples are not so much converging around the same values as they are sharing a greater ability to recognize and articulate their values. Thus, this parametric change is global in scope because it has enabled Islamic fundamentalists, Asian peasants, and Western sophisticates alike to better serve their respective orientations. And thus, too, the commotion in public squares has not been confined to cities in any particular region of the world. From Seoul to Prague, from Soweto to Beijing, from Jakarta to the West Bank, from Belgrade to Rangoon—to mention only a few of the places where collective demands have recently been voiced—the transformation of the micro parameter has been unmistakably evident.

Equally important, evidence of the skill revolution can be readily discerned in trend data for education, migration, television viewing, computer usage, travel, and a host of other situations in which people are called upon to employ their analytic, emotional, and imaginative skills.[7] And hardly less relevant, in a number of local circumstances— from traffic jams to water shortages, from budget crises to racial conflicts, from flows of refugees to threats of terrorism—people are relentlessly confronted with social, economic, and political complexities that impel them to forego their rudimentary premises and replace them with more elaborate conceptions of how to respond to the challenges of daily life.

This is not say that people everywhere are now equal in the skills they bring to bear upon world politics. Obviously, the analytically rich continue to be more adept than the analytically poor. But although the gap between the two ends of the skill continuum may be no narrower than in the past, the advance in the competencies of those at every point on the continuum is sufficient to contribute to a major transformation in the conduct of world affairs.

The Macro-Micro Parameter:
A Relocation of Authority

This parameter consists of the recurrent orientations, practices, and patterns of aggregation through which citizens at the micro level are linked to their collectivities at the macro level. In effect, it encompasses the authority structures whereby large aggregations, including private organizations as well as public agencies, achieve and sustain the cooperation and compliance of their memberships. Historically, these authority structures have been founded on traditional criteria of legitimacy derived from constitutional and legal sources. Under these circumstances individuals were habituated to compliance with the directives issued by higher authorities. They did what they were told to do because, well, because that is what one did. As a consequence, authority structures remained in place for decades, even centuries, as people unquestioningly yielded to the dictates of governments or the leadership of any other organizations with which they were affiliated. For a variety of reasons, including the expanded skills of citizens as well as a number of other factors noted below, the foundations of this parameter have undergone erosion. Throughout the world today, in both public and private settings, the sources of authority have shifted from traditional to performance criteria of legitimacy. Where the structures of authority were once in place, in other words, now they are in crisis, with the readiness of individuals to comply with governing directives being very much a function of their assessment of the performances of the authorities. The more the performance record is considered appropriate—in terms of satisfying needs, moving toward goals, and providing stability—the more are they likely to cooperate and comply. The less they approve the performance record, the more are they likely to withhold their compliance or otherwise complicate the efforts of macro authorities.

As a consequence of the pervasive authority crises, states and governments have become less effective in confronting challenges and implementing policies than they were in the past. They can still maintain public order through their police powers, but their ability to address and solve substantive problems is declining as people find fault with their performances and thus question their authority, redefine the bases of their legitimacy, and withhold their cooperation. Such a transformation is being played out dramatically today in the former Soviet Union, as it did earlier within all the countries of Eastern Europe. But authority crises in the former Communist world are only the more obvious instances of this newly emergent pattern. It is equally evident in every other part of the world, although the crises take different forms in different countries and in different types of

private organizations. In Canada the authority crisis is rooted in linguistic, cultural, and constitutional issues as Quebec seeks to secede
or otherwise redefine its relationship to the central government, an effort that in turn has fostered the emergence of demands for rights by
women, new ethnic groups, and indigenous peoples (and subsequent
legislation on these issues). In France the devolution of authority was
legally sanctioned through legislation that privatized several governmental activities and relocated authority away from Paris and toward
greater jurisdiction for the provinces. In China the provinces enjoy a
wider jurisdiction by, in effect, ignoring or defying Beijing. In the former Yugoslavia the crisis led to violence, civil war, and ultimately international war. In the crisis-ridden countries of Latin America the
challenge to traditional authority originates with insurgent movements, human rights, and the drug trade. In Japan and Mexico the
decades-long predominance of a single party has come to an end.
And in those parts of the world where the shift to performance criteria of legitimacy has not resulted in the relocation of authority—such
as the United States, Israel, Argentina, the Philippines, and South
Korea—uneasy stalemates prevail in the policy-making process as
governments have proven incapable of bridging societal divisions
sufficiently to undertake the decisive actions necessary to address
and resolve intractable problems. Indeed, in the United States the
government twice in late 1995 was forced to close down because of an
inability to agree on a budget for the next year.

Nor is the global authority crisis confined to states and governments. It is also manifest in subnational jurisdictions, international organizations, and nongovernmental transnational entities. Indeed, in
some cases the crises unfold simultaneously at different levels: Just as
the issue of Quebec's place in Canada became paramount, for example, so did the Mohawks in Quebec press for their own autonomy.
Similarly, just as Moldavia rejected Moscow's authority, so did several ethnic groups within Moldavia seek to establish their own autonomy by rejecting Moldavia's authority. And, to cite but a few conspicuous examples of crises in international and transnational
organizations, the United Nations Educational, Scientific, and Cultural Organization (UNESCO), the Palestine Liberation Organization
(PLO), and the Catholic Church have all experienced decentralizing
dynamics that are at least partly rooted in the replacement of traditional with performance criteria of legitimacy.

The relocating of authority precipitated by challenges to states and governments at the national level occurs in several directions, depending in good part on the scope of the enterprises people perceive as more receptive to their concerns and thus more capable of meeting their increased preoccupation with the adequacy of performances. In many instances this process has involved "downward" relocation toward subnational groups—toward ethnic minorities, local governments, single-issue organizations, religious and linguistic groupings, political factions, trade unions, and the like. In some instances the relocating process has moved in the opposite direction toward more encompassing collectivities that transcend national boundaries. The beneficiaries of this "upward" relocation of authority range from supranational organizations like the European Union to intergovernmental organizations like the International Labor Organization, from nongovernmental organizations like Greenpeace to professional groups such as Medecins sans Frontiers, from multinational corporations like IBM to inchoate social movements that join together environmentalists or women in different countries, from informal international regimes like those active in different industries to formal associations of political parties like those that share conservative or socialist ideologies—to mention but a few types of larger-than-national entities that have become the focus of legitimacy sentiments. Needless to say, these multiple directions in which authority is being relocated serve to reinforce the tensions between the centralizing and decentralizing dynamics that underlie the turbulence presently at work in world politics.

Associated with the crises that have overcome the macro-micro parameter is an undermining of the principle of national sovereignty. To challenge the authority of the state and to then redirect legitimacy sentiments toward supranational or subnational collectivities is to begin to deny that the state has the ultimate decisional power, including the right to resort to force. Since authority is structurally layered such that many levels of authority may have autonomy within their jurisdictions without also possessing sovereign powers, there is no obvious relationship between the location of authority and sovereignty. Nevertheless, trends toward the relocation of authority are bound to contribute to the erosion of sovereignty. If a state is thwarted in its efforts to mobilize effective armed forces, then its sovereignty is hardly a conspicuous feature of its existence as an independent collectivity. If a state cannot prevent outside actors from calling attention to its human rights record and thereby intervening on behalf of political prisoners, then the reach of its sovereignty is certainly reduced.[8]

The Macro Parameter: A Bifurcation of Global Structures

For more than three centuries the overall structure of world politics has been founded on an anarchic system of sovereign nation-states that did not have to answer to any higher authority and that managed their conflicts through accommodation or war. States were not the only actors on the world stage, but traditionally they were the dominant collectivities who set the rules by which the others had to live. The resulting state-centric world evolved its own hierarchy based on the way in which military, economic, and political power was distributed. Depending on how many states had the greatest concentration of power, at different historical moments the overall system was varyingly marked by hegemonic, bipolar, or multipolar structures.

From the perspective of the postinternational paradigm, however, the state-centric world is no longer predominant. Due to the skill revolution, the worldwide spread of authority crises, and several other sources of turbulence (noted below), it has undergone bifurcation into two increasingly autonomous worlds. Alongside the traditional world of states, a complex multi-centric world of diverse actors has emerged, replete with structures, processes, and decision rules of its own. The sovereignty-free actors (SFAs) of the multi-centric world include multinational corporations, ethnic minorities, subnational governments and bureaucracies, professional societies, political parties, transnational organizations, and the like. Individually, and sometimes jointly, they compete, conflict, cooperate, or otherwise interact with the sovereignty-bound actors (SBAs) of the state-centric world.[9] Table 4.2 delineates the main differences between the multi-centric and state-centric worlds.

Unlike the state-centric world, where most interactions involve events that unfold reciprocally and bilaterally between SBAs, the multi-centric world entails sequences of action that take the form of cascades, of fast-moving flows of action that not only precipitate reactions on the part of their immediate targets but that also stimulate

TABLE 4.2   Structure and Process in the Two Worlds of World Politics

	State-centric World	Multi-centric World
Number of essential actors	Fewer than 200	Hundreds of thousands
Prime dilemma of actors	Security	Autonomy
Principal goals of actors	Preservation of territorial integrity and physical security	Increase in world market shares and maintenance of integration of subsystems
Ultimate resort for realizing goals	Armed force	Withholding of cooperation or compliance
Normative priorities	Processes, especially those that preserve sovereignty and the rule of law	Outcomes, especially those that expand human rights, justice, and wealth
Modes of collaboration	Formal alliances whenever possible	Temporary coalitions
Scope of agenda	Limited	Unlimited
Rules governing interactions among actors	Diplomatic practices	Ad hoc, situational
Distribution of power among actors	Hierarchical by amount of power	Relative equality as far as initiating action is concerned
Interaction patterns among actors	Symmetrical	Asymmetrical
Locus of leadership	Great powers	Innovative actors with extensive resources
Institutionalization	Well established	Emergent
Susceptibility to change	Relatively low	Relatively high
Control over outcomes	Concentrated	Diffused
Bases of decisional structures	Formal authority, law	Various types of authority, effective leadership

Source: James N. Rosenau, *Turbulence in World Politics: A Theory of Change and Continuity* (Princeton: Princeton University Press, 1990), p. 250.

new actions on the part of as many SFAs and SBAs as happen to get caught up in the causal networks that crisscross the two worlds of world politics. Cascades, in other words, are the processes whereby the energies of parametric change are sustained and carried through the global system. That the course of cascades can vary from one system or situation to another is amply illustrated in Tables 4.3 and 4.4. Here a sample of decision rules that SFAs and SBAs follow in their in-

TABLE 4.3   Some Decision Rules Underlying the Conduct of Sovereignty-Bound Actors (SBAs) in the Multi-Centric World

1. States yield jurisdiction, fully or partially, to transnational sovereignty-free actors when

    a. governments in a conflict situation are paralyzed by prior commitments and sovereignty-free actors may be able to break the stalemate;
    b. the initiatives of private actors or transnational collectivities do not intrude upon prior commitments and may yield desirable results;
    c. there is merit in a new course of action, but a public commitment to it prior to a demonstration of its merit runs the risk of public opposition;
    d. an issue has acquired such extensive momentum in a particular direction that to attempt to curb the involvement of multi-centric actors is to risk unacceptable consequences in other policy areas.

2. States allow domestic demands to take precedence over external requirements when

    a. the domestic economy stagnates;
    b. a major subsystem becomes agitated;
    c. domestic opinion coalesces and aggregates around a specific perspective;
    d. internal divisiveness and strife seriously threaten governmental effectiveness.

3. States respond to or seek out relations with sovereignty-free collectivities abroad when

    a. they seek to bring pressure on governments abroad and the collectivities are seen as having potential influence on the issues involved;
    b. they are under pressure to do so from domestic groups at home;
    c. they perceive the foreign actors as helpful in building a policy consensus at home;
    d. they seek to find and promote their shares of foreign markets.

4. States coordinate both with other states and with sovereignty-free actors abroad when

    a. sudden crises or disasters occur in the world economy, the physical universe, or the social world that bear immediately upon the welfare of private groups in several countries.

5. States coordinate with other states as a means of moving more freely in the multi-centric world when

    a. their governments agree on a course to follow, but one or more are severely constrained by the opposition of domestic groups;
    b. transnational interactions among sovereignty-free actors begin to impinge upon the stability of two or more governments.

6. States avoid contacts in the multi-centric world when

    a. their involvement would catch them up in cascades that run counter to their values and policies;
    b. to do so would be to set precedents for future contacts deemed risky.

7. States initiate covert policies and actions when

    a. desired outcomes of international situations are not amenable to action under the norms of the multi-centric system;
    b. private groups or individuals have goals or resources that cannot be mobilized through conventional diplomatic channels or accepted practice in the multi-centric world.

Source: James N. Rosenau, *Turbulence in World Politics: A Theory of Change and Continuity* (Princeton: Princeton University Press, 1990), p. 306.

TABLE 4.4   Some Decision Rules Underlying the Conduct of Sovereignty-Free Actors (SFAs) in the State-Centric World

1. SFAs seek to enhance their relations with states by

    a. being quick to defend the legitimacy of their organizational status and the worthiness of the activities and values from which their existence derives;
    b. avoiding a reputation as an ineffective or unreliable transnational actor;
    c. demonstrating as often as possible a capacity to act independently of the government in which their headquarters are located;
    d. expanding their memberships as widely as possible among citizens and organizations abroad and establishing local affiliates through whom those in other countries can work;
    e. seizing opportunities to intrude themselves into situations where their values and competence can be relevant to the course of events;
    f. maintaining a multiplicity of ties to other transnational actors in their own and related fields.

2. SFAs seek to enhance their internal coherence by

    a. proffering support, financial as well as moral where possible, to affiliates and counterparts abroad whenever the latter get embroiled in conflicts with their own governments or other adversaries;
    b. avoiding situations that may require their memberships to attach a higher priority to their transnational than their national loyalties;
    c. stressing their transnational ties and the benefits derived from them;
    d. resisting efforts by governments to narrow the scope of their activities.

3. SFAs seek to enhance their relationships with the state in which they have their main headquarters by

    a. establishing a multiplicity of links to states and counterparts abroad, thereby increasing the costs to the host state for any effort to curb their activities;
    b. publicizing the contributions their transnational activities make to the welfare of communities in the host state.

Source: James N. Rosenau, *Turbulence in World Politics: A Theory of Change and Continuity* (Princeton: Princeton University Press, 1990), p. 308.

teractions with each other are presented, and their diversity and range suggest the intensity that can ensue when actors in the two worlds have occasion to respond to each other.

In sum, although the bifurcation of world politics has not pushed states to the edge of the global stage, they are no longer the only key actors. They still form alliances and blocs that resemble the bipolar or multipolar structures of the past, but today they are also faced with the new task of coping with disparate rivals from another world as well as the challenges posed by counterparts in their own world. The macro parameter is thus perhaps most incisively described as sustaining the two worlds of world politics.

The Sources of Global Turbulence

Given a world with the new parametric values represented by the skill revolution, the relocation of authority, and the bifurcation of global structures, it is hardly surprising that politicians, publics, and pundits speak of a new global order. For it is a new order—not so much because the Cold War has ended or because a successful coalition was mobilized to oust Iraq from Kuwait, but because the fundamental underpinnings of world politics, the parameters that sustain it, have undergone transformation.

Thus far, however, the discussion has been more descriptive than explanatory. We have defined turbulence and indicated the sites at which its consequences are likely to be most extensive and enduring, but we have not accounted for the dynamics that underlie the parametric transformations. What drives the turbulence? This question needs to be clarified, at least briefly, if we are to compare and assess the turbulence, liberal, and realist paradigms.

Although a variety of factors have contributed to the onset of turbulence, several stand out as particularly salient and worthy of elaboration. As can be seen in the enumeration that follows, some of these sources are external to the processes of world politics and some are internal to them. That is, some of the sources are endogenous in the sense that they are inherent in the political processes, whereas others are exogenous in the sense that they derive from demographic, technological, economic, and cultural processes. Together the endogenous and exogenous sources go a long way toward explaining why what once seemed so anomalous now appears so patterned.

The Proliferation of Actors

Perhaps few facts about world politics are better known than those describing the huge increase in the human population since the end of World War II. Whereas the world's population was in excess of 2.5 billion in 1950, by 2000 the figure had reached 6 billion, and it continues to grow at a rapid rate. This demographic explosion lies at the heart of many of the world's problems and is also a continual source of the complexity and dynamism that has overtaken the parameters of the global system. Ever greater numbers of people have exerted pressure for technological innovations in a process that has brought about larger, more articulate, and increasingly unwieldy publics. These populations have contributed to the unmanageability of public affairs that has weakened states, stimulated the search for more responsive collectivities, and hastened the advent of paralyzing authority crises. And the sheer weight of numbers has created new and intractable public issues, of which famines and threats to the environment are only the more conspicuous examples.

But the proliferation of relevant actors is not confined to the huge growth in the number of individual citizens. No less important for present purposes is the vast increase in the number and types of collective actors whose leaders can clamber onto the global stage and act on behalf of their memberships. Indeed, this deepening density of the global system is due not so much to the unorganized complexity fostered by the population explosion as it is to the organized complexity consisting of millions of factions, associations, parties, organizations, movements, interest groups, and a host of other kinds of collectivities that share an aspiration to advance their welfare and a sensitivity to the ways in which a rapidly changing world may require them to network with each other.[10]

The dizzying increase in the density of actors that sustain world politics stems, of course, from a variety of sources. In part it is a product of the trend toward ever greater specialization that is the hallmark of industrial and postindustrial economies and the greater interdependence that they foster. In part, too, it is a consequence of widespread dissatisfaction with large-scale collectivities and the performance of existing authorities, a discontent that underlies the turn to less encompassing organizations that are more fully expressive of close-at-hand needs and wants. Relevant here also are the expanded analytic skills of citizens, which enable them to appreciate how they can join in collective actions that serve as avenues for expressing their discontent. Whatever the reasons for the proliferation of collective actors, however, their sheer number has been a prime stimulus to the evolution of new loci of authority in the multi-centric world[11] and to the authority crises that have wracked the state-centric world.

Although on a lesser scale, the state-centric world has also undergone substantial enlargement, with the number of member states in the U.N. having more than tripled since its inception in 1945. Indeed, this growth has contributed to the exponential increase of actors in the multi-centric world, since each new state carved out of the former colonial empires spawned its own array of nongovernmental actors who contribute to the formation of new transnational networks. The organized complexity and deepening density of the global system, in other words, has derived from formal state-making dynamics as well as the multiplication of activities within societies.

The Impact of Dynamic Technologies

The technological explosion since World War II is no less impressive than its demographic counterpart. In a wide number of fields, from agriculture to transportation, from communications to medicine, from biogenetics to artificial intelligence, huge leaps have been made in humankind's ability to cope with the laws of nature. As a result, geographic distances have been shortened, social distances narrowed, and economic barriers circumvented. The world gets smaller and smaller as its peoples become more and more interdependent, processes that have had enormous consequences for the skills of individuals, their relations with higher authorities, and the macro structures through which their affairs are (or are not) managed. It is highly doubtful, in short, whether world politics would have been overtaken by turbulence had major technologies not exploded in the past forty years.

Two of these explosions, the nuclear and communications revolutions, stand out as especially relevant to the complexity and dynamism that have inundated the three prime parameters. The extraordinary advances in military weaponry subsequent to World War II, marked by nuclear warheads and the rocketry to deliver them, imposed a context on the conduct of world affairs that, in effect, increasingly inhibited recourse to military action and reduced the probability of a major global war. The nuclear revolution thus had the ironic consequence of depriving states of one of their prime instruments for pursuing and defending their interests. To be sure, the arms race and nuclear proliferation (see Chapter 6) infused world affairs with a high degree of volatility that often made them seem very fragile indeed. Even as the arms race emphasized the extraordinary capacities several states had acquired, however, so did it point up the limits of state action and thereby open the door for challenges to the authority of states. It is no accident that a series of transnational, large-scale, and powerful social movements—in the realms of peace, ecology, and women's rights—acquired momentum during the same period as states added substantially to their nuclear arsenals. Greenpeace, a major nongovernmental actor in the multi-centric world, for example, reflects the dual concern with war and the environment.

The communications revolution is hardly less central as a source of global turbulence. The rapidity and clarity with which ideas and information now circulate through television, VCRs, computer networks, fax machines, satellite hook-ups, fiber-optic telephone circuits, and many other microelectronic devices have rendered national boundaries ever more porous and world politics ever more vulnerable to cascading demands. Events that once took weeks and months to unfold now develop within days and hours. Financial transactions that once were mired in long delays can now be consummated in seconds. Diplomats, adversaries, military commanders, and publics who once had to wait long periods before reaching conclusions are now able to act decisively. Today the whole world, its leaders and its citizenries, instantaneously share the same pictures and descriptions, albeit not necessarily the same understandings, of what is transpiring in any situation.[12]

Examples of the cascading effects of the communications revolution abound. Most conspicuous perhaps is the impact of the Cable News Network (CNN), which is said to be on and continuously watched in every embassy and every foreign office of every country in the world and which, during the Gulf War, served as the basis for diplomatic and military action on both sides of the conflict.[13] Hardly less telling is the example of the French journal *Actuel,* which was so upset by the crackdown in Tiananmen Square that, having compiled a mock edition of the *People's Daily* that contained numerous accounts that the Chinese leadership did not want their people to read, sent it to every fax machine in China in the fall of 1989.[14] In a like manner, Chinese dissidents outside China have been sending articles on human rights and other issues via the Internet to China in a weekly newsletter that went to more than 250,000 addresses in 1998,[15] just as more recently the Serbs and Albanian Kosovars sought to stay in touch with the outside world through e-mail during the war in that troubled part of the world. Or consider the explosive implications of the fact that 5 percent of Brazil's households had television receiving sets when its 1960 presidential election was held and that this figure had swollen to 72 percent at the time of the next presidential contest in 1989.

Given the magnitude of these communications dynamics, it is hardly surprising that people everywhere have become more analytically, emotionally, and imaginatively skillful, more ready to challenge authority, and more capable of engaging in collective actions that press their demands. Their information may be skewed and their understanding of the stakes at risk in situations may be loaded with bias, but the stimuli to action are now ever present. Today individuals can literally see the aggregation of demands—that is, the coming together of publics and the acquiescence of governments—and how the participation of their counterparts elsewhere can have meaningful consequences. Likewise, the availability of high-tech communications equipment has enabled leaders in the public and private sectors to turn quickly to their memberships and mobilize them in support of their immediate goals in the multi- and state-centric worlds.[16]

The Globalization of National Economies

If the communications revolution has been a prime stimulus of the tendencies toward decentralization through the empowering of citizens and subnational groups, the dynamics at work in the realm of economics are equally powerful as sources of centralizing tendencies. Starting in the technologically most advanced sectors of the global economy, and following the sudden increase in oil prices that prompted the economic crisis of 1973–1974, a new kind of production organization geared to limited orders for a variety of specialized markets began to replace the large plants that produced standardized goods. Consequently, the products of numerous semi-skilled workers in big plants were no longer competitive with the outputs of a large number of small units that could be tailored to shifting demands, and business became concerned about restructuring capital so as to be more effective in world markets. As capital became increasingly internationalized, so did groups of producers and plants in different territorial jurisdictions become linked in order to supply markets in many countries, all of which fostered and sustained a financial system global in scope and centered in major cities such as New York, Tokyo, and London.

In short, capital, production, labor, and markets have all been globalized to the point where financiers, entrepreneurs, workers, and consumers are now deeply enmeshed in networks of the world economy that have superseded the traditional political jurisdictions of national scope. Such a transformation was bound to have an impact upon the established parameters of world politics. Among other things, it served to loosen the ties of producers to their states and workers to their firms, to expand the horizons within which citizens pondered their self-interests, and to foster the formation of transnational organizations that could operate on a global scale to protect and advance the economic interests of their members. The rapid growth and maturation of the multi-centric world can in good part be traced to the extraordinary dynamism and expansion of the global economy. And so can the weakening of the state, which is no longer the manager of the national economy and has become, instead, an instrument for adjusting the national economy to the exigencies of an expanding world economy. Of course, as will be seen in the account of the Asian financial crisis presented in Chapter 6, the globalization of national economies has increased their vulnerabilities as well as their opportunities.

The Advent of Interdependence Issues

The evolution of the world economy is not the only source of centralizing tendencies at work in global life. There are also a number of new, transnational problems that are crowding high on the world's agenda and forcing the globalization of certain kinds of issues. Whereas the political agenda used to consist of issues that governments could cope with on their own or through interstate bargaining, conventional issues are now being joined by challenges that by their very nature do not fall exclusively within the jurisdiction of states and their diplomatic institutions. Six current challenges are illustrative: environmental pollution, currency crises, the drug trade, terrorism, AIDS, and the flow of refugees. Each of these issues embraces processes that involve participation by large numbers of citizens and that inherently and inescapably transgress national boundaries—following the explosion of the nuclear plant at Chernobyl, for example, the winds carried the pollution into many countries and intruded upon many lives—thus making it impossible for governments to treat them as domestic problems or contain them within conventional diplomatic channels.

Since these challenges are essentially the product of dynamic technologies and the shrinking social and geographic distances that separate peoples, they can appropriately be called "interdependence" issues. And, given their origins and scope, they can also be regarded as important centralizing dynamics in the sense that they impel cooperation on a transnational scale. All six issues, for instance, are the focus of either transnational social movements or ad hoc international institutions forged to ameliorate, if not to resolve, the boundary-crossing problems they have created. To be sure, such issues may originate in local settings that are addressed by local or state authorities, but the fact that their consequences are global in scope means that transnational authorities have to address them as well. The World Health Organization (WHO), for example, is a key actor in the struggle to limit and reduce the incidence of AIDS throughout the world.

The advent of interdependence issues has contributed to the present era of turbulence in world politics in several ways. First, as in the case of the economic changes, such issues have given citizens pause about their states as the ultimate problem solvers, and in the case of those who join social movements, the issues have reoriented people to ponder a restructuring of their loyalties. Equally important, given their diffuse, boundary-crossing structure, these types of issues are spawning a whole range of transnational associations that are furthering the density of the multi-centric world and, as a result, are likely to serve as additional challenges to the authority of states.

The Weakening of States and the Restructuring of Loyalties

Before noting the ways in which states have suffered a loss in their authority, we must stress that we are referring to a relative and not an absolute loss. Postinternationalists do not view states as becoming peripheral to global affairs. On the contrary, states are seen as continuing to maintain their world—as forming alliances and seeking to balance power and otherwise enhancing their international system and infusing it with vitality and a capacity for adapting to change. More than that, states have been and continue to be a source of the turbulent changes that are at work. After all, it was the state-centric, not the multi-centric, world that created multilateral organizations such as the United Nations, that developed the arrangements through which the nuclear revolution has been contained, that responded to the demands for decolonization in such a way as to produce the hierarchi-

cal arrangements that have enabled the industrial countries to dominate those in the Third World and that framed the debate over the distribution of the world's resources—to mention only a few of the more
obvious ways in which states have shaped and still shape the ongoing realities of world politics. To discern a decline in the capacity of
states, therefore, is not to suggest or in any way imply that they are no
longer relevant actors on the world stage.

At the same time, however, it is just as erroneous to treat states as
constants as it is to view the skills of citizens as invulnerable to
change. States are not eternal verities; they are as susceptible to variability as any other social system, and thus the possibility exists that
they could suffer a decline of sovereignty as well as an erosion of their
ability to address problems, much less of their ability to come up with
satisfactory solutions to them.[17]

Viewed from the perspective of vulnerabilities, the growing density
of populations, the expanding complexity of the organized segments
of society, the globalization of national economies, the relentless pressure of technological innovations, the challenge of subgroups intent
upon achieving greater autonomy, and the endless array of other intractable problems that form the modern political agenda, it seems
evident that world politics have cumulated to a severity of circumstances that lessens the capacity of states to be decisive and effective.
And added to these difficulties is the fact that citizenries, through the
microelectronic revolution, are continuously exposed to scenes of authority crises around the world—scenes that are bound to give rise to
doubts and demands in even the most stable of polities and thus to
foment a greater readiness to question the legitimacy of governmental policies.[18]

Accordingly, although states may not be about to exit from the political stage, and they may even continue to occupy the center of the
stage, they do seem likely to become increasingly vulnerable and im-
potent. And as such, as ineffective managers of their own affairs, they
will also serve as stimuli to turbulence in world politics. Their difficulties in responding to local and global challenges will prompt more
autonomy in the multi-centric world as more skillful citizens demand
more effective performances from their leaders and thus further
weaken the capacity of states to respond to problems.

But this argument for diminished state competence is subtle and
depends on intangible processes for which solid indicators are not

easily developed. Perhaps most notable in this regard are subtle shifts in loyalties that accompany the globalization of national economies, the decentralizing tendencies toward subgroup autonomy, and the emergence of performance criteria of legitimacy. Such circumstances seem bound to affect loyalties to the state. That is, as transnational and subnational actors in the multi-centric world become increasingly active and effective, as they demonstrate a capacity to deal with problems that states have found intractable or beyond their competence, citizens will begin to look elsewhere than the national capital for assistance. Examples abound. Even prior to the dissolution of the Soviet Union, for instance, citizens had to make difficult choices between their long-standing orientations toward Moscow and the "downward" pull of the particular republics or ethnic minorities of which they were also members. With Moscow unable to halt and reverse a steep economic decline, and with subnational attachments being thereby heightened, individuals all over that troubled land had—and are still having—to face questions about distant attachments that they have long taken for granted. Bankers in Russia, for instance, had to confront a difficult situation in 1990 when the republic's parliament voted to cut its share of the Soviet budget: Normally the taxes for the Soviet Union were deposited in the republic banks and transferred by them to the coffers of the central government, but in this instance the bankers were told not to transfer the full amounts despite pressure from the Kremlin to do so.

It would be a mistake, however, to regard the loyalty problem as confined to multiethnic systems. Relatively homogeneous societies are beset with the same dilemma. Consider the situation of Norway, where the people have a deep emotional and historical attachment to the idea of independence: In 1972 they voted, by a small margin, not to join the European Community (EC), but by 1990 they were faced with the possibility of being the only West European country outside the EC as Sweden, Austria, Finland, and even Switzerland either applied for membership or indicated a readiness to forego their traditional neutrality and seek admission to the EC. Norwegian loyalties, in other words, were being pulled in an "upward" direction as the economic advantages of membership in a supranational organization increasingly seem to outweigh the psychologically satisfying and historically demonstrated virtues of being a member of an autonomous national community.[19] When the decisive vote was held in 1994, however, the upward pull faltered and the Norwegians became, by a vote of 53 to 47 percent, the only eligible nation to reject membership in the European Union.[20] Or ponder the unfolding malaise in France, where a mood of pessimism is widespread and where "many Frenchmen have doubts about the capacity of their country to meet successfully the dangers, opportunities, and uncertainties which the future holds." Put even more succinctly, France is presently marked by a pervasive impression that "something is breaking apart, that society is decomposing," and that, indeed, "all the institutions built over the past 40 years are in crisis and are therefore incapable of responding."[21]

This is not to say that traditional national loyalties are being widely abandoned. Plainly, such attachments do not suddenly collapse. Rather, it is only to take note of subtle processes whereby what was once well established and beyond question is now problematic and undergoing change. Even more relevant, it seems reasonable to presume that the diminished competence of states to act decisively, combined with the processes of loyalty transformation, serves as a significant source of the dynamics that are rendering more complex each of the three prime parameters of world politics. Clearly, the viability of the multi-centric world, the persistence of authority crises, and the analytic skills of individuals are all intensified the more the capabilities of states decline and the more the loyalties of citizens become problematic.

Subgroupism

Since there is a widespread inclination to refer loosely to "nationalism" as a source of the turbulent state of world politics, it is perhaps useful to be more precise about the collective nature of those decentralizing tendencies wherein individuals and groups feel readier to challenge authority and reorient their loyalties. As previously noted, the authority crises that result from such challenges can be either of an "upward" or a "downward" kind, depending on whether the aspiration is to relocate authority in more or less encompassing jurisdictions than those that operate at the national level. In a number of instances of both kinds of relocation, the motivation that sustains the change is not so deeply emotional as to qualify as an "ism." The creation of subnational administrative divisions, for example, can stem from detached efforts to rationalize the work of a governmental agency or private organization, and the process of implementing the decentralized arrangements can occur in the context of reasoned dialogue and calm decisionmaking. Often, however, intense concerns and powerful attachments—feelings and commitments strong enough to justify using terms like "transnationalism," "supranationalism," or "internationalism"—can accompany the press for new arrangements. The downward relocations marked by comparable intensities are perhaps best labeled by the generic term "subgroupism."

The postinternational paradigm posits subgroupism as arising out of those deep affinities that people develop toward the close-at-hand associations, organizations, and subcultures with which they have been historically, professionally, economically, socially, or politically linked and to which they attach their highest priorities. Subgroupism values the in-group over the out-group, sometimes treating the two as adversaries and sometimes positing them as susceptible to extensive cooperation. Subgroupism can derive from and be sustained by a variety of sources, not the least being disappointment in—and alienation from—the performances of the whole system in which the subgroup is located. Most of all perhaps, its intensities are the product of long-standing historical roots that span generations and get reinforced by an accumulated lore surrounding past events in which the subgroup survived trying circumstances.

That subgroupism can be deeply implanted in the consciousness of peoples is manifestly apparent in the resurfacing of strong ethnic identities throughout Eastern Europe and the former Soviet Union when, after decades, the authoritarian domination of Communist parties came to an end. In those cases, the subgroups were historic nations and the accompanying feelings can thus be readily regarded as expressions of nationalism. Not all, or even a preponderance, of decentralizing tendencies attach to nations, however. Governmental subdivisions, political parties, labor unions, professional societies, and a host of other types of subgroups can also evoke intense attachments, and it would grossly understate the relevance of the decentralizing tendencies at work in world politics to ignore these other forms of close-at-hand ties. Accordingly, it seems preferable to regard the emotional dimensions of generic decentralizing tendencies as those of subgroupism and to reserve the concept of nationalism for those subgroup expressions that revolve around nations and feelings of ethnicity.

The Mobility Upheaval

Hardly less central as a transformative dynamic underlying the persistence of global turbulence is the vast movement of people around the world. Using the notion of mobility in the broadest possible sense so as to include any movement for any length of time and for any purpose—from business to professional travel, from tourism to terrorism, from political asylum to the search for jobs, from legal to illegal migration—the boundary-spanning activities of people in recent decades have been so astounding as to justify regarding them as a veritable upheaval. Statistics for every form of travel depict sharp and continuous growth, and the trend shows no sign of letting up.[22] Not only is tourism among the world's largest industries, but the data on business travel also portray a continuing and growing flow of people around the world. And then there are the migratory flows that are driven largely by a search for employment and involve mostly people from the developing world moving into the industrial and financial centers of the developed world. All of these flows have been facilitated by transportation technologies—particularly the jet aircraft—that have had and will continue to have a profound impact on diverse institutions throughout the world.

Among the numerous consequences of the mobility upheaval, perhaps the most significant are its deterritorializing impacts. Those who move across borders often, as well as those who move their belongings for a more permanent stay abroad, not only loosen their ties to the homeland of their birth, but they also serve as conduits for the transmission of values and practices back and forth from one culture to another—with the result that peoples' sense of attachment to a particular geographic space has diminished. And the spectacle of this diminution on a worldwide scale adds to the momentum with which deterritorialization has accelerated in recent years.

It should be noted, however, that deterritorialization also involves what might be called "reterritorialization"—those processes whereby migrants converge in neighborhoods, publish their own newspapers, maintain their own television programs, found their own churches, and open their own restaurants, thereby creating homes away from home, diasporas that through generational time become combinations of old and new homelands, subcultures in increasingly multicultural societies. In other words, the mobility upheaval is marked by normative implications that are both good and bad. On the positive side are all the benefits that follow from people being exposed to new ways of thinking, new cultural premises, and alternative lifestyles as they move around the world. But on the negative side are the diverse ways in which the presence of travelers from abroad, especially those who do not return home, often pits subculture against subculture and poses questions as to the degree to which "foreigners" are tolerated.

The Spread of Poverty and the Third World

Underlying the bifurcation of world politics into state- and multi-centric worlds has been another split—between industrially developed and underdeveloped countries—that has also contributed substantially to the onset of turbulence. This regional split between the North and the South—known during the Cold War as the First and Third Worlds—is a gulf that seems destined to widen and sustain, even extend, the processes of turbulence: The terrible problems and thwarted aspirations of peoples in the South are not going to be ameliorated in the foreseeable future and will thus continue to roil global waters. Among other things, the diverse and numerous countries of the South have added to the complexity and dynamism of global structures; sharpened the performance criteria of legitimacy; enriched the skills of the underprivileged; hastened the transnationalization of economies, corporations, and social movements; limited the authority of northern states over their production facilities; intensified the flow of people from South to North; lengthened the list of interdependence issues; and strengthened the tendencies toward subgroupism.

The impact of the split fostered by the breakup of Europe's colonial empires is perhaps most obvious with respect to global structures. Not only did decolonization result in the proliferation of actors in the state-centric world, but it also had the consequence of rigidifying the degree of hierarchy in that world. The process whereby ever greater power accompanied the emergence of industrial states in the North was not matched when statehood came to Africa and Asia. The newly established states of the South acquired sovereignty and international recognition even though they lacked the internal resources and consensual foundations to provide for their own development, a circumstance that led one astute observer to call them "quasi-states"[23] and led the states themselves into a deep resentment over their depen-

dence on the industrialized world for trade, technology, and many of
the other prerequisites necessary to fulfill their desire for industrial
development. Their sovereignty, in effect, is "negative" in that it protects them against outside interference but does not empower them to
address their problems successfully.[24] The result has been a pervasive
global pattern in which the industrial world has continued to prosper
while Africa, Latin America, and parts of Asia have languished in a
system endlessly reinforcing the inequities underlying the hierarchical structures of world politics.

In addition, resentments in the developing world, the legitimacy
problems of quasi-states, and their attempts to use their majority in
the General Assembly to alter the U.N.'s agenda and priorities have
extended and deepened the global authority crisis. Indeed, the U.N.
has become a major site of the authority crisis as the South has challenged the legitimacy of its actions and as the North, fearful of dominance by the sheer number of developing countries, has also questioned its legitimacy by periodically failing to meet its financial
obligations to the U.N.

Even as the developing countries have rigidified the hierarchical
structure of the state-centric world, so have they added to the decentralizing tendencies in the multi-centric world. Composed of tribes
and ethnic groups artificially brought together under state banners by
First World decolonizers, besieged by multinational corporations
seeking to extend their operations and markets, and plagued with internal divisions and massive socioeconomic problems, Third World
countries have added greatly to the breadth and depth of the multi-
centric world. Their quasi-sovereignty keeps them active in the state
system, but the multi-centric world has been hospitable to their frag-
menting dynamics and thereby has contributed to the process
wherein subgroup networks are proliferating.

Conclusion

Given the various sources that are fostering and sustaining the dynamic transformations of the basic parameters subsumed by the turbulence model, the question arises as to where world politics may be
heading in the foreseeable future. Is the bifurcation of global structures likely to continue? Will it end because states will regain their
earlier capabilities and effectiveness? Or might these structures frag-

ment further as the multi-centric world becomes even more central to the course of events? The questions cannot be answered with certainty under present circumstances, but at the same time postinternationalists see no reason to believe that the skill revolution is soon to peter out or that the authority crises are likely to diminish in frequency and intensity. Hence the probabilities seem high that the present bifurcated structures will endure and become more deeply seated with the passage of time. If one subscribes to the postinternational model, one can be assured that more turbulence will, for better or worse, pervade the conduct of world affairs.[25]

5

Realism, Liberalism, and Postinternationalism Compared

It does not take a close reading of the three previous chapters to appreciate that one's understanding of world politics is highly dependent on the paradigm one employs to interpret the course of events. This is a profound insight. It highlights, as already noted, that the facts do not speak for themselves, that world affairs are not self-evident, that what we know depends on how we go about organizing all the events and trends to which we attach significance. Moreover, the solutions designed to cope with global challenges are likely to be as sound as one's grasp of how and why world politics unfold as they do.

It follows that both citizens and policymakers will be best equipped to assess and respond to the course of events when they have been explicit about the premises that underlie their understandings of international relations. Thus, it is useful to undertake a comparison of the realist, liberal, and postinternational paradigms, identifying both their differences and similarities, in order to demonstrate how the same events could have diverse meanings and implications for different observers. Such is the task of this chapter: to contrast the realist, liberal, and turbulence paradigms without taking a stand as to which of the three approaches is "best." The reader must weigh the validity of the views for himself or herself. There is no "right" paradigm, and we have sought not to load the analysis in favor of any of them. We care only that readers be sufficiently aware of the differences between the three paradigms to be able to choose between them. The reasons for preferring one of them—or some variant or combination of them—may vary greatly from reader to reader, but in the end readers will have a preference, and it is important to be conscious of what that preference is.

The first column of Table 5.1 sets forth the dimensions along which the three paradigms may be contrasted. By reading down the other three columns one can discern the coherence of each paradigm, and by reading across the rows one can sense the points at which the realist, liberal, and turbulence models are similar or different. A quick perusal in this fashion affirms the central thrust of the ensuing discussion, namely, that the differences between the three paradigms are far more pervasive and significant than the similarities.

The Appeal of Theory

The first three rows of Table 5.1 sum up the overall aspects of each paradigm that their adherents find so appealing. Although realism and liberalism are elegant theories because they are founded on a few simple and familiar premises that can be readily grasped and widely applied, the postinternational model can hardly be called elegant, inasmuch as it is based on several interrelated premises that its supporters find compelling precisely because they see the world as marked by high degrees of complexity. As previously noted, postinternationalists aspire to elegant theory through a few universal rules that govern world affairs, but they have yet to figure out how to accomplish this goal without abandoning the conviction that ambiguities and contradictions are crucial and pervasive aspects of the course of events.

Units of Action

Although none of the three paradigms classify the units of action on which their model is founded, the differences between them can be readily inferred from the foci of their concerns. Being organized around only a few basic premises and the actions of states, realists tend to posit discrete events as their basic unit of analysis. The concern of liberal theorists with societal structures leads them to treat issues as the essential analytic units. The more complex, interdependent world posited by postinternationalists, on the other hand,

TABLE 5.1 Comparison of the Realist, Liberal, and Postinternationalist
Paradigms

	Realist Model	*Liberal Model*	*Postinternationalist Model*
Appeal of theory	Simplicity	Familiarity	Complexity
Number of organizing premises	Few	Few	Several
Paradigmatic complexity	Low	Low	High
Units of action	Events	Issues	Cascades
Global structures	Anarchical interstate system	Diverse institutions	Bifurcation of state-centric and multi-centric worlds
State sovereignty	Unchanging	Eroding	Eroding
State structures	Unitary actors	Pluralistic	Fragmented
Societal structures	Irrelevant	Central	Central
Role of citizens	Irrelevant	Limited	Central
Concerns of collectivities	Security dilemma	Authority dilemma	Autonomy dilemma
Competitive orientation	Relative gains	Absolute gains	Absolute gains
Conceptions of power	Primarily military	Knowledge and access	Multiple sources
Use of force	Always possible	Supplemental	Inhibited
Domestic-foreign boundaries	Firm	Porous	Porous
Technology and media of communications	Facilitate state controls	Differentiate access to state structures	Diminish state controls
Law	Exclusionary	Inclusionary	Inclusionary
Coalition formation	Alliances	Overlapping interest groups	Loose aggregations
State management of economy	Governments collaborate at summits	Restrain govern-ments through specialized NGOs	Collaboration between state- and multi-centric actors
State's role in protecting individuals from globalization	States should exercise control over trade and money to protect jobs	States should do nothing, as all will eventually benefit from free markets	States should provide safety net and protect those who suffer as globalization expands
Sensitivity to change	Low	Moderate	High

orients them toward sequences of interactions, or cascades, as the units around which their empirical inquiries are organized.

Global Structures

It is important to stress that in certain respects the realist, liberal, and turbulence paradigms overlap. All three posit an interstate system in which states possess sovereignty and are not formally responsible to a higher authority. In other words, none of them posits an overarching governmental body empowered to make authoritative decisions with which international actors must comply. In this sense, all three paradigms presume an anarchical global structure. To a large extent, however, this similarity is offset by a major structural difference: The realist paradigm allows only for the interstate system and presumes that it pervades and dominates the course of events, whereas the liberal model attaches importance to diverse international institutions (such as the IMF and the World Bank) and regimes as well as states. The postinternational paradigm goes even further and delineates a multi-centric system of sovereignty-free actors that exists independently of the interstate system and competes, conflicts, cooperates, or otherwise interacts with it. This bifurcation of world politics adds extensive layers of complexity to the anarchical structure. According to the postinternationalist, power and authority are much more dispersed and decentralized than is presumed by the realist, and, under these turbulent conditions, achieving coordinated policies designed to address and alleviate global problems is much more difficult and time consuming.

State Sovereignty

Although all three paradigms presume that states possess sovereignty, which accords them the exclusive right to employ coercive force at home and renders them free of higher authority abroad, they differ considerably on the extent to which the principles of sovereignty are carried out in practice. Realists presume that these principles remain intact, that states do not and will not knowingly accept any diminution in their sovereign rights as independent actors. Liberals and postinternationalists, in contrast, perceive a continuing erosion in the sovereignty of states. They argue not only that states have lost some control over the inviolability of their borders (as the discussion of the domestic-foreign distinction stresses below), but also that the language of diplomacy has witnessed states interpreting fewer and fewer situations as posing challenges to their sovereign privileges.

State Structures

The difference in the complexity of world politics posed by the three models is extended further by their respective conceptions of how states are constituted. In the realist model states are viewed as strong unitary actors, as so consensual or hierarchical that they speak with only one voice, that of the chiefs of state who occupy the highest positions of authority. Under the turbulence model, in contrast, states are conceived of as weak, fragmented, and undergoing authority crises, with the result that they speak with many voices, of which the chief of state is only one. Indeed, postinternationalists hold that, more often than not, it is unclear whether the official pronouncements of states are reliable guides to their future actions. Liberals fall somewhere between the realists and postinternationalists on the issue of state structures. Unlike the former, they see the state as an organized pattern of pluralism, which means a state can have different policies on given different issues. Unlike the latter, liberals do not think the plurality of voices must result in weak states, because democratic procedures generally organize the voices into patterned access to government policymaking.

Societal Structures

Given the presumption of states as unitary actors, the realist model accords little salience to the internal structures of societies. Realists view states as responding to political and economic challenges and circumstances arising out of the interstate system and, accordingly, it matters little to them what the histories, values, and social structures of any state may be. Both the liberal and the turbulence paradigms proceed from quite the opposite perspective. Since both presume that the policies of governments are shaped by a plurality of interests, they both accord considerable salience to societal structures. On the other hand, liberals and postinternationalists differ on the ways in which such structures play a central role. The former posit the plurality of interests as balanced and thus as sufficiently ordered to sustain continuity in the external behavior of states. But postinternationalists do not presume that the diverse interests are a balanced source of orderly and coherent conduct. They do not preclude consistent policies, but given the existence of aroused and active citizens, not to mention extensive subgroupism and weakened governmental authority, they perceive states as capable of external behavior that is very much a consequence of internal tensions and thus marked by variability and complexity.

Role of Citizens

It follows that the three paradigms adhere to very different, even exactly contrary, postures toward the role that citizens, both as individuals and as publics, play in world affairs. Inclined to confine causal power to the conduct of states, realists largely ignore individuals who do not occupy high government positions. Either they take publics for granted or they see them as easily manipulated and ever ready to acquiesce to the policies of their state's leaders. Liberals, in contrast, accord a limited role to citizens by stressing the various ways in which their diverse interests generate collective organizations that press a plurality of demands on public officials. Postinternationalists go even further in this regard. For them, individuals are central. Persuaded that a skill revolution is transforming how people relate to public issues, postinternationalists assume that citizens, their skills, and their orientations are consequential; that macro collectivities and institutions derive their sustenance from the individuals they embrace; and that therefore any significant transformation at the micro level is bound to find expression in the aggregated dynamics that give shape and direction to global life.

Concerns of Collectivities

Given its focus on international threats and challenges, the realism paradigm centers on the security dilemma. States are seen as ready to achieve territorial and economic security either through cooperation with other states or, if need be, through a readiness to go to war. Realists do not argue that military preparations are a constant or exclusive preoccupation of the leaders of states. They acknowledge that other policy goals are pursued and that, lately, some security threats—such as the availability of oil imports—have become increasingly economic in nature. At the same time they are also inclined to view war as the ultimate response to threats and thus believe that weapons stockpiles and the readiness of armed forces to enter combat are never far from the center of state concerns. For liberals, however, the concerns of states are viewed as marked by greater variability. For them, security dilemmas are no more crucial than those associated with the state's acquisition and maintenance of authority. Since the liberal paradigm posits states as weak in relation to the plurality of voices and interests demanding to be heard and heeded, state officials are continuously confronted with an erosion of their authority—not a usurpation of their authority, but an erosion in the sense that they are ever subject to yielding to, or at least compromising with, the powerful special interests that press claims upon them. Liberals accept that state leaders are not unmindful of the need for territorial integrity or of the existence of threats from foreign enemies, but their readiness to maintain military preparedness is located in a more encompassing context, one that promotes cooperation abroad as a means of serving and meeting domestic challenges to their authority. Because states are seen as faced with divisive subgroups and skeptical publics, they are, in other words, viewed by liberals as devoting as much energy to sustaining their internal strength as to maximizing their external capabilities.

In contrast to the thinking of realists and liberals, the main concerns of postinternationalists focus less on the security and authority of actors in the state-centric world and more on the autonomy of collectivities in the multi-centric world. Put differently, by positing a diversity of significant actors in the multi-centric world, the turbulence model extends well beyond the security dilemma. Whatever the bases of their organizations, the salient collectivities in the multi-centric world are conceived as concerned with maximizing their independence and that of their fellow sovereignty-free actors so that they can realize their aspirations without being hostage to the complexities that mark public affairs. To be sure, like states, the actors in the multi-centric world are ever ready to cooperate with like-minded counterparts, but this readiness does not extend to policies that might result in irremediable jeopardy to their autonomy.

Competitive Orientations

Whereas the realist paradigm posits states as preoccupied with other states not gaining at their expense—that is, with relative gains that do not diminish their power vis-à-vis their competitors—both the liberal and postinternational models focus on absolute gains, on actors moving toward their goals irrespective of what their competitors may be accomplishing. The latter two models focus on the competitive concerns of different sets of actors, but they share an inclination not to worry about whether any of the actors are improving their position in relation to each other. Liberalism concentrates on the absolute gains accruing to states as they cooperate with each other, and being sensitive to the needs of domestic interests, they assess a state's gains in terms of the benefits it secures for the corporations and other organizations that make the most intense demands on it. Postinternational theory, on the other hand, assesses the absolute gains achieved by actors in the multi-centric world as well as those in the state-centric world. The theory even allows for situations in which a state may not realize gains even though bargaining between sovereignty-free actors results in absolute movement toward their goals.

Conceptions of Power

The three paradigms differ considerably in what they regard as the crucial elements of power. Where realism stresses the military and tangible dimensions of power, liberalism and postinternationalism conceive of power more in terms of intangibles. For liberals the intangibles consist mainly of knowledge and money and the access that such resources accord to those actors who have them to advance and protect their interests. Postinternationalists have an even broader approach to the nature of power. For them, the intangibles also include such dimensions as the size and commitment of an organization's membership, the universality of its appeal, the skill of its leaders, and its reputation for keeping promises. Indeed, given the autonomy of its collectivities and the decentralized nature of its structures, the multi-centric world is seen less as an arena of power struggles than as a shifting set of locales in which coalitions are formed and reformed through subtle influence processes. Charts comparing countries by the number of their men in uniform, the size of their agricultural output, and the

output of their oil wells are commonplace in realist analyses of international politics, but similar diagrammatic displays are rare in liberal
and postinternational inquiries. Why? Because for both the latter models neither states nor collectivities rely so much on power bases to affect each other directly as they do on the indirect routes through which
they have access to attentive publics, markets, bureaucracies, and
other arenas where authority is diffuse and informal. Of course, realists also view states as concerned with influencing these arenas, but
mostly their policies and actions are seen as following direct routes to
the concentrated and formal centers of decisionmaking in other states.

Use of Force

Given different conceptions of power and sovereignty, it is hardly surprising that adherents of the three paradigms take quite different positions on the role of force in world politics. Realists posit that states
are always prepared to resort to force to protect or advance their interests. After all, states have the sovereign right to use coercion, and since
they are beholden to no higher authority, they must be ready to go to
war if their interests cannot be protected in any other way. Liberals
and postinternationalists do not deny that states work hard at maintaining their war-making potential and indicating a readiness to use it,
but they contend that the probability of states actually warring on
each other has declined. At the very least, liberal theorists are likely to
contend, states use force as supplemental to other, less violent means
of exercising power. Their postinternational counterparts are even
more dubious about the relevance of force in the present era. They perceive states as increasingly inhibited in their readiness to conduct war
against other states. The mounting inhibitions are seen as stemming
from an appreciation of the devastation that nuclear weapons could
wreak as well as from a realization that modern societies are too complex to be easily conquered. In addition, such analysts stress that
publics have become increasingly wary of situations involving battle
casualties and thus much less mobilizable for war-making purposes.

Domestic-Foreign Boundaries

Virtually by definition, the realist paradigm diverges widely from the
other two in how it views the boundaries that divide foreign and do-

mestic affairs. For those who subscribe to realism, the boundaries setting off states from their external environments are firm and immutable, guarded by troops, customs officers, tariff walls, and a host of other barriers. Leaders of states thus distinguish between challenges abroad and those at home, and their policymaking arrangements fully reflect this distinction. Thus, foreign and defense departments assume responsibility for the challenges from abroad—and for ensuring that the country responds as a unitary actor—and problems arising at home are handled by interior, labor, transportation, and other such departments.

For liberals and postinternationalists concerned with the dynamics at work in the multi-centric world, domestic-foreign boundaries are seen as sufficiently porous to enable a continuous flow of people, goods, money, and ideas to pass through them. Why? Because these collectivities, whether transnational corporations, ethnic minorities, scientific associations, political parties, religious organizations, or subgovernmental bureaucracies, derive much of their purpose and strength from their links and interactions with affiliates or counterparts abroad. Because such groups are not confined within national boundaries, the multi-centric system is in important respects a world without borders—or, more accurately, a world with borders that are traced by the autonomous reach of each of its diverse collectivities. Moreover, each collectivity has internal needs and problems but must also function in an external environment. This internal-external balance is far different from the domestic-foreign boundaries that crisscross the state-centric world. Among other things, it is a balance that is continuously shifting as the multi-centric collectivities expand or contract their goals, resources, and activities.

Technology and Media of Communications

Given the importance postinternationalists attach to citizens and their SFAs, it is hardly surprising that they are sensitive to the role that technology and the mass media of communications play in diminishing the centrality of states. Indeed, they tend to stress that neither the skill revolution nor many authority crises would have occurred without the world's new capacities for transmitting ideas and pictures speedily to all corners of the earth. Because they are not ready to accord significance to the flow of ideas and their impact on the orientations of publics, realists are not especially attentive to the dynamics of technology and widening channels of communications. If anything, realists are inclined to view these factors as facilitating the control of states and thus as reinforcing the dominance of the state-centric world. The liberal view of technology and communications media falls between the perspectives of the postinternationalists and realists. Liberals differentiate between those states that afford publics access to governmental policymaking and those that do not. If wealthy citizens have much better access to the media, however, the representational basis for the state's authority may erode.

Law

As realists see it, only relatively recently has the scope of international law broadened beyond a selected range of topics that were of particular interest to states. Historically, this range was confined mostly to issues of territory, recognition of other states, treaties, the initiation and conduct of war, and treatment of diplomats, foreign nationals, and dependent peoples (colonies). Not until the latter half of the nineteenth century did international law begin to include rules on trade and communications. In the twentieth century, other arenas—such as economics, labor standards, and the environment—were touched by international law. Essentially, realists contend, international law is what states agree it is and only states can use the system directly. Any protection of citizens (i.e., of citizens traveling or stationed abroad) is due to reciprocity between states. When violations occur, citizens' interests might be advanced by their respective countries on the grounds that their mistreatment constitutes an "insult" to the country of citizenship.

States are viewed as taking international law seriously, if only because it is one way to manage conflict. But realists note three characteristics of international law to further illustrate the integrity of their argument. First, as noted above, international law embraces only a limited number of topics. Second, by the nineteenth century states generally rejected claims of "justness" in formulating law and instead favored the positive acceptance of rules; in other words, states feel they are bound to abide by only those rules that they have explicitly agreed to (they want to sign on the dotted line, so to speak). Third, international law long excluded citizens, firms, and other organizations from direct access to these rules. This exclusionary perspective largely remains the case today. Unless a treaty specifically provides a citizen or nongovernmental organization "standing," only international organizations and states are subjects of public international law. Indeed, it took a 1949 advisory opinion by the International Court of Justice to give international organizations the right to bring a claim against a state. The decision (for the United Nations) was considered a landmark change and provoked a dissenting opinion by J. Hackworth, who argued, "There is no specific provision in the United Nations Charter, nor is there any provision in any other agreement conferring upon the United Nations authority to assume the role of a state."[1]

The strict boundary between domestic and international actions is very much present in the legal realm. National courts (called "municipal" under international law) will defer making a judgment on many topics until they have received guidance from the foreign office. In some cases, courts (in Anglo-American systems) have refused a case on the grounds that it is a political question beyond the competence of a national court.

In contrast, the liberal and postinternational paradigms posit international law as inclusionary. They emphasize four aspects of the law in world politics. First, there has been a vast growth of rule making by international organizations. Second, advocacy groups advance their aims through a proliferating set of legal strategies. The widely accepted land mine treaty, for example, can be readily attributed to the pressures exerted by advocacy groups. Third, many actors in world politics now couch their legal claims in language emphasizing an underlying normative base of "justness" and reason. This philosophical orientation, in essence, draws on natural rather than positive legal traditions. Last, citizens, firms, and other organizations are increasingly successful in gaining direct access to the rule making that has been traditionally left to states alone.

States may well set up international organizations, but once in place, these organizations often set the rules for states. Liberals and postinternationalists stress that one need not even turn to the most dramatic instance of this process, the European Union, which lies somewhere between an international organization and a territorial state. Rather, they note, one need only consider how the rules for civil air travel, trade, labor, and a host of other functional areas are deeply structured by international organizations. Obligations set out by international organizations often lead to changes inside states as new departments are created to meet the obligations. Viewed from a liberal or postinternational perspective, therefore, international rule making can serve as an important source of internal political change.

The same perspective, moreover, stresses that advocacy groups or networks—those clusters of activists "distinguishable largely by the centrality of principled ideas or values in motivating their formation"[2]—such as Amnesty International or Greenpeace now have sophisticated strategies for using domestic and international legal forums to advance their organizational interests. Human rights organizations in developing nations—although not yet as important as those in developed countries—exemplify this point. Human rights organizations take cases into national courts primarily to educate judges on international law regarding human rights. In the United States, they also lobby Congress to influence the shape of the law. In Europe, the European Court of Human Rights, although still closely tied to states, hears complaints. In many Latin American countries, grassroots groups of mothers formed in the 1980s to protest "disappearances"; human rights organizations from other countries often supplied information to these groups and carried their message to the world. A number of regional international organizations concerned with human rights now solicit reports from nongovernmental organizations (NGOs).

Claims on behalf of human rights, the environment, or economic justice (and the NGOs in these areas increasingly go into "alliance" with each other) often lie outside existing international treaty frameworks. As liberals and postinternationalists see it, however, such organizations also tend to threaten the authority of states in general by basing their claims on natural law, according to which there is a law beyond anything written that can be accessed to reason about social problems. The essence of the theory of natural law, one observer notes, is that "law was derived from justice."[3] By appealing to justice, actors in the multi-centric world can begin to challenge existing rules.

The fact that SFAs have increasingly gained access to the organizations used by states to solve problems highlights the important roles they can play in decisionmaking on global problems. As consultative NGOs to the United Nations and its specialized agencies, they may be actively consulted by U.N. members in their areas of expertise. At home, these same groups can pressure both for legal and policy changes. Thus, the liberal and postinternationalist concludes that subgroups are using a combination of legal strategies and newly won access to state and international organizations to form a complex web of legal processes and thus expand their influence in shaping world politics.

Coalition Formation

At times it is in the interests of a single actor to associate with others or to build a following. In the realist view, alliance between states is a solid basis for advancing interests when going it alone will not suffice. An alliance is a formal pact, usually concluded after lengthy negotiations, between two or more states that outlines a relationship between the contracting parties and is generally directed against specified actions by other states. States would prefer to pursue their interests by themselves, using solely their power base. Alliances are thus a second-best strategy. Generally, states use alliances to maintain the balance of power. Very powerful states, especially in bipolar structural situations, may weave a web of alliances, thereby creating a followership of states.

Viewed from a liberal or postinternational perspective, coalition processes are far less formal and much more spontaneous than the realist would concede. Indeed, sometimes the processes are virtually out of control as members join, bargain, defect, or use other unpredictable strategies. This informality derives, in other words, from the involvement of numerous groups and the participation of individual citizens, all of whom associate with the coalition for their own reasons and thus have varying degrees of commitment and may remain involved for as long or as short a time as they wish. Although liberals tend to view such coalitions as comprising overlapping interest groups, the identity of which varies from issue to issue, postinternationalists regard them as loose aggregations, only parts of which are mobilized into advocacy on particular issues. In other words, coalitions in the multi-centric world undergo continual transformations as issues come and go, whereas alliances in the state-centric world are ordinarily enduring and fixed features of the relationships among their members.

States' Management of the Global Economy

The globalization of national economies, a process that has a dynamic of its own that is not readily controlled, poses a severe challenge to those attempting to grasp world affairs. Realists meet this challenge by stressing that control over currency crises and the other distortions of economic globalization is sought through summit meetings of the chief executives or finance ministers of the most powerful states. Since global economic crises are often variable in their origins and location, collaboration among governments at the summit occurs on an ad hoc basis as well as on an annual schedule among the G-7 (the United States, Canada, the United Kingdom, France, Germany, Italy, and Japan). In addition, realists stress that since governments have votes in the deliberations of the International Monetary Fund (IMF) proportionate to their contributions to the IMF's resources, the largest states, and especially the United States, can exercise indirect control over the global economy through international organizations (IGOs) created by the interstate system to manage such matters.

The challenge of the global economy is perhaps even more severe for the liberal paradigm. This is especially the case for those liberals who believe that markets work better and yield greater benefits the less governments intervene in their functioning. Those liberals who hesitate to accord a central role to states on economic issues tend either to remain silent in the face of economic crises or to record agreement with other liberals who recognize that distortions can and do occur in the global economy and that some remedial actions are therefore desirable. Their solution to this need is to emphasize the cooperative efforts of trade, investment, environmental, and other specialized IGOs to address the problems and restrain excessive responses on the part of national governments.

Unlike liberals, postinternationalists do not resist the idea of governments playing key roles in coping with global economic problems. But for them the challenge of such issues is viewed as best met through collaboration between the relevant actors in the state- and multi-centric worlds. They regard multinational corporations, labor unions, groups of private experts (often labeled "epistemic communities"), and other affected organizations in the multi-centric world as no less relevant to remedial actions than IGOs. Accordingly, postinternationalists point to global economic crises as prime stimuli to co-operation between the two worlds of world politics.

States' Role in Protecting Individuals from Globalization

As the Asian financial crisis that began in 1997 poignantly demon-strates (see Chapter 6), the processes of globalization can harm as well as benefit the well-being of people. Adherents of the three para-digms argue along very different lines as to how the negative conse-quences of globalizing dynamics for individuals can and should be offset. Realists highlight the role states should play by stressing that governments need to exercise control over foreign trade and invest-ments to protect workers and their jobs. In effect, their solution is to contain globalization by resurrecting barriers to the free flow of goods and money. Liberals, on the other hand, stress quite the opposite line of reasoning. Those liberals who believe free markets, if left unre-strained, will eventually eliminate their irregularities and bring bene-fits to everyone contend that states should do nothing to protect indi-viduals from any untoward effects of globalizing dynamics. Other liberals—those who focus on individual rights and international co-operation—and postinternationalists take a stance between these two extremes. Their position is that states should engage in limited inter-vention not by raising barriers to trade and investments but by pro-viding safety nets for citizens who need protection from those conse-quences of globalization that result in a loss of jobs and income.

Sensitivity to Change

Perhaps the sharpest difference between the three paradigms con-cerns the role each ascribes to change dynamics. Realists cite the cen-turies-long history of the interstate system to bulwark their premise that institutions are firmly in place and essentially impervious to any major changes that could recast fundamental structures. They readily acknowledge that war, revolution, and shifting alliance formations have periodically altered the degree to which the interstate system is organized along bipolar or multipolar lines, but such alterations, they say, occur in the context of an unchanging system rooted in the anarchical arrangements wherein states seek to maximize their interests in terms of the power available to them. Neorealists concede that transnational organizations have become increasingly relevant to the day-to-day developments that mark world politics, but at the same time they presume that this greater relevance is not so great as to alter the underlying nature and predominance of the interstate system. In the words of one leading realist, states "may choose to interfere little in the affairs of nonstate actors for long periods of time," but they "nevertheless set the terms of the intercourse. . . . When the crunch comes, states remake the rules by which other actors operate"[4]— which is another way of asserting that states are capable of resisting change dynamics and thereby maintaining the continuities on which their system rests.

In contrast, the liberal paradigm, being committed to the rule of law and the open marketplace, allows for moderate degrees of change, with legal institutions serving to contain the types and degrees of change even as markets allow extensive transformations. On the other hand, postinternationalism is highly sensitive to the forces of change that are unfolding at local, national, and global levels. Since it locates the sources of transformation in underlying processes, such as those driven by new technologies and restructured authority relations, rather than in events such as war and revolution, the turbulence approach posits a number of points at which change can be initiated, the more so as the dynamics of technology and authority relations quicken in pace and broaden in scope. To be sure, those who employ a postinternational perspective do not ignore the pervasiveness of continuities and historical patterns in global life. They acknowledge that people are rooted in habitual ways and that organizational inertia is widespread. Still, on balance, they conceive of the continuities as under constant siege by a variety of forces that turn people, institutions, and societies in new directions. Indeed, it is the uncertainties that attach to the multiplicity of change dynamics that are conceived to render world affairs so turbulent.

Conclusion

In short, it matters a great deal which paradigm one chooses to infuse order into the welter of phenomena that make up world politics. The realism model is compelling in its simplicity, the liberal model is persuasive in its stress on open markets and inclusionary law, and the postinternational approach forces one to come to grips with the complexities of global life. Each thus has its virtues and its drawbacks even as all three offer a coherent means for advancing understanding. As a result, readers must make their own choices as they ponder the world in which they live, choices that are bound to shape what they regard as salient and crucial in the course of events. And as stressed at the outset, the more self-conscious they can be about the paradigmatic choices they make, the more they are likely to grasp and clarify what is at work in world politics as a new century dawns.

6

Interactive Crises: International, Domestic, and Individual

As stated earlier, we approach everything we encounter with some sort of theory, be it simple or complex, more or less accurate, learned in an academic sense or acquired through experience. The clearer one can get in identifying the working propositions and abstract concepts one applies to the "real world," the better the theorist one will be. The facts never speak for themselves. The moment one puts one fact before another, as in writing history, one is making crucial decisions about what matters at a more abstract level. One's more abstract images of the world shape what the facts say.

We have found, however, that students often dislike learning about and using "theories." At one level, this is because students feel theories are artificial, that facts are being forced to confirm to theories rather than being allowed to "speak for themselves." At another level, students want to create their own models to explain the facts. Our response to these concerns is twofold. First, part of learning any field is learning about the theories, models, concepts, and methods used by its specialists. How specialists organize information and argue about explanations is crucial to learning in any field. Second, one can sharpen one's own theoretical explanation of the facts by practicing with more developed paradigms. A theory is nothing more than an organized way of asking, "What makes this tick?" in the absence of empirical proof. The use of existing theories can help students grasp what is involved in describing and analyzing the events transpiring all about them.

The next three chapters are designed to facilitate learning the logics of the three theories presented in the previous chapters more thoroughly through the use of cases. Each chapter offers a different way of using theories to organize cases. A case sets out an account of a real problem or event.

This chapter offers the most difficult challenge to broad theories like realism, liberalism, and postinternationalism. It illustrates how the theories assess sequences of events that culminate in crises. Broad theories do not typically explore those moments in global life where time seems compressed, influence and power are shaken up, and danger lurks nearby. Our three crisis cases—the proliferation of nuclear weapons by India and Pakistan, the Asian financial crisis, and the flows of refugees from Rwanda and Kosovo—show this need not be the case. Broad theories can highlight features of a crisis as well as its immediate causes and consequences.

Chapter Seven takes up the United Nations. Here the case is about a particular organization important to global politics rather than a historical sequence of events. The three theories fundamentally differ, however, on the nature of the organization and its proper role in world affairs. This should not be surprising, because liberalism and realism are founded on very different premises about cooperation and because postinternationalism goes beyond either of the other theories in according the U.N. autonomy to act in many areas.

Chapter Eight takes a different tack using the case of the Antarctica Treaty. It uses the theories to state explicit hypotheses about a set of questions. The hypotheses are then evaluated against various kinds of empirical evidence. Or, more correctly, the theories send the researcher off in search of different kinds of evidence. The theories operate powerfully in some respects and not so well in others. In so doing they demonstrate how one's theory can generate very good explanations for why things turned out the way they did while ignoring other enticing explanations. This is because, to repeat, theorizing involves selecting some facts as important and dismissing others as trivial.

Essential Characteristics of Crises

Perhaps no sequence of events is more challenging to one's theoretical perspective than those that fall under the general heading of "crisis." Such situations arise suddenly; they collapse the time frame for decision; they transform nuanced differences into raw clashes of power over crucial values; they move relentlessly toward deadlines; and at some point they may well elude or slip beyond the control of high-level officials. Thus, many crises are described as putting their participants on a seemingly uncompromisable "collision course" in which the actors differ so intensely over the disputed issues that they feel obligated to press for outcomes that can be neither avoided nor postponed.

Whether or not crises culminate in violence—and some do—they usually result in severe dislocations and loss for the people and collectivities caught up in their swift flow of events. These attributes of crises challenge our theories because they unfold so quickly that many of the variables out of which our models are constructed may not appear to be operative, thereby seeming to deprive us of our theoretical perspectives and confounding our grasp of what is transpiring. To be sure, decisionmaking theorists allow for choices made under crisis conditions and thus can readily analyze the key turning points and outcomes of crises. But such theories are concerned primarily with policymaking processes and do not attempt to account for the dynamics of more fundamental societal and systemic variables. The realist, liberal, and postinternational models, in contrast, are more encompassing. They sweep across longer time spans and they concentrate on the ways in which conflicts derive from underlying forces at work within the competing societies and the larger international systems of which the adversaries are a part. Such models are best suited to explain the patterning of events rather than the specific event, so that normally they do not address particular actions that are taken when time is short and deadlines loom.

What, then, can realist, liberal, and postinternational analysts do when confronted with crises that evolve quickly and culminate soon thereafter? Do they hold off undertaking interpretations until the more fundamental forces at work can be retrospectively assessed long after the crisis has ended and either normal patterns have been restored or new patterns established? Or do they conclude that waiting for the advantages of hindsight suggests their theories are profoundly flawed and that thus they had better cope as best they can by fitting whatever dynamics are manifested by the crisis into their theoretical framework? Do international crises lend themselves more readily to realism, whereas domestic crises are best interpreted through liberal lenses, and individual crises are more conducive to probing through application of the postinternational model? Or do crises tend to spread across all three levels, no matter the level at which they originate? And if they do spread in a crazy-quilt fashion, what does the theorist do? Try to fit the international, domestic, and individual dimensions of a crisis under the same theoretical umbrella or, in effect, use three umbrellas to comprehend the developments at each of the levels? To ask the question differently, if the actions and interactions observable in a crisis do not seem to be explicable by their preferred theory, can theorists shift to another model that appears to fit better within the contours of the crisis? Or, given the ability of theories to account for any form behavior may take, are we not so locked into our preferred theory that it is virtually impossible to shift back and forth between models as circumstances warrant and our interests change?

Although these questions amount to a serious and vigorous challenge to theorists, we have already indicated in Chapter 1 the basis of our response to them. We see a paradigm as locking an observer into a particular view of the world under most conditions, but we recognize that some observers have enough curiosity to allow for events that occur outside the scope of their paradigm. This means, as will be seen, that on occasion we may move to another model of world politics to explain different types of crises. And it is also the case that some analysts might change to another model as their understanding deepens and their existing perspectives seem obsolete. But such shifts tend to be enduring and thus occur rarely rather than repeatedly. Given the thoroughgoing nature of theories as systems of thought—especially their capacity to account for virtually any event or trend that may arise in a situation—normally we do not have reason to look to another model for guidance. Put more emphatically, usually we are locked into the theory with which we are most comfortable. It gives meaning to any and all discrepancies. It infuses order into seemingly disparate developments, highlights the central actors, clarifies their motives, and explains their successes and failures. It accentuates the relationships that matter and anticipates their likely evolution. Thus it is hardly surprising that analysts ordinarily adhere to a single model as they observe, ponder, and interpret the unfolding world scene.

Crises in world politics, in short, are also crises for theorists. At the most basic level crises test the premises, logic, and flexibility of our theories, and the more severe, intense, and abbreviated the crises are, the more stringently do they test our understanding. Hence it is important that the challenge of interpreting crises be addressed by determining how well realism, liberalism, and postinternationalism do in offering meaningful accounts of specific crisis situations. Such is the purpose of this chapter. We shall take on the challenge in three stages, first by inquiring further into the general characteristics of crises that render them theoretically difficult; second, by outlining the turning points of several recent crises; and third, by using these cases to explore the difficulties they pose for realists, liberals, and postinternationalists.

In addition to shortening the time frame so sharply as to inhibit or (in some cases) prevent the discernment of key underlying variables, crises are distinguished by several other characteristics that hinder the effort of theorists to fit the flow of events into their models. One involves the large degree to which crises revolve around deadlines. The specific day and hour at which the collision course will come to an end may not become clear until a crisis is well along—though sometimes it is set well in advance—but the fact that the actors are bound to collide in the near future is known to all concerned. Why? Because one or more (or all) of the parties to the crisis has specified that the adversary has to undertake certain actions in the near future, or else remedial and (often) violent steps will be taken to resolve the situation. Whether it be the cessation of nuclear proliferation, the adoption of measures to prevent or ameliorate financial crises, or the curbing of unmanageable flows of refugees—to mention only a few of the more conspicuous demands that have marked modern crises— deadlines for specified actions are set in the immediate future and it only remains to determine whether the challenging adversary will carry through on the threat or the challenged party will comply before the deadline expires. If no deadline is set or if no remedial actions are specified as having to be taken by a target date—as is the case in a preponderance of the situations on any political agenda—then the parties interact as they must to resolve their differences in due time without recourse to the urgent rhetoric of crisis. But deadlines render situations into tests of will and thereby generate last-minute negotiations or otherwise intensify the unfolding conflict.

Put differently, it is not until a call for a specified action is set in an immediate time frame—or an unexpected flow of events creates an urgent time frame that must be met if untoward outcomes are to be avoided—that officials, publics, journalists, academics, and other interested parties are inclined to attach the word "crisis" to a situation. Consider, for example, the British agreement to turn Hong Kong over to the People's Republic of China on July 1, 1997. In the mid-1990s that date was still felt to be so far off that tensions associated with the takeover had yet to reach crisis proportions, but it was reasonable to anticipate that as the date got closer and closer, the situation would be increasingly characterized as one of crisis. No matter that the outcome was predetermined; the situation was viewed as a crisis because it was far from clear how much change the Chinese would impose on Hong Kong and how far the residents of that city would go in accepting or protesting any new policies the Chinese adopted when they took over. Similarly, although the possibility of India and Pakistan developing nuclear weapons always loomed on the horizon, only when a nationalistic government was elected in India and announced in 1998 that it would proceed to test a nuclear device was the situation in South Asia quickly upgraded to a crisis by leaders, the press, and publics throughout the world.

It follows that uncertainty is another characteristic of crises. No political situation is free of some degree of uncertainty, of course, but given the immediacy of the time frame within which action must be taken, uncertainty about the outcome of a crisis is especially intense and fully experienced by all concerned. Of course, uncertainty is no stranger to theorists. It is, rather, a pervasive condition with which they must endlessly cope and serves, in effect, to infuse their theorizing with probabilistic forms of reasoning. Knowing that there can be no assurances as to how events will turn out, good theorists have long been accustomed to allowing for uncertainty by founding their hypotheses on likelihoods, on central tendencies from which deviations can be expected to occur.

Most crises are also marked by the adversaries having opposite goals in a situation, with one favoring the status quo and the other eager to alter it. Their conflict may appear to be over land, rights, privileges, procedures, or security. The main gulf that separates them, however, has to do exclusively with change. Are new arrangements with respect to land, rights, privileges, procedures, or security to be welcomed or prevented? Needless to say, the parties start down the collision course when the one seeking to alter the status quo—

whether it be nuclear proliferation by India or Pakistan, the sharp downturns of economies in Asia, or the flight of refugees in Africa—initiates actions on behalf of the desired changes. The actions may or may not be justified, depending on the perspective employed, and they may or may not be recognized as initiating a crisis (since the initiating party does not know whether the adversary will contest or yield to the actions), but the first step on the road to collision is discernible when the status quo is challenged.

More often than not, the first step is taken by a collective actor—say, a government, a political party, an NGO, or a corporation—but some crises have the added complexity of arising out of similar actions being taken by individuals. The gathering of protesters, the flow of refugees, and the collapse of markets are illustrative in this regard. Once the first steps are taken by individuals at the micro level, of course, such crises quickly escalate to concern governments and other relevant collectivities.

After the first step is taken and a counterreaction evoked, the long-run goals of transforming or preserving the status quo recede into the background and, as noted, the situation becomes a test of wills, a test of which party to the crisis has the greater power to prevail. Indeed, it is axiomatic that there can be no crisis unless efforts to exercise power are involved. The act of implementing a law is not considered a crisis because authority is evoked to achieve compliance. Authority is legitimate power; people accept the application of what might, in other circumstances, be called power because they think they ought to or because they believe the person or agency asking for a given behavior has the right to do so. Nor are the day-to-day decisions of states and other collectivities regarded as exercises in crisis decision-making. Again, legitimate authority may be involved or simple bargaining among the players may be at work. But what about situations where a legislative majority adopts a new law that is subsequently implemented by the government? Is not the implementation of the law an exercise of power even though administrative routines of this sort are standard governmental operations and not the first step toward crisis conditions? How, then, to distinguish situations in which the exercise of power can give rise to crises? If the newly enacted law dramatically alters the status quo, why is it not regarded as provoking a crisis?

A useful way of responding to these questions is to differentiate between situations in which the risks and benefits of a particular change are distributed among all (as is the case when laws are adopted by accepted constitutional procedures) and those in which one or more groups perceive an impending and unfair shift in who will bear the new risks and who will enjoy the new benefits (which may give rise to crises).[1] Examples abound. A family may experience a "crisis" when a child or spouse suddenly wants to do things not done before. Business firms often reach a fever pitch during a crisis over leadership. States consider themselves in crises when impending changes seem likely to increase their risks and lessen their benefits in substantial ways. In everyday political life, much can be achieved and many can be "empowered" to take action, but in a crisis the actors are dominated by the sense that an impending loss may lie ahead.

Still another attribute of crises is that they can culminate in calamitous outcomes and severe losses, even violence and death. Having become ever more committed to the exercise of power as they move down the collision course on behalf of cherished values, the adversaries can be too committed to back off and end the crisis. Like the game of chicken, one party may veer off and accept defeat by calling for negotiations, but sometimes neither party changes course, with the result that violent conflict will ensue when the deadline is reached.

It follows that if the adversaries in a crisis are institutional structures—such as states, the U.N., corporations, or terrorist organizations—then analysts will be encouraged to focus on decisionmaking processes. At every point along the collision course, not to mention a number of points during the earlier interactions that gave rise to the crisis conditions, the parties to the situation are faced with choices—with having to decide what demands to make, what resources to mobilize, what compromises are feasible, what alternative courses of action are possible, and so on across a multitude of choice points. For those who employ decisionmaking theories, therefore, crises offer marvelous opportunities for testing and revising propositions. And this is especially so when—as happened in the case of the Cuban missile crisis—subsequent years witnessed the publication of memoirs and interviews in which the participants recalled what they did and why they did it.

Crises seem to look solely like decisionmaking problems because they collapse the time in which the key variables interact. In this abbreviated "space," they highlight decisionmaking processes while masking the underlying systemic dynamics that brought about the collision course. Indeed, it is not far-fetched to observe that often crises are seen as emphasizing the salience of choice to the virtual exclusion of everything else. But treating crises as though they were unique and not susceptible to broad theorizing is like saying we should ignore words if punctuation occurs in a sentence. It is the logic of the string of words that demands the punctuation, not the other way around.

In short, it would be surprising if broad theories such as realism, liberalism, or postinternationalism, all of which focus on big structures, large processes, and huge comparisons,[2] drew a blank in their effort to interpret crises. Curiously, however, crises have rarely been thought of in terms of systemic variables. Rather, given the short time frame in which they are conceived, they are usually depicted in terms and logics drawn from psychological theory or bureaucratic politics.[3] The focus of this chapter is thus hardly characteristic of most writing about crises.

The first task is to confront the fact that realist, liberal, and postinternationalist theories are far more encompassing than those that focus on decision phenomena. Rather than anticipating the behavior of individuals in choice situations, the theories of concern here seek to explain large societal and systemic patterns that subsume the underlying dynamics that narrow and guide the choices open to decisionmakers. What, then, do these broader theoretical perspectives have going for them when crises arise? The answer is provocative: At first glance crises appear to offer very little that facilitates theorizing by realists, liberals, and postinternationalists, which is why earlier we stressed that crises amount to severe tests for these more systemic approaches.

Good theorists, however, are not prepared to back away from severe tests. Not only are their frameworks abstract and thoroughgoing enough to permit explanation of any development, but their commitments to their theories are also so strong that they are unlikely to abandon them just because, at first glance, only decisional phenomena are discernible or because much seems otherwise unfamiliar. On the contrary, the challenge of severe empirical tests enlivens theorists to stretch their imaginations and clarify theoretical nuances that they had not previously recognized. Consequently, and more important, when they turn to a close inspection of a crisis, they find that appearances can be deceiving, that both the actions and attributes that characterize the crisis—as well as those that are conspicuously absent as the collision course evolves—can be interpreted as indicative of the dynamics on which their theories are founded.

Generally speaking, the theoretical antennae of realists tend to be especially sensitive to situations in which the territorial sovereignty of one or another state is threatened. Such threats can evoke counterthreats and quickly escalate into a full-blown crisis in which the parties to the conflict progressively harden their positions and intensify their demands. The theoretical antennae of liberals, on the other hand, tend to be aroused either when issue area boundaries are threatened—that is, when national or transnational groups seek to extend or contract the scope of an issue at each other's expense—or when the boundaries of one issue area begin to overlap with those of another, as most typically occurs when the rise and fall of markets has serious consequences for the stability of governments and societies. For liberals the spread of such crises is often marked by shifting coalitions of societal actors within and between issue areas. As for postinternationalists, their theoretical antennae tend to crackle when the boundaries between the state- and multi-centric worlds are violated. Such situations often arise when the aggregation of people in the multi-centric world pose challenges for actors in the state-centric world and the institutions of the latter are lacking in the capacity to absorb and cope with the challenges.

International, Domestic, and Individual Crises

To facilitate comparisons of the capacity of realists, liberals, and postinternationalists to interpret and explain crises, we turn now to outlining briefly the major stages of several types of collision courses the world has witnessed in recent decades. One case focuses on the testing of nuclear weapons by India and Pakistan in 1998, a development that can be regarded as an international crisis not only because it involved the interaction of two adjacent states, but also because the addition of members to the nuclear club of states makes the dangers of devastating war seem all the greater. A second case portrays the Asian financial crises that began in 1997, a series of cascading events that can be viewed as a domestic crisis because it involved an upheaval in one country's economy and quickly spread throughout the Asian region and beyond. The third case draws from the flow of migrants and refugees around the world, a pattern that can be treated as an individual crisis because it originates with a large number of persons each deciding to leave or flee his or her homeland at the same time and for essentially the same reasons. Taken together, these cases are sufficiently differentiated to serve as good tests for any systemic theorist.

Although these three cases involve unique circumstances, it should be stressed that they are only recent instances of recurring patterns. Indeed, in our first edition of this book we analyzed the Cuban missile crisis of 1962 as illustrative of an international crisis, the 1989 massacre of students in China's Tiananmen Square as exemplifying a domestic crisis with widespread repercussions elsewhere in the world, and a series of simultaneous refugee flows in 1994 as representative of individual crises. We have replaced these cases to demonstrate that crises are not isolated events but occur in any contemporary period.

Nuclear Proliferation

In 1962 the Soviets started putting nuclear weapons in Cuba, much to the alarm of the United States. This action led to the most dangerous few days of the nuclear age and stands as a classic international crisis. Recently, India and Pakistan had their own nuclear crisis, which shook both countries and the rest of the international community. It began when the newly elected government of India tested three types of nuclear weapons on May 11, 1998, only two months after the conclusion of an election campaign in which the successful candidates promised that they would go nuclear. Countries around the world quickly condemned the action, slapped economic sanctions on India, and urged the Pakistanis to show restraint. Pakistan, with which India had gone to war three times in the past, eventually chose to ignore the international pressure and detonate its own device. It joined the nuclear club on May 28, 1998. Again, some countries imposed economic sanctions, this time on Pakistan.

The Indian and Pakistani resort to nuclear weapons meet the main criteria for a crisis. India's detonation was unexpected, despite clues that it might be on the way. It posed a significant alteration in power, with Pakistan the potential immediate loser and efforts to limit the global spread of nuclear weapons the long-term loser. Pakistan did not have a clear deadline placed on it to respond, but it did have to respond in some fashion. Delays in the response were a consequence of international pressure to "just say no" and, perhaps, the time it takes to finish off the essentials of such a complex technical feat. There was at least a strong prospect of violence (although renewed skirmishes over Kashmir a year later were handled with conventional forces). Uncertainty over the significance of the event was extremely high for Pakistan and very high for other nations in the region and the world. In one sense, the end date for the crisis is May 28, 1998, when Pakistan responded with its own bomb, thus restoring the strategic status quo with India.

As researchers warned in the 1970s, "Even a minimum size, inefficient and unreliable 'bomb' could result in a local disaster and an international crisis of immense proportions."[4] And indeed, the crisis extended well beyond India and Pakistan because it threatened the entire international structure designed to prevent nuclear proliferation. The International Atomic Energy Agency expressed concern and along with many others wondered if the Non-Proliferation Treaty (NPT) and the recently negotiated Comprehensive Test Ban Treaty (CTBT) were dead letters. Soon after detonating its device, India began talking about how it would be willing to sign and ratify the CTBT, providing other nuclear powers did so, including Pakistan. Perhaps this was in response to international pressure. But just as likely it reflected changed public sentiment. The initial elation in India (and later in Pakistan) over the detonations shifted to regret. As one ditty went at the time in India, "What has been tested can be detested but not de-tested."[5] Just a year later, in the spring of 1999, the Hindu-nationalist political party, Bharatiya Janata Party (BJP), which had campaigned successfully on a plank of going nuclear, lost support and had to call new elections (which they won). In this sense, the crisis has had no formal end either within Indian politics or among nations who seek to build a nonproliferation system.

To understand the proliferation crisis, one needs to see the larger context. When the United States launched the nuclear age with its atomic attack on Hiroshima and Nagasaki in 1945, it also opened the door to the spread of nuclear weapons. Within five years Great Britain,

France, and the Soviet Union had joined the club. China became a nuclear power in the early 1960s. Along with nuclear weapons came the promise of cheap power through nuclear reactors. By the mid-1950s, the promise of civilian uses of nuclear energy and the military danger of nuclear weapons opened a window to curb the further spread of nuclear weapons and eventually led to the Limited Test Ban Treaty in 1963 (which outlawed atmospheric tests) and to the Non-Proliferation Treaty (NPT) of 1968. The NPT offered this deal: The nuclear-weapons states would attempt to limit and reduce their nuclear arsenals and they would not sell or give nuclear weapons to nonnuclear states, but they would provide nonnuclear countries with help on the civilian uses of nuclear energy. In exchange, the nonnuclear countries would agree to forgo nuclear weapons. This agreement was further backed up by giving the International Atomic Energy Agency (IAEA), an agency of the United Nations, a role in monitoring the treaty.

Many nations signed the NPT, although crucial ones such as India and Pakistan did not. Some countries, like India, detonated peaceful nuclear explosions; others, notably South Africa and Brazil, started and then terminated weapons programs. At least one, Israel, was an unconfirmed, bomb-in-the-basement nuclear power. Nevertheless, the agreement seemed to work to prevent proliferation. Except as a result of the breakup of the Soviet Union, no new *official* nuclear weapons states came on the scene until the Indian detonation in 1998. Many of the heirs to Soviet weapons chose to dismantle them entirely and leave the "club" as quickly as they could. This was yet more evidence of a norm—and a political reality—opposing the spread of these weapons.

As the Cold War ended, however, NPT signatories and nonsignatories alike were increasingly upset with the behavior of the nuclear powers. The nonnuclear states said there had been precious little progress by the five club members in eliminating nuclear weapons, and the flow of civilian aid had tapered to a trickle. Thus, there was talk of ending the agreement, although it was ultimately extended indefinitely. The Comprehensive Test Ban Treaty was a response to the complaints, although the U.S. Senate continued to drag its feet on ratification. Two longtime national security advisers, Paul Nitze and Sidney Drell, stressed that U.S. inaction would prove disastrous, especially relative to Pakistan and India. Taking action would have a good effect: "U.S. ratification would remove any excuse for inaction on the part of these nations and would strengthen their resolve."[6]

Realists were likely to be comfortable with the basics of this crisis. A state, recognizing growing threats on its borders and an incapacity to stand up to great powers in some future setting, chose to go nuclear. The *Jakarta Post* said India's reason for going "overtly nuclear was the growing military asymmetry with China and the latter's continuing covert nuclear and missile assistance to Pakistan."[7] Not surprising, India's nearby nonnuclear enemy, Pakistan, responded in kind. Pakistani Prime Minister Sharif argued that the strategic balance and deterrence between the two countries had been destroyed.[8] Explained Sharif, "India is an expansionist power. We have settled the score with India."[9] In what can only be described as the classic logic of a security dilemma, India's Prime Minister, Atal Bihari Vajpayee, pointed to the Pakistani detonations and said India was "vindicated" in building its own program.[10] For both countries, in sum, concerns over relative power mattered.

That the United States would urge Pakistan not to respond—and attempt to injure India economically—also makes sense from a realist perspective. Why would the United States want to see a new member in the nuclear club? India itself also saw nuclear weapons as a way to even the field with a country like the United States. As one Indian general said at the end of the Gulf War, "The lesson of Desert Storm is don't mess with the United States without nuclear weapons."[11]

The origins of the crisis, however, suggest a possible error in U.S. policy. One reason Indian officials offered for breaking the moratorium on nuclear weapons development was their belief that India was not being rewarded by the United States for its restraint. The contrast to China was clear. "Indians have been peeved that the Clinton administration has been rewarding the world's largest autocracy, China, with supercomputers and space and missile technology, while penalizing the world's largest democracy, India, through a rising tide of US-inspired national and multinational technology sanctions."[12] U.S. policy might have been one of trying to moderate and contain an existing nuclear power—China. But the consequence was to provide a regional disincentive to nonproliferation. If so, the security dilemma that prompts arms racing is about to begin anew, not just in this region but elsewhere.

Conceivably, on the other hand, the proliferation on the South Asian subcontinent may prove a boon to the United States. Just as China was happy to advance the nuclear programs of Pakistan to balance India (which also had ties with China's then-mortal enemy, the Soviet Union), perhaps the United States will benefit from the extra balancing provided in the region by India and Pakistan. It may be that the two detonations will tie China down militarily, thus reducing the burden on the United States to deter Chinese aggression.

As for liberals, they are likely to interpret the proliferation as a crisis for international efforts at cooperation on nuclear matters. Although neither country had actually violated the NPT, because neither was a signatory, many nations thought the aim of the nonproliferation treaty had become a broadly controlling international norm. The norm of the treaty had been given strong teeth by domestic legislation in different countries. For example, the United States had passed the Nuclear Proliferation Prevention Act of 1994, which requires the president to impose economic sanctions on any state that transfers to a "non-weapons state a nuclear explosive device" or when a nonnuclear state receives or detonates such a device.

But the norm did not stop the proliferation. All the power of states and international organizations to influence the two countries seemed to fail. Pakistan had been offered Can$14 million in aid by Canada—the amount of aid withdrawn from India after its blasts—but the measure was to no avail.[13] Even threats of stopping aid from the multilateral development banks failed to deter the two countries. That both India and Pakistan, in full awareness of the likelihood of sanctions, still went ahead was a blow to the entire system. But the problem may lie in inadequate and untimely application of sanctions. Liberals could say the effort to balance and moderate China, even though the country was no democracy, was in error. India may have seen matters this way, and later Pakistan said India's nuclearization should have prompted even more stringent sanctions than it did.

Within the new nuclear nations, critics of the decision questioned the cost of nuclear weapons to the economy. Consider this comment from Pakistan's former prime minister, Benazir Bhutto: "Did the subcontinent want to build peace or become another Soviet Union which, 'despite possessing huge nuclear arsenals and the largest land mass, ended up having to beg for food from the European Commission.'"[14] Although it is true that the bulk of the Pakistani nuclear program was built under Bhutto's rule, perhaps in an effort to keep the military from seizing power again, it is equally true that she never officially weaponized the program. Her concern with power is quite different from that of the realists. What matters is building the possibilities for cooperation in the region to develop sounder economies. Cooperation makes for wealth, arms racing makes for poverty. Traditional elements of power, such as military force, were no guarantee the national power fundamentals would be sound.

Postinternationalists would admit the two new nuclear powers posed a crisis for the state-centric world, but their theoretical attention would be drawn first to the sources of the political decision in India, second to the way India and Pakistan thought of the sanctions, and third to the cascading effects that gripped the region and the world. Until the March 1998 election, the political parties that had governed India had stuck to the no-nuclear-weapons policy they established in the 1970s. With the 1998 election, this changed. The idea of being a nuclear power may have held considerable fascination for the voting public, or perhaps few of the voters actually believed the BJP's party platform. Either way, the initial response by the public to the detonations was surprise and jubilation. "Now every Indian can walk taller," commented one citizen.[15] Pakistan's leader had hawks in his own party demanding a response. The hawks argued that there was a Jewish bomb (although Israel has not officially acknowledged as much), a Hindu bomb, and many Christian bombs; therefore there should be an Islamic one. Realists are unlikely to put religion into their calculations and liberals will seek to protect religious freedom as a path to peace. Neither view readily accepts that religious sentiment may have fueled the decision or at least fired up public support.

Public opinion polls showed strong support for nuclear tests, even if the result was sanctions,[16] a puzzling pattern for both realists and liberals. The sanctions generated few fears, according to some Pakistani and Indian cynics, because corruption already took most of the foreign aid given the countries. People in both countries thought the sanctions would pose few problems among the poor, who never saw the money anyway. Nor did people on the street think the sanctions would last. As *The Economist* summarized the mood in New Delhi, "Who cares, national pride can't be counted in dollars. And remember, nothing much happened to China, despite Tiananmen Square."[17]

Publics used their knowledge of recent world affairs and, at least temporarily, lent their support to their leaders.

Both countries took action to cope with the economic realities of the sanctions. Realists would say this response proves their point that states can exercise control when they want to. And India, realists might note, could take some comfort in the economic power differential represented by the two countries' foreign currency holdings: Pakistan's $1 billion left far less economic wiggle room than India's $30 billion. But the realist image runs into difficulty because the two countries, faced with very similar international strategic and sanction situations, reacted in radically different ways. Sharif spent much of the two weeks between the Indian and Pakistani explosions preparing his citizens for hardship. The Pakistani stock market crashed.[18] On the day of the detonations, Pakistan declared a state of emergency and imposed currency exchange controls. In contrast, the day of the detonation in India evoked an uproar from the opposition in parliament, but no state of emergency was declared. Liberals might say this was because India was much more of a democracy than Pakistan.

The story continues with its complications for theorists. India's leaders changed part of their nationalist party platform: Instead of rejecting foreign investment as they had promised in their campaign, they rapidly approved pending contracts to foreign firms—including some major U.S. oil firms—and invited more investment by allowing foreign firms to hold 100 percent equity in some companies.[19] Indian diplomats in Europe told businesses and governments that now was the time to invest in India, while the Americans were focused on sanctions. This soon did the trick, as firms in the United States and Europe quietly urged their governments to loosen the sanctions. Realists would emphasize government control over the economy. Postinternationalists would point out the oddity of an internationally sanctioned and domestically weak government using sovereignty-free actors to solve its domestic economic problem by changing U.S. security policy. Liberals might note that democracy and economic liberalization go together and, moreover, the capacity of a weaker democracy to influence the stronger actually enhances the power of the stronger.

From a postinternationalist perspective, the cascade of events immediately following the Indian detonation shows how difficult it is for states to live alone in their own world and how coping with publics strongly influences their capacity. Even a major security decision like going nuclear has its roots in waves of intersecting cascades from publics, other states, international organizations, and the market. The consequences of the crisis continue to propagate across the state- and multi-centric worlds. Pakistan and India continue to fight over Kashmir.

Thus far, in short, the nuclear crisis seems to have changed nothing. Other states may be contemplating going nuclear now that the nonproliferation norm has been breached. Within India, the "American sanctions imposed after India's nuclear tests have undoubtedly pushed economic liberalisation forward."[20] At the same time, however, the BJP government has fallen due to economic problems and publics that now doubt the nuclear decision was reasonable or responsible. The incapacity of the United States and India to resist international corporations has once again raised the question of authority in both countries. The crisis may be over, say postinternationalists, but the confusion has just begun.

The Asian Financial Crisis

It has been written that "if the Cuban missile standoff was a quintessential cold-war crisis, then today's global economic upheaval may be a landmark crisis of the post-cold-war era."[21] The upheaval began on July 2, 1997, when a loss of confidence in Thailand's currency resulted in the government's decision to allow the baht to float (rather than supporting it with governmental reserves). The baht's value quickly declined, which precipitated an avalanche across Asia that sent local currencies into a free fall, with stock prices collapsing, real estate prices plummeting, and investors transferring their money to safer havens. In turn, new loans dried up; companies went bankrupt; workers were laid off; and borrowers failed to make their payments on old loans with the result that banks that had borrowed in hard currencies (the dollar, mark, and yen) to make questionable loans were unable to repay their debts and hastened further decline as they called in the loans they had made to their borrowers. Panic set in as investors, fearing disaster in the emergent markets of Asia, Brazil, and elsewhere, sold their stocks in milliseconds and reinvested their money in U.S. bonds or other less vulnerable securities.[22] Summarizing measures of the severity of these interrelated dynamics are provided by these data: Between the onset of the crisis and late September 1998—some fourteen months—South Korea's economy shrank by 45 percent; Thailand's by 50 percent; and Indonesia's by nearly 80 percent;[23] with the Indonesian currency, the rupiah, dropping from 2,500 to the U.S. dollar in August 1997 to 16,000 in January 1998.[24]

To cope with these diverse developments the International Monetary Fund (IMF), an agency created by states in 1944 to maintain a modicum of global financial stability, arranged "rescue packages" for several Asian countries, packages that provided substantial loans in exchange for the imposition of harsh economic reforms such as fiscal austerity, open markets, regulated banks, and a host of other measures consistent with the premises of neoclassical economics and capitalism practiced in the West. But whatever their merit, the packages did not stem the tide of unwanted change. In Indonesia riots in the streets swept a dictator from office; in Korea strikes became commonplace; in Thailand poverty became pervasive; in Hong Kong real estate prices declined precipitously; in Japan economic problems multiplied and Japanese banks suffered enormous setbacks; and as sales and travel to Asia slumped, oil prices fell and companies and stock markets in the West began to experience the repercussions. So did Latin American countries, especially Brazil, as borrowers defaulted, banks failed, inflation increased, and unemployment soared. These problems were compounded even further for economies highly dependent on the export of oil, such as those of Venezuela and Mexico. In Russia the decline of oil prices and the loss of Asian business, reinforced by extensive corruption and a devaluation of the ruble, underlay a rapidly expanding inflation, a surge of unemployment, a severe paralysis of the central government, and eventually a canceling of foreign debts (i.e., bankruptcy).

To some extent this summary of the Asian crisis is misleading. It does not account for either the multiplicity of factors that brought on the crisis or the different circumstances of the affected countries and the varying ways they responded to it. Least of all does it begin to hint at the extensive dislocation and sufferings experienced by individuals who were at the receiving end of the crisis. A few examples may help to convey the consequences at the micro level. In less than a year after the onset of the crisis, in May 1998, the suicide rate in Korea was up 30 percent.[25] Millions of Asian children dropped out of school and many started working long hours for tragically little money under sweatshop conditions.[26] Hospitals went bankrupt, their nurses and medical aides working without salaries even as medical equipment was removed to offset the costs of bankruptcy.[27] Infant mortality in Indonesia was estimated to have jumped 30 percent subsequent to July 1997, after being lowered by two-thirds in the previous twenty-five years.[28] In Thailand 2,000 people a day lost their jobs; in South Korea the total who lost their jobs exceeded 1 million; in Indonesia the figure was estimated to approach 20 million.[29] No less horrendous, many of the newly unemployed were migrant workers, thus causing the governments of the host countries to deport hundreds of thousands of migrants back to their countries of origin and even larger numbers back to the village homes within their countries—back to rural villages that had come to rely on the money the workers sent back during the boom years.[30] As one observer put it, the nations in recession "are sending home those who built their skyscrapers and toiled in their factories."[31] In the case of South Korea, "Nearly 100 times a day somewhere in the country, someone's dream—a tennis shoe factory, a corner grocery store, a giant automaker, a promising fashion house, even a hospital—is crushed under the weight of economic collapse. Unpaid bills are piled too high, the 'closed' sign is posted, workers are dumped, and the nation's economy slips a little lower."[32] Stated more starkly: "Short of a massive asteroid strike from outer space, no natural disaster could destroy this much wealth or plunge this many people into misery [as did the Asian crisis]."[33]

At the macro level, however, there is a crucial respect in which the foregoing summary of the crisis is adequate, namely, it indicates that the developments in the various countries impacted on each other and thus portrays the high degree to which Asian and other economies have become interdependent. Viewed in this way, it is hardly surprising that despite the variabilities it was not long before the many complex dynamics were reduced to a single label: Calling it everything from the "Asian flu" to the "Asian contagion," from the Asian financial crisis to the global financial crisis"—to mention only the more widely used labels—people everywhere began to appreciate that perhaps an era of prolonged prosperity may be giving way to an uncertain future. But although such labels may capture the cascading nature of a serious challenge confronting societies and states alike, they do not begin to explain why such an overlapping sequence of events occurred or how they may evolve in the future.

In each case a major part of the explanation can be traced to domestic economic and political factors—such as, for example, Japan's
history of unregulated banks and a politics subservient to bureaucratic agencies, Indonesia's autocratic institutions that allowed for the
accumulation of great wealth on the part of its leaders and their fam-
ilies, and South Korea's dominance by a few huge corporations—that
were deeply ingrained and not fully responsive to the external pressures exerted by the IMF, the United States, and other Western powers. Stated differently, Asian countries like Japan and South Korea
have long adhered to economic policies that deviate substantially
from the neoclassical economic model to which the United States and
other Western countries have subscribed. Whereas the latter rely on
free trade and markets to achieve progressive economies, the version
of capitalism practiced in Asia has depended less on the market and
more on government planning and long-term relationships. Thus the
Asian model presumed that bureaucrats were better able to allocate
capital and goods than markets were, with the result that historically
Asian economies were subject to strict regulations that limited foreign
imports and investments. At the same time these practices enabled
companies to maintain a tradition of not laying off workers and, instead, of assuring them they could count on a lifelong job. It was these
premises of the Asian model that the West, mainly but not exclusively
through the IMF, sought to alter as the crisis made it increasingly
clear that the global repercussions of the Asian contagion were so extensive that the problem was rife with international as well as domestic dynamics. And indeed, to some extent the pressures from the
West did begin to make the Asian countries take on the coloration of
Western forms of capitalism, making future political crises in these
countries all the more likely.[34]

Unlike its onset, no single date can be cited as indicative of when
the Asian crisis came to an end. But assuming that by the crisis is
meant the financial instabilities occasioned by the collapse of currencies and stock markets and the unavailability of credit, then it can be
said to have ground to a halt in the latter months of 1998 as the currencies, markets, and banks of the region stabilized rather than continuing to decline. As one report put it, the crisis changed "from a
panic inducing meltdown of currencies and government reserves to a
more chronic, grinding recession."[35] Indeed, by the summer of 1999 it
was possible to speak of "the remarkable speed of the rebound," a

pace that was in some ways too great inasmuch as it "drained the political urgency out of many reforms that seemed so vital during the
darkest days of the crisis—and may still be essential to Asia's future."[36]

Yet, to note the end of the financial crisis is not to imply that its consequences also came to an end. The fallout in greater unemployment,
poverty, and societal disarray continues unabated in many countries,
with perhaps Russia being most mired in—and most unable to recover from—the severe downturn its economy and polity suffered.
Indeed, although the financial crisis may be over and the international community may develop mechanisms to minimize the chances
of its recurrence, numerous experts anticipate that its consequences in
human misery will continue for a long, long time. Put more succinctly, "The pain that is invisible on traders' screens, but striking in
the villages where unemployment and misery still lurk, will not ease
any time soon."[37]

Whatever the future may hold, the three theories contrasted in this
book can serve, at least partially, as explanations for what happened.
Such explanations must perforce be partial in two respects. Not only
are domestic factors highly relevant, but so much of what occurred
can be traced to the productivity of workers, the flow of trade, the
practices of banks, and the shifting of currencies that a substantial
part of the explanation also lies in the field of economic theory, thus
further limiting the interpretations that realism, liberalism, and
postinternationalism can offer.

In reacting to the Asia crisis, realists are likely to focus on its implications for national power and the possibility that states will cope
with the decline in their economies by resorting to policies that seal
their boundaries more securely against the consequences of free trade
and currency flows. For them free trade and open economies are not
principles to be served; rather, depending on whether a country's interests are or are not advanced, free trade is either a useful or not useful instrument of national policy. Consequently, viewed from a U.S.
perspective, realists do not regret the problems besetting Japan in the
1990s. For them relative gains are what count, and the fact that the
U.S. economy thrived in recent years while the Japanese economy did
not amounts to a relative gain of considerable importance, especially
when it is recalled that in the 1980s it was Japan that was regarded as
on its way to becoming the world's economic superpower. On the

other hand, realists are likely to be troubled by the economic decline of Russia: In that case the greater relative decline is offset by the abundance of nuclear weapons in Russia that could fall into the wrong hands if the country's stability continues to decay and gets replaced by political paralysis and social collapse. Realists purport not to be concerned about domestic developments, but in the case of Russia they are likely to make an exception because of the severe international threat that attaches to the potential misuse of nuclear materials.

Similarly, realists are likely to anticipate that other countries will follow the path of Malaysia the more the Asian contagion spreads and underlies domestic dislocations. Led by Prime Minister Mahatir Mohammad, Malaysia's response to the contagion was to advance its national interest by ending the convertibility of its currency and imposing sweeping capital controls over its markets. "We told you so," realists are likely to assert. "If state controls over the economy are substantially reduced, political instability will eventually set in and states will act to recover their capacity to steer their own economic development." For realists, in other words, the Malaysian reaction is hardly surprising inasmuch as they view the Asian flu less as a set of interdependent processes and more as another form of competition among states, with each state pursing the policies most likely to enhance its relative gains.

The realist paradigm, however, leaves much to be desired in this case. It fails to penetrate to the heart of the Asian crisis. So much of the paradigm is rooted in the conduct of states as unitary actors for which social structures and citizens are essentially irrelevant—and for which reliance on force and military action is viewed as the prime way of coping with crises (see Table 5.1)—that the breakdown of markets and economies involves developments with which realists cannot adequately cope. Besides taking note of any tendencies to retreat from policies that facilitate open economies, they can highlight how the IMF as an interstate agency dominated by the sole remaining superpower imposed strict reforms on countries with troubled economies in exchange for loans designed to promote economic stability and solvency. Indeed, a realist might conclude that U.S. hegemony saved Asia from even greater calamities by using its economic clout to manage its own economy carefully and by giving both extra money and detailed instructions to the IMF. On the other hand, this explanation breaks down the more the IMF and the liberal policies it espoused failed to reverse the decline of Asian economies and the spread of its repercussions around the world. Preoccupied with the exercise of state power, realists tend to be nonplussed when markets dictate the course of events and present states and governments with few techniques of effective control other than those of retreating from involvement in the global economy. In effect, the Asian flu highlights a blind spot of realist theory, a blind spot that is not particularly worrisome to realists because they tend to view economic issues as secondary to those of military defense and security.

Quite the opposite is the case for liberal theory. Since so much of the onset and subsequent evolution of the Asian flu reflects the high degree to which the world has become interdependent and in need of cooperation across national boundaries, liberals may well be inclined to view this case as a vindication of their theoretical perspective. Unlike the realists, they are inclined to view Malaysia's withdrawal from the global economy—and the possibility that this action might be emulated by other countries—with considerable distress. Their presumption that the central tendencies in world affairs are founded on cooperation leads them to view open economies and free trade as involving other than zero-sum outcomes. For liberals absolute gains are preferred to relative ones; they do not care who gains the most as long as all gain the maximum possible. Hence, for them, Japan's problems are U.S. problems as well. Stated more generally, liberals see the Asian contagion as a threat to global interdependence and harmony that needs to be contested through efforts by the IMF and other agencies and countries to minimize the dislocations that have followed. Any doubts they may have about the wisdom of promoting capitalism through neoclassical economic policies focus on the need for safety nets to ease the transition to open economies and offset their sharp downturns, so that trading in markets and not fighting in streets becomes the arena of competition.

Stated differently, the various forms of liberalism share a conception in which economic dynamics are no less relevant than political and military power. They tend to see governments as interfering too extensively in economic affairs, as not enabling market forces to play themselves out in a way they believe will eventually benefit all citizens. Such reasoning leads to support for policies designed to limit inflation, reduce interest rates, collect taxes, stimulate consumer spending through lowered tax rates, control government spending,

lower tariffs, and otherwise enable markets to allow for the free inter-
play of supply and demand—measures that taken together have been
referred to as the "economic adjustment policies" of previously gov-
ernment-dominated economies. Accordingly, viewed through the
lenses of the liberal paradigm, the Asian flu is readily explicable even
though the absence of sufficient regulation of banks and markets allowed it to spread unnecessarily.

But the resistance of liberals to governmental interference focuses
mainly on national governments. Being mindful that markets and the
interdependence of economies require a modicum of authoritative supervision and support, they look to cooperation among governments—to international institutions—for these necessities. Thus it is
hardly surprising that a number of ideas have been voiced as to how
the IMF and other international mechanisms might be reformed,[38]
and that, indeed, high-level officials of a number of governments
have met in search of a vaccine for the Asian flu.[39] That these efforts
in international cooperation have yet to yield meaningful results can
be traced to cultural and intellectual differences among liberals as to
how to solve the problem as well as political resistance to policies on
the part of some governments.[40]

The postinternational paradigm seems especially suited to account
for the rapid-fire sequence of events through which the Asian flu
spread. More than any variants of realism or liberalism, this model
stresses the role of individuals—in this case, investors, bankers, busi-
nesspeople, consumers, and workers—as agents that sustain the
processes of contagion. There is no magical wand wielded by an invisible hand that accounts for the rise and collapse of markets, no
guiding principle of economic development that steers prices to new
highs and lows, no conception of power that posits economic forces
as subservient to the influence of elites. Rather, the postinternationalist would argue, markets, bankruptcies, corrupt institutions, and fragile currencies are the product of thousands upon thousands of individuals making choices that collectively generate price fluctuations,
inflationary pressures, bank failures, patterns of consumption, and
the many other outcomes through which economies prosper or
founder and governments persist or fall. To be sure, governments
make the decisions to devalue or otherwise protect their currency, just
as the IMF frames the policies designed to check inflation and facilitate growth and just as corporations decide to open or close factories.

Yet, these macro forces are unleashed because those responsible perceive the collective tendencies of individuals and publics who consume goods, sustain markets, manage banks, and invest abroad as having compelled macro shifts in one direction or another—or at least that is how postinternationalists would begin to explain the sequence of events. For them the Asian contagion is not a mystical force that descended on Asian countries and then spread around the world; rather, they see the contagion as the result of individuals interpreting their circumstances and futures in similar ways.

Nor are postinternationalists taken aback by the speed with which the Asian flu spread throughout the world. Not only do they emphasize the relevance of microelectronic technologies—which in this case allowed for the hasty withdrawal of investments from the emergent economies—but they also stress that global affairs are marked more by overlapping cascades that move swiftly across national boundaries and less by discrete events that occur in one country and are subsequently the focus of reactions elsewhere.

Least of all are postinternationalists surprised by the inability of states, either singularly or collectively, to contain and contest the spread of the Asian flu. They view their conceptions of states and the limited extent to which governments can exercise control in a bifurcated world of ever more skillful citizens as amply—and regrettably—vindicated by global financial crises.

Refugee Flights from Rwanda and Kosovo

During the summer of 1994 three widely separated sequences of events—each with its own roots and yet in some important respects similar to the others—escalated into crisis proportions. In Rwanda, Haiti, and Cuba thousands upon thousands of citizens felt compelled to flee their homeland and seek refuge in safer havens. In all three cases the numbers of refugees were so extensive—in Rwanda the figure eventually exceeded 1 million—that crisis conditions evolved not only for those fleeing but also for the agencies and countries that sought to cope with the tragedies to which such instantaneous and massive migrations give rise. Five years later, in 1999, another set of refugee crises challenged the world. Hundreds of thousands of ethnic Albanians fled from Kosovo. Meanwhile, renewed civil war in Angola made getting aid to the 1.6 million Angolans displaced by decades of civil war extremely difficult. Meanwhile, in the Great Lakes region of Africa, millions already in camps were joined by hundreds of thousands of new people, who had been displaced by a heightened regionalization of the conflict that began in Rwanda in 1994.

Given the complexity of world politics in the present era, it is perhaps not surprising that these crises became, in curious and circuitous ways, inextricably linked to each other by the profound humanitarian questions they commonly posed and by their consequences for the peace and security of entire regions. Here we assess when and why refugees create political crises by considering two grave flows of refugees: Rwanda in 1994 and Kosovo in 1999. Both originated when national governments launched deadly attacks on one of their ethnic groups: In Rwanda, Tutsis attacked Hutus; in Kosovo, Serbs attacked ethnic Albanians.

Although in 1998 the U.N. High Commission for Refugees (UNHCR) reported that the ranks of refugees numbered 22.3 million persons, the plight of this many people (and the figure is probably an underestimate) does not necessarily constitute a crisis. Or at least so little interest exists in the continuing problem of refugees that the U.N.'s relief agencies and nongovernmental organizations (NGOs) such as Africa Watch had to beg for funds from states and individual donors. While the United States spent over $40 million in the investigation of President Clinton, the World Food Program (WFP) tried—unsuccessfully—to get $8.8 million to continue an airlift of food to refugees in Angola. The Netherlands pledged a half million dollars.[41] One analyst put the expenditure by states on African refugees at 11 cents per person per day (the figure was $1.10 in Kosovo).[42] Indeed, just as starvation and new influxes of refugees flooded African refugee camps, the WFP was directed by Western states to redirect personnel and food to Kosovo. Once housed, it seems, refugees stop being a crisis, especially if those people live in places with large refugee populations (such as Africa). The everyday struggle for millions of individual refugees is, apparently, no crisis for anyone but the people experiencing it and perhaps the poorer nations of Africa and Asia.

Our focus, therefore, is on the more acute phase of refugee flows rather than the everyday catastrophe that is the global refugee problem. The acute phase starts when massive numbers of people decide the risk of staying at home is worse than the uncertainty and danger of going to a new country. Without a doubt, such moments amount to a personal crisis of the highest magnitude. The individual must leave home, friends, work, and familiar landscapes for a very unsure future. Parents are often separated from their children in the confusion. Husbands, brothers, and sons may be killed along the way or forced to join military units. Coping with all the people may tax relief organizations, both NGOs and international governmental organizations (IGOs), such as the UNHCR and UNICEF.

Refugee flows may turn into crises for states as well. First, for the receiving state the influx may be dramatic and sudden; it may threaten capacities to govern, especially in poorer countries in the developing world where 80 percent of refugees currently live. Refugees may exacerbate local and national ethnic rivalries, thus further burdening weak governments. Or they may be used by rival factions within and between states, as happened in Africa's Great Lakes region in the aftermath of the 1994 Rwanda refugee crisis. Typically, the sending state is in deep civil turmoil. States may announce deadlines for closure of borders to refugees, thereby increasing the pressure on other states and further internationalizing the crisis. Attacks on people by governments may prompt ultimatums and even war, as happened in Kosovo. Once the bombing campaign against Serbia began, refugees in Kosovo posed an acute military problem. It appeared the massive influx of ethnic Albanians into surrounding countries was part of Serbia's strategic plan to cleanse and control the region. At one point it seemed Serbia had achieved its aim of reducing the Albanian population and it looked as if NATO's cohesion might waver. Although clear deadlines may not typically characterize refugee flows, other attributes of crises were readily apparent in Kosovo and indicate that states may even create a refugee crisis as an instrument of policy.

Rwanda. The Rwandan crisis began with a major turn in a four-year-old civil war that triggered an enormous flow of humanity in 1994. This flow precipitated a sense of emergency that virtually demanded innovative responses from IGOs, NGOs, and states. Real urgency attended efforts on the ground to cope with all the people; perceptual urgency mounted elsewhere in the world as television images and newspaper photos depicted huge movements of people that could not be ignored.

In all crises, the specific triggering decision or event springs from a series of prior developments that infuse a logic into the actions of those who precipitate and sustain the crisis. In the case of Rwanda, the outlines of a collision course became evident after a suspicious plane crash in April killed the country's president, a member of the majority Hutu tribe. This event led to a sharp escalation of a four-year-old civil war between his tribe and its longtime rival, the minority Tutsi tribe. Hutu extremists in the government used the plane crash as an excuse to provoke and launch large-scale killings of Tutsis throughout the country. Subsequently, the Tutsi-led Rwandan Patriotic Front turned the tide in the civil war and routed the Rwandan army. As rebel offensives moved across the country, hundreds of thousands of Hutus, along with their government, fled out of fear that the Tutsis would seek revenge for the large numbers of Tutsis who had been massacred by Hutu mobs in what was widely called a genocidal campaign.

By July 15 the flight of the Hutus crossing the Rwandan border into Zaire had reached the rate of at least 2,000 persons per hour, with some estimates ranging as high as 10,000 an hour.[43] At that time the International Red Cross was the only organization in Zaire with food for refugees, and it had only enough for 150,000 people. The number of fleeing Hutus began to exceed 0.5 million, and in the several days that followed the figure surpassed 1.2 million as international relief agencies pleaded with the Tutsi rebels to call a cease-fire, hoping that such an action would also halt the flood of refugees. Wanting to catch the government officials and militias who had conducted the genocidal campaign against their people, leaders of the rebel Patriotic Front did not announce a cease-fire until July 18. On July 19 the Tutsi-dominated victors installed a new government of reconciliation, named a moderate Hutu as president and prime minister, and pledged to protect all Rwandans except those who had participated in the earlier massacre of Tutsis.

In the meantime, the U.N. undertook to mobilize a global relief effort for the refugees. The United States began sending relief flights into Zaire carrying food, oil, and shelters. Yet, the crisis worsened. An estimated 2.4 million fled Rwanda by July 21, and the crowded, makeshift refugee camps in Zaire were soon overwhelmed by a cholera epidemic. Within two weeks refugees were dying at the rate of 1,800 a day. Bodies began piling up by roadsides as the death rate exceeded the capacity of relief officials to dig mass graves. Although it received permission to burn the corpses, the U.N. was reluctant to do so because such a procedure would violate Rwandan religious and cultural customs.

To end the crisis, the new coalition government, the U.N., and the relief workers urged, even pleaded with, the refugees in Zaire to return home. But many refused to move, their fear of death at the hands of the Patriotic Front exceeding their fear of death by cholera.[44] Even the new Rwandan prime minister was unable to persuade his family to return. From his point of view, in fact, the crisis had no end:

> I am sincerely fed up for not having a future for my children, for the people from my generation or for the people of the generations to come. . . . A child who is 7 years old now can live maybe 60 years. When they are 67 years old, they will still remember what has happened in this country. Just imagine a whole generation that for about a half century is going to remember this. What do we do for people to forget? I think that we can only start by teaching children that we are one people.[45]

Although it is analytically confounding to conceive of a crisis lasting a half century, the exact point at which the Rwandan situation returned to "normal" is not easily fixed. Possibly August 31, 1994, is an appropriate date, since that is when the new Rwandan government was allowed to have its delegate take his seat at the United Nations even as the refugees began to straggle home; or perhaps September 6 might be considered the turning point, as that is when the man who led the rebel Patriotic Front to victory publicly vowed that Rwanda would become a multiparty democracy in which ethnic origins would be irrelevant, an announcement that appeared to one journalist to be consistent with a pattern in which "Rwanda does not have the feel of a military dictatorship."[46]

Or, perhaps it is possible to have a fifty-year crisis sustained by the minds and muscles of individuals. By August 1994, there were 1.7 million Hutus seeking refuge in eastern Zaire and the western United Republic of Tanzania, including those who had launched the original genocide against the Tutsis. The camps became the source of what is now a violent, well-organized, and heavily armed body of men. They have destabilized the entire region, gotten some governments in the region to broadcast radio messages of hate against the Tutsis, and managed to tie in to the illegal arms trade from southern and central Europe. According to a U.N. report, "Tens of thousands of the former Forces Armees Rwandaises trained, rearmed and plotted to retake control of their country."[47] The U.N. Commission of Inquiry estimated in 1998 that armed Hutu groups, once largely confined to two countries, had spread to ten, including Rwanda. A large contingent of them were fighting for the government of the Democratic Republic of Congo, which overthrew the former leader of then-Zaire, President Mobutu Sese Seko. The government of Rwanda, objecting to attacks from the Congo, launched its own attacks in response, all of which prompted, by July 1999, 1,500 to 2,500 people a day to leave the violence in the Congo for the relative peace of Tanzania.

At the same time, efforts were under way under the auspices of the Southern African Development Community and the Organisation of African Unity to broker a peace between the Democratic Republic of Congo government and rebels in the region, as well as to pacify and repatriate the Hutus who left Rwanda in 1994.[48] Surveying the region in 1998, the U.N. Commission of Inquiry concluded that the Hutu refugees from the original Rwandan crisis (along with others since displaced from other countries) ought to be disarmed, demobilized, and reintegrated into their societies, even though this would be difficult and expensive. They "are so harmful to the security and stability of African States and Governments, so threatening to human rights and so destructive to economic growth, that such an effort ought to be contemplated."[49]

Kosovo.   The earliest signs of trouble in Kosovo began with Serb government attacks on ethnic Albanian citizens in the Kosovo region of the Federal Republic of Yugoslavia (FRY). On March 31, 1998, the Security Council of the U.N. condemned the violence used by Serbs against ethnic Albanians. Intense diplomacy by individual states and by U.N. and NATO representatives ensued. Then came more ominous news: People were starting to move away from the terror. "The offensive that began in late May," noted an article in *The Economist*, "has so far killed at least 50 people and sent 65,000 fleeing from their homes."[50] Eventually this internal movement of people would go international and inundate other semiautonomous regions of FRY, as well as Albania, an independent country. Both the U.N. and NATO were interested in the problem. As early as June 24, 1998, U.N. Secretary General Kofi Annan reminded NATO that pursuant to the U.N. Charter, NATO needed Security Council approval before launching a military intervention—a warning partially ignored later. By September 29, the UNHCR estimated 200,000 people had been displaced. Peace talks between Serbs and Kosovar Albanians took place in the winter of 1998–1999 and led to a peace agreement.

At this point, NATO participation was consistent with Security Council resolutions, but FRY objected to the use of NATO in peace-keeping in Kosovo and rejected the agreement. FRY massed troops and police near the Kosovo border. On March 20, 1999, just a day after the peace talks in Paris were suspended, FRY troops crossed the border to reclaim and "cleanse," or "rebalance the ethnic composition" of the province.[51] In response, NATO gave the Yugoslav president, Slobodan Milosevic an ultimatum to comply with the peace agreement. On March 24, NATO air strikes began without U.N. Security Council approval. On the twenty-fifth, FRY broke diplomatic relations with the United States, Britain, France, and Germany.

The relative trickle of ethnic Albanians into nearby regions and countries started swelling on March 27. By the twenty-ninth, 60,000 were in Albania and nearly 50,000 in Montenegro. In early April, Macedonia had 30,000 and Albania over 100,000. By April 12, Albania had 300,000; and the UNHCR announced on April 18 that half a million had fled to other countries. The movement of people to Montenegro and to Macedonia on trains and buses seemed so smooth that NATO thought it was planned by Milosevic. On April 29, FRY filed suit against ten NATO countries at the International Court of Justice (ICJ) claiming NATO had committed war crimes in attacking a sovereign country. Much of this suit was rejected in June by the ICJ and, indeed, Milosevic was indicted as a war criminal on May 27. Meanwhile, poor intelligence led U.S. aircraft to bomb the Chinese embassy in Belgrade, seriously eroding relations between the United States and the People's Republic.

Talks between NATO and FRY resumed while the bombing continued and aid agencies coped with the refugees. NATO and the Serbs finally found a way to end the conflict. Serb forces had to start leaving before the bombing would end, but NATO agreed to obtain a U.N. Security Council Resolution authorizing entry by the NATO forces into Kosovo to restore peace. On June 10, 1999, the bombing stopped upon evidence of Serb withdrawals. A few tense days followed when, without prior consultation, Russian troops took control of the Pristina airport in Kosovo. The potential conflict was resolved—although part of the resolution involved Hungary and other central European nations refusing to let the Russians use their airspace to resupply troops.

Meanwhile, Kosovar refugees were returning home and, in some cases, taking revenge on Serbs. Serbs as well as Gypsies (who were deemed collaborators with the Serbs) went on the move themselves. U.N./NATO forces were often under attack by both sides, as they attempted to clear mines, maintain order, and help resettle Kosovars. In June, the top religious leader in Serbia called for Milosevic to resign, and by July 1999, tens of thousands of Serbs were calling for Milosevic's resignation as well.[52] Regardless of the degree of success in resettlement and the restoration of order, the return of refugees seems destined to contribute to future administrative difficulties and huge reconstruction problems.

In the Kosovo situation and in the enduring problems engendered by the Rwandan exiles, realists would note the continuing importance of states and high-level decisionmakers. Much was at stake for NATO countries as they tried to establish order in Europe. Realists, however, would be uneasy with the very idea of NATO risking war for humanitarian reasons. There were few power reasons to care about Yugoslavia's internal affairs. Despite protestations to the contrary, it seemed NATO wanted to destroy the territorial sovereignty of an independent state. Realists might admit the need for neighboring nations to balance against Serbia, but they would be likely to view turning a domestic issue into an international crisis as unwise.

Once the war was under way, the idea that Milosevic planned the removal of the Kosovars makes sense to realists, as did Milosevic's apparent calculation that the inability of air power to protect the Kosovars would break up the NATO alliance. In explaining the peace deal that ended the bombing, realists presumed that Milosevic relied on Russian assurances of support, an assumption that also accounts for the sudden arrival of the Russian troops in Pristina.

In the Rwanda case, realists could say that perhaps there were no genuine sovereign states in the region after all. No states, no crisis. Instead, events in the region were early state-building efforts. Independence had been a sham; the new countries were sovereign only in name. Now, through the fire of civil war, real independent states will emerge, just as millions died to create the West. For realists with less apocalyptic visions of events, the efforts of the states in the region to police themselves and broker peace agreements paralleled the European case in earlier centuries. Each region secures its own peace and deals with its own crises.

Liberal theorists are likely to be uncomfortable with the Kosovo affair and the refugee crisis it precipitated. They may be uncertain whether peace will ensue as individuals are secured from their government's violence or whether it will prove a disaster for international organizations or a political fiasco of the first order (as realists fear). Realists might argue that in advancing the rights of individuals, liberals have turned a domestic crisis that would be ignored elsewhere in the world into an international one. Liberals would point out that the very first signs of crimes against humanity by Serbian forces came with the movement of people, that it does matter what a country does at home to the political and economic rights of people, and that countries should stop the aggressor government when people protest brutal behavior at home by fleeing. By translating this reasoning into decisive action, NATO averted a larger war.

That it was accomplished through multilateral cooperation between democracies is all to the good from a liberal perspective. Democracies can and should lead on humanitarian policy. The massive flow of refugees presented a major humanitarian crisis, but it enhanced the credibility and determination of NATO to finish the job. Where realists would advise ignoring early warning signs of refugees' flight but escalating with ground troops when the refugees made the air operations look like a failure, NATO's successful use of consultation among allies, many diplomatic channels to the Serbs, and adherence to a clear humanitarian goal produced an important victory for human rights and democracy in Europe. True, the disregard of the U.N. Security Council at the outset of the bombing was a direct violation of the U.N. Charter. But in the end the U.N. Security Council did unanimously approve the deal (with one abstention). The war has clarified how regional security organizations can take decisive action to prevent threats to the peace. Communications between states are thereby enhanced. A similar policy might well work in Africa, especially since many of the states in the Great Lakes region of Africa are democracies. It is not war that makes for genuine sovereign states, but rather the promotion of the well-being of citizens. Attention to the well-being of people will, as the U.N. Rwanda report[53] indicated, make for stronger, not weaker, states.

Realists and liberals miss the micro dynamic of refugee crises, say postinternationalists. Both realist and liberal theories assume the refugee crises are rooted in the collective management problems of states, whereas postinternationalists contend that the real sources of the crisis involve the choices made by huge aggregations of people. True, liberals point to the internal circumstances of states to distinguish better friends from foes, but they fail to consider whether new authority patterns can be reestablished between citizens and those who govern on their behalf. The aftermath of the Rwanda example should be sobering in this regard. The refugees from Kosovo must go home; they must not be allowed to scatter or they will destabilize countries. Meanwhile, back at home, an arduous process of reconciliation looms and there are no nostrums on how to succeed. Emergent authority patterns among states, individuals, and the U.N. may also have been deeply changed by the events in Kosovo. Have states actually rejected global collective security through the U.N.? Are refugees outside the bright light of NATO out of luck as U.N. agencies fail to get cash from states?

Postinternationalists would also predict a long series of conflicts and new refugee flows as individuals learn different lessons from the Kosovo and Rwandan/African cases. Perhaps people will see the events on TV or hear accounts on the radio and misjudge entirely their prospects. Individuals in the developing world may decide there is no future in asking for their rights; or governments and peoples alike will decide that the costs of constant civil war are such as to require more authority and stronger communications. Perhaps ethnic and religious groups will be bolder about their demands in regions with many democratic nations but insufficiently bold elsewhere. The response from governments might well lead to enhanced individual rights and stronger democracies. On the other hand, such an expectation might prove risky. For example, Turkish troops joined their NATO allies in Kosovo as peace enforcers. Yet, at home, a brutal repression of Kurds is going on. Does the Kosovo situation mean Turkey is next for enforced liberal democratization—and the new flow of refugees that would follow? And what if the increased demands by subgroups reduce the capacity of existing democratic governments to deliver the performances people expect? Mistakes in policies designed to cope with subgroup demands could provoke violence and renewed refugee flows as communications and authority relations between all parties break down.

Rwanda itself has managed to begin to rebuild by starting an arduous community-building process and protecting both Hutu and Tutsi citizens. Whether this effort can displace memories of genocide remains to be seen. Tens of thousands of Hutus displaced by the earlier civil war seem ready to disrupt this progress and to undermine difficult ethnic and tribal relations in other countries of the region. For reasons like these, postinternational theory urges us to look for the early signs of micro organization, disorganization, or dislocation. It will be the collective actions of individuals that impede or enhance the capacity of governments and organizations to provide secure communities for people.

Interpreting Crises

It seems doubtful whether many observers would differ substantially with the foregoing outlines of the raw facts of the crises described. Presumably, realists, liberals, and postinternationalists would, despite their disparate interpretations of the events, agree that none of the situations were minor incidents. Realists may be dubious about classifying the unraveling of Asian economies and refugee episodes as "true" crises, but they would probably concede that these events were of sufficient importance to require efforts at theoretical explanation. In addition, proponents of all three schools of thought would be likely to concur that the crisis of the Indian and Pakistani entry into the nuclear club, lasting as it did only several months and with the leaders of both countries indicating a readiness to sign the test ban treaty, was the shortest and most clear-cut of the crises described and that it reminded the world that the end of the Cold War did not extinguish the dangers of a nuclear holocaust. Presumably, too, they would agree that the Asian financial crisis—or what realists might call a series of "domestic upheavals"—was the most prolonged and least clear-cut (since traces of its repercussions could still be discerned several years after the Thai currency collapsed). Similarly, the flight of Rwandan and Kosovar refugees would likely be interpreted by the three types of theorists as the crises most difficult to control (since they sprang largely from the common action of people whose fears and plight were not amenable to the formation of new institutions within either the state- or multi-centric worlds capable of ameliorating, much less resolving, either situation).

In all likelihood, moreover, there would not be much dispute over where the situations originated. Realists, liberals, and postinternationalists would surely agree that the nuclear proliferation crisis had its origins in the world of states, that the Asian financial crisis began with a state decision by the Thai government to devalue its currency and then spread quickly through the markets and investing communities of the multi-centric world, and that the refugee crises were initiated at the micro level of disparate and desperate people who were provoked into flight.

But these agreements on the raw facts do not tell us much. They are merely empirical summaries and not explanations of why the crises unfolded as they did. They do not account for what happens once analysis moves beyond mere description and confronts the theoretical tests posed by the crises: How is each case to be interpreted? What underlying dynamics of world politics do they reflect? In what respects, if any, do realists, liberals, and postinternationalists differ as to the meanings they attach to the cases? And, whatever their explanations, can these cases be regarded as meeting the severe challenges that crises pose for theorists?

Our method for exploring these questions is to turn for guidance to Table 5.1, which sets forth differences between realism, liberalism, and postinternationalism along several crucial dimensions, and then to extend the list of dimensions to those that are more specifically relevant to crisis conditions (see Table 6.1). The ensuing analysis highlights a number of ways in which adherents of the three paradigms are likely to disagree sharply on the nature and meaning of each crisis.

Global Structures and the
Exercise of Coercive Power

Perhaps the most obvious explanatory divergence derives from the conceptions of global structures held by realists, liberals, and postinternationalists. Realists are likely to question whether the financial and refugee situations were "true" crises, citing the fact that they did not involve direct confrontations between states. Given a conception

TABLE 6.1 Comparison of Likely Realist, Liberal, and Postinternationalist
Interpretations of Crises

	Realist Model	*Liberal Model*	*Postinternationalist Model*
Essential nature	Simple	Bounded	Complex
Number of situations classified as crises	Few	Limited	Numerous
Identity of key actors	States	Groups	SFAs and SBAs
Locale of crises	High government decisionmaking bodies	Transnational coalitions	Collective actions of citizens and governments
Onset of crises	When states set deadlines	When coalitions break in issue areas	Variable stimuli
Duration	Short, with definitive endings	Sequential as action moves through issue areas	Possibly lengthy, sometimes with ambiguous endings
Nature of power employed	Military	Economic and mass communications	Nonmilitary as well as military capabilities

of the world as organized around an anarchical interstate system, realists tend to regard as critical only those conflicts occurring between
states. Sure, a realist might concede, the United States and other states
reacted immediately, both individually and collectively, to the onset
of the Asian financial crisis and, yes, institutions in the state-centric
world, especially the IMF and the World Bank, were quick to suggest
mechanisms that might contain the crisis and prevent similar situations from breaking out in the future; nevertheless, the core of the situation was essentially a matter of domestic economies and their interdependence. Hence, realists conclude, the collapse of Asian
economies and their political repercussions, however serious and
long lasting they might prove to be, did not amount to a "true" crisis.
For similar reasons, they assert, the refugee situations cannot be regarded as crises. They were tragic, yes; unspeakable horror, yes; but
not crises, because they did not involve an eyeball-to-eyeball confrontation of states. On the contrary, in many respects, their main ac-

tors were masses of people and international organizations. Then, eager to drive home the tightness of their logic, realists might well add a comparison to the nuclear proliferation crisis: That was a "true" crisis, not only because it pitted state against state, but also because it involved a confrontation in which the rawest form of power could now be used by both sides. The realist might well ask how can one treat the proliferation crisis in the same breath with the others? "Surely, you are not going to argue that those brief weeks were a crisis for the multi-centric world! Why, the crisis petered out before actors other than states could even begin to mobilize!"

Not a problem, those committed to the turbulence model would be likely to respond. The bifurcated conception of global structures readily accommodates the different crises: The conflict over nuclear tests occurred in the state-centric world; those involving the flight of refugees emanated from the multi-centric world; and the spread of financial chaos entangled actors in both worlds. In other words, postinternationalists do not deny that interstate crises exist or that they are important. Quite to the contrary, their analytic antennae are tuned in to such developments and the losses and violence they may involve. But at the same time, their notion of a bifurcation that allows for serious and meaningful conflicts to occur among sovereignty-free actors or between them and states makes it possible for proponents of postinternationalism to treat the financial and refugee situations as no less "true" crises than the testing of nuclear weapons by India and Pakistan. Realist theory can envision wholly state-centric crises but tends to downplay crises that arise wholly in the multi-centric world or in interactions between the state- and multi-centric worlds. It may acknowledge the occurrence of the other two types of situations, but it will view them as events with little lasting importance.

The spread of nuclear weapons was not as troubling for liberals as were the financial and refugee crises. Problems in the nonproliferation regime had long been apparent, so the India-Pakistan decisions were not entirely unexpected. But the liberal view that cooperation among states improves the prospects for individuals and markets to realize their potentials is called into question when either or both become unruly and unstable. Under these circumstances, interstate institutions that facilitate cooperation tend to be undermined. And that is precisely what occurred when the Asian markets collapsed. The collapse directly challenged the IMF and the capacity of industrial states to moderate the chaos. Similarly, Kosovar refugees taxed NATO and the European human rights regime in Europe, just as Rwandan refugees shook the capacity of the U.N. to respond to the humanitarian disaster. These kinds of crisis are disconcerting for liberals because they can augur a decline in the authority of states and their established patterns of cooperation.

As indicated in both Tables 5.1 and 6.1, since realists are preoccupied with power in military confrontations, whereas liberals and postinternationalists are concerned with its operation in diverse circumstances, it is hardly surprising that the three are likely to differ in the kinds of situations that provoke them to attach the descriptor "crisis." For realists, crises refer primarily to time-compressed situations where vital national interests are at stake or where there is a significant prospect of war.[54] Thus they would be unlikely to characterize intense conflicts over trade, money, environmental, or human rights problems as crises. Not so for liberals and postinternationalists. Viewing power as generated by multiple sources, they are prepared to view various situations as giving rise to intense crises. For liberals such crises are likely to be limited in number and bounded in scope by the sequences of interaction to which fluctuating economies give rise, whereas postinternationalists, not being confined by their paradigms to situations springing from economic considerations, are likely to attach the "crisis" label to numerous, complex, and prolonged situations that end ambiguously. Thus, for example, postinternationalists might well characterize President Nixon's sudden decision to take the United States off the gold standard on August 15, 1971, as a crisis in the same way they are likely to discern the presence of crisis in a cholera epidemic among Rwandan refugees who fled to Zaire or in the initial rejection of the European Union's Maastricht Treaty by Danish citizens.

Boundaries, Sovereignty, and the Identity of Actors

A number of the differences between the three theories revolve around the boundary between foreign and domestic affairs and the identity of the key actors in world politics. As indicated in Table 5.1, the nature of sovereignty provides the crucial lever in this set of theory characteristics. Since realists are inclined to view the sovereignty of states as undiminished, they can also assume that states are unitary actors, that citizens are not relevant to foreign affairs, and that the line between domestic and foreign affairs is quite clear and solid. These interconnected propositions have important implications for how realists are likely to interpret the dynamics of crises. For them, states make decisions and take actions. Individuals matter only in the sense that as officials they speak for the state and can act on behalf of its interests. Concrete and identifiable persons "stand in" for the country, but ordinary citizens are of no consequence except as tokens of a state's power—as soldiers or as productive workers who can advance their country's economic power. When the leadership of a country announces that forces will be sent somewhere, realists presume that the forces will be sent. Put differently, realists view crises as occasions when the participation of citizens is likely to be minimal. Because the time horizon narrows so sharply, publics and transnational groups, which are generally deemed irrelevant by realism in any event, are left as mere bystanders. All the key decisions get made at the highest level—state to state—as the military and diplomatic arms of governments swing into action, while domestic agencies, whose voices are unlikely to penetrate the crisis deliberations, stay out of the picture.

Inasmuch as authority is most effectively backed up by the threat or use of force, realists tend to presume that military maneuvers are indicative of the buildup of crises. If a currency collapses and finance ministers quickly gather in a cooperative effort to stem the changing monetary values, realists would be hard pressed to describe such a situation as a crisis—a problem, yes; an imbalance, yes; but not a crisis in the sense that states are on a collision course.

Since those who employ the turbulence model are inclined to conceive of the sovereignty of states as undergoing erosion and the foreign-domestic boundary as thus porous and endlessly in flux, they are unlikely to treat states as unitary actors. To be sure, the decisions that get made in the state-centric world are those of leaders who act on behalf of their countries, but postinternationalists are too sensitive to the operation of societal variables to ignore evidence that governmental decisionmaking processes consist of bureaucratic and top-level conflicts fueled by groups within the society. In instances such as the nuclear proliferation crisis, they would concede, these groups may be mostly bystanders; they are unable to exert direct influence, either because of a shortage of time or because the crisis deliberations are conducted in secret. Even under these circumstances, however, postinternationalists might contend that the leaders are not unmindful of the political and societal implications of their decisions. In the proliferation crisis, for instance, neither Indian nor Pakistani leaders could be insensitive to the nationalistic sentiments of their aroused publics. Even in dire diplomatic and military crises, postinternationalists might thus argue, the policies adopted are not entirely those of a unitary actor.

This is not to imply, however, that postinternationalist theory is oblivious to territorial boundaries. Its adherents do not posit a borderless world so much as they conceive of its boundaries as fluctuating from issue to issue and as being crossed readily by a host of actors on both sides of the legally established lines that separate states.

As for liberals, they assert that good fences make good neighbors and that governments should take care not to thwart markets or the capacities of individuals, else they will create problems for themselves, the market, and civil society. At the same time, sovereignty matters for liberals because, through international law, it is the prime means by which states identify their rights and obligations. Maintaining distinctions between actors enhances the development of their identities and their potential for adding to human welfare. Thus once again liberals would be less preoccupied with the proliferation crisis even as they worried that the other two crises would introduce a measure of ambiguity into the loci of sovereignty and the identity of key actors.

Citizens, Publics, and Societal Institutions

It is not difficult to deduce from the foregoing why realists focus on decisionmaking processes in their interpretations of crises. Since they view crises as occurring exclusively between states as unitary actors, they need not be concerned about publics or societal institutions and can concentrate on how and why officials converged around a plan for action as the collision course neared a climax. In contrast, it is precisely because liberals and postinternationalists attach importance to the orientations and collective actions of public and societal institutions that they are not especially preoccupied with decisional processes. In focusing on the Asian financial crisis, for example, liberals would probably not investigate who in the Thai government first decided to devalue the currency, how the decision was made, or what form the decisionmaking process took. Rather, their analyses are likely to stress the cascading dynamics that flowed from the decision.

Far from being bystanders, investors, workers, bankers, and the many other individuals whose actions sustained the cascade of events across Asia are seen as occupying the center of the world stage. Likewise, although predisposed to attach the crisis label to sudden and massive movements of people across national boundaries, postinternationalists are unlikely to probe for any collective decisions that may have led to flight on the part of hundreds of thousands of Rwandans and Kosovars. What counts is not the decisionmaking process of discrete individuals but the convergence and aggregation of innumerable individuals around the same choices.

Thus, for those who employ the turbulence model, the crises generated by the collapse of currencies and mass migrations highlight the underlying tensions at work in national and international systems. These tensions affirm the premise of postinternationalists that the skills of individuals have undergone transformation to the point where individuals are prepared to act decisively. To withdraw from a market or to flee a tyranny is to engage in deep and serious calculations—estimates that require a readiness to reverse direction or to pull up roots and leave all that has meant home and tradition—and to reach conclusions that are painful and profoundly unsettling. The turbulence model allows for actions reflecting these calculations and posits their aggregation as part of the pervasive authority crises that mark world politics in this era.

Similarly, the aggregation of individual decisions that lead to a run on a country's currency and subsequently to a hasty meeting of finance ministers is likely to affirm the liberal perspective that crises need not evolve in a military context. On the other hand, whereas postinternationalists emphasize the centrality of micro actions and the capacity of those decisions to disrupt authority, liberals argue that the function of states is to facilitate and organize avenues for micro actions. An extreme run on the market is disruptive to the markets, individuals, and states, so it demands decisive state action. Refugees represent a failure of internal order and require a comprehensive approach that brings the state as well as society back to health. Again, the proliferation crisis was unfortunate and worthy of actions to prevent further proliferation, but it did not greatly disrupt patterns between states or between governments and citizens. The disruption-of-authority concern sets up a contrast between liberals and the other two theoretical perspectives. Unlike postinternationalists, liberals care about decision processes, but, in contrast to the concerns of realists, the decision processes of interest to liberals are those that facilitate rule making through either international or even societal institutions. When states, markets, or even individuals move far out of normal range from the process rules for making decisions, they prompt crises.

Realists might counter that even if one was to stretch the word crisis to cover the currency and refugee situations, it makes sense to do so only at a crucial stage when states are obliged to step in. After all, they would reiterate, neither the currency nor the refugee situations began to ameliorate until governments and international organizations entered the picture and undertook efforts to halt the flow of money in the former case and the flow of people in the latter instance. Only by severely distorting the dynamics of such situations, realists might conclude, can financial and refugee situations be interpreted as unfolding outside the context of interacting states. Not at all, retort postinternationalists; the underlying dynamics involved restless investors and migrants engaging in collective actions that were widely reported by the television media. Only as the situations entered their final phases did states and their international organizations become involved. Indeed, they had no choice: The dynamism of the skill revolution and the global authority crisis forced their hand and left them to take mopping-up roles that were essentially peripheral to the central problems posed by the flight of money and people.

Sensitivity to Change

Underlying the different responses of the three theories to crisis conditions is a huge gap in their understanding of the dynamics of change. Being inclined to presume that the course of events springs from the constancy of national goals and power distributions, realists are much less ready to discern change factors at work in world politics than are those who subscribe to the liberal or turbulence models. Realist theory anticipates little change, and thus its practitioners notice little change. To the extent that policymakers view the world through realist lenses, this tendency to perceive constancy has the paradoxical consequence of heightening the probability of crises in the state-centric world. Why is this? It is because policymakers may ignore underlying indicators of pending conflict and then be surprised and threatened when deeply embedded tensions surface into full-blown and unmanageable discord.

In contrast, at the other extreme postinternationalist theory rests on the presumption the world is undergoing vast transformations. Constancy is acknowledged, but it tends to be treated less as a central tendency and more as a set of restraints that channel, hinder, and delay the playing out of the transformations. Consequently, being readier to probe the underpinnings of surface tranquillity than their realist counterparts, postinternationalists discern the onset of crises earlier and thus tend not to be surprised as the likelihood of a collision increases. Indeed, given their perspective that change is a worldwide phenomenon and that global repercussions can flow from localized conflicts, postinternationalists are likely not only to anticipate many more crises than realists but also to look for them as emanating from a wider variety of sources—from newly empowered citizens, from financially paralyzed international organizations unable to act decisively, from governmental agencies in the domestic arena pursuing goals that take them across fluid foreign-domestic boundaries, from the worldwide and intense coverage of news media that brings distant events close to home, and from the many other SFAs that an increasingly fragmented and turbulent world has accorded roles on the global stage. Thus it is, to cite concrete illustrations, that the U.S. Department of Commerce provoked a trade crisis over construction contract rules in Japan and that humanitarian organizations were drawn into crisis by the huge flow of Rwandan refugees; it was as a result of these events that the organizations pressed their crises onto the agenda of the state-centric world. No less important, the turbulence model encourages its adherents to look to the role played by the mass media of communications in hastening the pace of movement along the collision course of crises. It is not coincidental that television coverage of the tragic circumstances of fleeing refugees is viewed by postinternationalists as part and parcel of the cascades that sustain such crises.

Given the orientation of realist theory toward constancy and that of turbulence theory toward change, it is not surprising that the two perspectives differ in the degree to which they see complexity as relevant to the onset and unfolding of crises. For example, whereas realists tend to view a crisis as an event that comes to some particular end (and that's that), postinternationalists are likely to discern the makings of a crisis as arising out of complex streams of action—out of cascades rather than events—that may not have clear-cut terminations. They are inclined to see crises as occurring at those points where multiple cascades coalesce, clash, and then resume until such time as they converge again. For postinternationalists, in other words, governmental decisions may precipitate crises, but these decisions are seen as springing from prior societal or transnational processes and as not necessarily bringing crises to climactic endings. For postinternationalists, therefore, the Asian financial crisis had its roots in developments that unfolded before the Thai government was moved to devalue its currency and it did not finally wind down for some seventeen months. Nor are postinternationalists deterred from viewing the movement of vast numbers of refugees as crises even though neither the plight of those who fled nor that of those who remained may show any sign of abating. To repeat, postinternationalists are disposed to measure crises by the persistence of specifiable conditions and not by specifiable decisions that lead to specifiable actions and interactions.

The turbulence model, in short, inclines its adherents to regard crises as having multiple origins and unfolding in multiple locales. Just as they perceive the Rwandan situation as a crisis for humanitarian organizations as well as states, so are they likely to regard, say, the strife in the former Yugoslavia as a crisis for Serbia, Bosnia, and Kosovo as well as the United Nations. Wherever circumstances turn sharply for the worse—whether it be in the areas of human rights, trade, money, or simply the dignity and well-being of people—postinternationalists are likely to speak of the onset of crises.

Staunch realists would interpret these events as merely the normal problems that mark the day-to-day routines and conflicts of world politics. For them, currency devaluations and mass migrations followed by subsequent governmental involvement are essentially inconspicuous developments in world politics, a presumption that those less wedded to the realist model tend to find questionable even as they concede that states do not ignore such situations and usually seek to infuse a measure of stability into them. For those who subscribe to the turbulence model, it does not seem logical to treat the pathos of suddenly dismissed Korean workers, riots in Indonesia, or fleeing refugees that come into view on global television screens as routine. For them, such crises are obvious instances of the micro and micro-macro parameters playing a central role in the course of events.

The orientation of liberals toward crises as sources of change lies somewhere between the realist and postinternationalist extremes. They have an evolutionary perspective on change and are thus inclined to ascribe change dynamics only selectively. Crises that involve the transformation or absence of effective institutions are likely to evoke their analytic concerns, whereas those that occur within the context of existing institutions do not particularly arrest their attention. The crisis resulting from the testing of nuclear devices by India and Pakistan, therefore, did not preoccupy them, whereas the Asian financial crisis was a matter of intense concern. Indeed, spurred by the IMF's concession that it erred in handling the crisis,[55] bothered by the failure of the G-7 finance ministers to agree on measures to promote global currency stability,[56] and troubled by the policies toward the crisis pursued by the United States,[57] liberals became deeply—although not consensually—engaged by the question of what kind of institutional mechanisms can be devised to prevent, or at least contain, future currency crises on a regional or global scale.

Similarly, the refugee crises proved problematic, because of a serious lack of humanitarian institutions. Refugee crises also trouble liberals because of the violence mass movements visit upon human freedom and dignity. Moreover, the crisis of individual freedom challenges the capacity of states to respond even incrementally to the problem. If states set individuals at the heart of their international relations, as some have done at home, then they may greatly destabilize a vast array of international institutions. If they do nothing, even larger numbers of people may be in distress. Perhaps the Kosovo case illustrates how humanitarian reform may evolve further. The norm may spread from Europe outward, gaining new state supporters. If this happens, states and their nongovernmental humanitarian allies will learn better how to manage the refugee flows that still occur.

Conclusion

Clearly, all three models are capable of meeting the tests that crises pose. Neither realists nor liberals nor postinternationalists need lose any sleep over how to interpret those moments in world politics that explode into crises. They all have conceptual tools that enable them to offer explanations that are meaningful and that preserve the integrity of their perspectives.

To be sure, the reader may find fault with how one or the other theory classifies and analyzes crises, but such conclusions are indicative of the reader's theoretical orientations and not of fatal flaws in the models. Indeed, if crises serve to provoke theoretical impulses on the part of readers, they are likely to value the effort in Chapter 9 to suggest how analysts might perfect their skills at thinking theory more thoroughly.

7

The United Nations

Most case studies describe processes wherein actors conflict as they seek contrary goals in an evolving situation. As such, they are narratives of how problems arise, persist, or get resolved with the passage of time. In this case, however, the focus is on an institution, the United Nations, and how it is adjusting to a wide range of challenges. Our concern is less with a single issue moving through time and more with the dynamics whereby numerous overlapping and simultaneous issues are addressed by a multipurpose organization at roughly a single point in time. Stated differently, we are interested in multiple narratives and how they interact to shape the authority, stability, resources, and structures of a vital instrument for the maintenance of international order.

The end of the Cold War in 1989 brought to the forefront of world affairs the question of what roles the U.N. can and should play in the course of events. The U.N.'s peacekeeping activities had been hidden deeply within the shadows of superpower rivalry during the prior four decades, but the collapse of the rivalry, along with a growing conviction that the world had become too complex for any country to predominate as a superpower, meant that the U.N. could no longer be viewed as a peripheral institution. A vacuum had been created. The demise of the Soviet empire and the surge of domestic preoccupations in the United States meant that the long-established mechanisms for preventing or coping with conflicts around the world were no longer available. And there were many trouble spots. Iraq invaded and conquered Kuwait. Ethnic groups in the former Yugoslavia resorted to civil war. Famine and intense tribal warfare struck Somalia. A democratic election was overturned by a military coup in Haiti.

Cambodia's warring factions quarreled over the format for a nation-wide election. A pro-independence election outcome in East Timor resulted in a massacre by paramilitary Indonesian forces. And so it went all around the globe as the world groped for a new order to replace the Cold War system to which it had become so accustomed. Under these circumstances the U.N. loomed as an institution suitable for generating the cooperation necessary to address many of the crises that were erupting within and between countries. Perhaps more accurately, in the absence of any alternatives, the world turned to the U.N. for remedial actions. Beginning in the mid-1990s, however, this trend seemed likely to result in a condition of system overload whereby the U.N. would be committed to remedying more conflict situations than it could manage or finance.

Given the U.N.'s expanded involvement in a multiplicity of conflicts, it is hardly surprising that the organization has become the focus of considerable controversy among governments, within bureaucracies, between political parties, in newspaper columns, and in the U.N. itself. And as each situation involving the U.N. develops, so do affirmations of its importance or criticisms of its role intensify. As will be seen, these varied reactions to the U.N.'s performances are partly dependent on whether a situation appears to be improving or worsening, but they are even more profoundly a consequence of whether the critic is looking at the situation from a realist, a liberal, or a postinternationalist perspective. Perhaps never before, in fact, have the distinctions between the three paradigms been more evident in the course of events. The differences can readily be discerned in conceptions of the U.N.'s history and development, in reactions to the question of an appropriate role for the U.N. in the many civil wars that have evolved since the end of the Cold War, in the policies pursued by the secretary general of the U.N., in the issue of whether U.S. troops should serve under foreign commanders in U.N. peacekeeping operations, in the emergent global concern with protecting and extending human rights, in the monitoring of domestic elections, in the administrative problems involved in coordinating the multiple agencies with overlapping responsibilities under the U.N. umbrella, and in the difficult problem of providing adequate financing for all the U.N.'s new assignments—to mention only the more prominent of the controversies that have surrounded the organization since the end of the Cold War.

History and Development

It is worth noting at the outset that despite its deep involvement in world affairs in recent years, the U.N. has not been a preoccupation of theorists. Aside from some early theorizing undertaken prior to the onset of the Cold War (see immediately below), most of the theoretical interpretations ascribed to the three paradigms in this chapter are derived more from inferences implicit in the logic of each theory than from explicit formulations. What it is about the U.N. that neither specialists in international organization nor general theorists have been inclined to make it the focus of theorizing in recent years is far from clear. Perhaps part of the explanation lies in the newness of the U.N.'s growing diversity of roles; that is, prior to the 1990s the U.N.'s activities did not seem significant enough to warrant theoretical exploration. Perhaps another part of the explanation is to be found in the predominance of states during the Cold War decades, a predominance that made the U.N. appear simply as a handy mechanism—rather than a primary instrument—for addressing problems states wished to avoid or for giving voice to the aspirations of weaker states. To some extent, the explanation may also lie in the early theoretical debates surrounding the founding of the U.N. in 1945, debates that were sustained at the time by the aspiration of diplomats and scholars to end the scourge of war through the structures and practices of international organizations. Whatever the reasons for the more recent theoretical neglect of the U.N., and doubtless there are many others, it remains perplexing that today's theorists have tended to ignore this major arena of global activities and that international organization specialists have treated its functioning as little more than an instance of public administration writ large. In short, to treat the U.N. as a major case study in a theoretically oriented book is to take on an important and puzzling challenge.

Since the postinternational model is of more recent origin, only the realists and liberals engaged in theorizing about the U.N. during and just after World War II. Then (and now) the realists saw the U.N. as a means for great powers to moderate each other and influence lesser powers though the Security Council. The leading postwar theorist, Hans Morgenthau, stressed the differences between the U.N. and its interwar predecessor, the League of Nations: "The tendency toward government by the great powers, which was already unmistakable in the League of Nations, completely dominates the distribution of functions in the United Nations."[1] The U.N. Charter as written took unity between the great powers "for granted" and focused on "the preservation of peace among the medium and small powers through the instrumentality of great-power government."[2] That it did not work as intended was due to the Cold War and the conflict between the great powers. With this conflict over, or at least considerably moderated, the U.N. had an opportunity to operate on the assumption of great-power unity—as it did during the Gulf War, thus conveying an impression that the U.N. was a powerful actor on its own. It is not, say the realists. Rather, the success of the U.N. depends on the great powers and especially on the United States. The U.N. was and remains beholden to great-power creativity, cooperation, or recalcitrance.

Nevertheless, said Morgenthau, the U.N., especially through the General Assembly,

> speaks with a voice which pretends and appears to be, and within certain limits actually is, different from that of the great powers. Thus nations in conflict with each other can afford to do vis-à-vis the United Nations what they think they cannot afford to do in their relations with each other—make concessions in the formulation, if not the substance, of their policies without losing face.[3]

Such concessions can be greatly enhanced if it is the secretary general who makes the initial proposal. To the degree the General Assembly or the secretary general are silenced through the operation of great-power government, then even this device for international cooperation tends to lose its utility. On the other hand, if the General Assembly and secretary general can continue to suggest solutions to mutual problems, then they might be able to balance the threats to sovereignty posed by a unified set of great powers.

Initial theorizing by liberals was based on the assumption that well-functioning sovereign states can cooperate on a wide range of issues, precisely because anarchy does not have to mean conflict. For liberals, a spreading culture of international institutions based on international law would enhance the domestic and international well-being of states. One scholar of international organizations put it this way: "The appropriate question to ask concerning international organizations is not whether they are succeeding in putting states out of business and taking the business for themselves, but whether they are contributing to the capacity of states to stay in business."[4]

Efforts to find institutional ways to promote peace, such as international arbitration of disputes, regular peace conferences, and even the League of Nations, all were consistent with liberal theory. At the same time, liberals developed another strand of theorizing about international organization, which came to be known as "functionalism." This approach advocated building international organization around non-war issues where states had strong reasons to cooperate. Thus the International Postal Union (1874) and the International Telegraphic Union (1865)—now transmuted into the International Telecommunications Union—came into being to organize the chaos of national rules and to set standards in these areas. Later the rise of labor movements in many democratic nations prompted the formation of the International Labor Organization in 1920. The functional logic that gave rise to these early international organizations also underpins the vast array of specialized agencies of the U.N. created since its founding in 1945. A form of functional theory even underlay the early efforts of what is now the European Union (a non-U.N. organization) and thereby also demonstrated the power of the liberal proposition that "cooperation is natural."

Let us now turn to theorizing since the end of the Cold War. Viewed from a realist perspective, the sudden burst of U.N. activity in recent years reflects the undoing of bipolarity in the international system. The civil wars in which the U.N. now tries to interject its peacekeepers were under way before 1989. Indeed, they were enhanced and prolonged by the U.S.-Soviet rivalry for spheres of influence. Once this rivalry ended, either the problems were soon corrected (as was the case in Namibia) or they flared out of control (as in Somalia, Bosnia, Kosovo, and East Timor). Thus it follows, the realists, ever skeptical about the centrality of the U.N. as an independent actor in world affairs, would stress that it is only because the present period is one in which the polarity of the system remains in doubt that the U.N. gives the illusion of playing its own game. But further reflection suggests a different line of reasoning. Realists contend that underlying the illusion is a developmental process wherein parts of the international system are becoming multipolar, thus allowing for the assertion of regional leadership, while other parts are tending toward unipolarity, thus enabling the United States to operate as first among equals in the security realm. The Euro-

pean Union's (EU) effort to take the lead in bringing peace to the former Yugoslavia is offered as one case of regional leadership, the continuing amenability of the Cambodian situation to Chinese policies is
cited as another, and Australia's leadership of U.N. forces in East Timor
is still another. For realists, the fact that the EU did not on its own succeed in bringing peace to Bosnia provides confirmation of the fact that
multipolar arrangements were at work, especially since the EU's efforts
suffered from disputes among its members and not from any inherent
inability to resolve the situation. The continuing centrality of the role of
states in the international system's developing structure is further vali-
dated by the method by which at least a tentative measure of peace
came to Bosnia: The bombing of the central market in Sarajevo brought
an end to the disputes among the EU's members and, reinforced by coordinated threats by the United States and NATO to bomb Serbian
guns surrounding the city, led to the withdrawal of the weaponry
around that beleaguered city.

U.S. leadership in NATO, along with the difficult and unsatisfying
course of affairs in Bosnia, may have prompted the use of NATO
rather than the U.N. in the dispute over the treatment of Albanian
Kosovars by the Serbs. Only as a way to end the conflict did the parties seek a Security Council resolution on the affair. Had NATO followed the rules of the U.N. Charter, it could have taken military action, but to do so required Security Council approval. Fearful of a
veto, NATO did not go down this path, thus suggesting to realists the
"true" nature of power in the security realm. The U.N. was useful
only in its aid for refugees and as a fig leaf at the end of the conflict.
What mattered was the fifty years of NATO cooperation and U.S.
leadership.

Realists might also argue that such situations highlight the unipolarity inherent in the relative power position held by the United
States, that the uncertainty that marks many of the more severe conflict situations around the world can be traced to U.S. confusion over
what to do and what to fight for as it reviews its core interests. Put
more succinctly, recent disputes on the role of the U.N.—on how and
where it should operate—have been led by U.S. concerns. Given the
relative strength of the United States, the sensitivity of the U.N. to
U.S. preoccupations will continue well into the future.

Irrespective of the degree to which the system is evolving in unipolar directions, realists would reason that the United States is unlikely

to lose interest in the U.N.—for the latter helps the former play its role as hegemon. That was the case in the early years of the U.N. and it remains the case today. Hegemons would not last long if they had to apply raw power at every turn. It is far better that they find ways of legitimating their power so that others will accept it more readily. The costs of the limited constraints placed on U.S. action due to membership in the U.N. are minor compared to the gains. In short, as it has from the outset, the U.N. must still proceed cautiously when U.S. interests and concerns are at stake.

Indeed, the realist historical perspective concludes, the U.N.'s original structure, especially its grant of the veto to the great powers, continues to underlie the organization's viability. The fact that use of the veto has declined in recent years is a measure not of the U.N.'s transformation but of changes in the world that have dissuaded the five permanent members of the Security Council from resorting to the veto. After all, it was the availability of the veto that encouraged the major powers to join the U.N. in the first place. And there is every reason to believe, realists would stress, that the United States and all the other permanent members of the Security Council would not hesitate to use their veto power again if they deemed circumstances warranted its exercise.

Liberals view the U.N. from a very different perspective. For them the U.N. is a beacon of hope—a sometimes-faded beacon, but nonetheless a beacon—in a strife-ridden world, an organization founded on cooperation among states that has the potential for ameliorating, if not resolving, the tensions that lead to or sustain wars. U.N. procedures facilitate discussion, reduce the costs of information about what matters to other states, and provide a mechanism for military leadership that does not force other states to choose the United States as their leader. Liberals concede that states use the U.N. for their own purposes and that thus recent history records a number of conflicts U.N. officials and agencies have failed to diminish. But, they stress, the U.N. offers a forum where states caught up in intense conflicts can air and discuss their differences, a stage of diplomacy that is seen as a necessary prerequisite to the kind of cooperation on which the resolution of long-standing disputes are founded. Besides, liberals note, not infrequently in recent years the U.N. has successfully contributed to the prevention or termination of conflicts, both within and between states. They point to the 1991 collaboration of thirty-two nations under U.N. auspices that compelled Iraq to withdraw from Kuwait in the Gulf War as illustrative of the organization's potential for successfully bringing interstate wars to an end, just as a commission of the U.N. was subsequently able for some seven years to monitor Iraq's dismantling of nuclear, chemical, and biological weapons of mass destruction. Indeed, liberals are quick to emphasize that as the concept of security has broadened beyond physical and territorial issues since the end of the Cold War, the U.N. has increasingly intruded upon the domestic affairs of states on behalf of humanitarian issues—for example, providing food, medicine, clothing, and shelter for Kurds in northern Iraq and needy people in Somalia and Rwanda.

Liberals would note that realists could hardly explain why NATO was worried about ethnic conflict within a sovereign country, with or without the U.N. They stress that the intervention makes more sense when viewed in the context of a U.S.-European security community. From a liberal perspective, democratic forms of government and respect for human rights dominate the NATO countries, whereas this is not the case in the U.N. Accordingly, liberals contend, the prospect of more ethnic violence by an outlaw state like Serbia/Yugoslavia could no longer be tolerated by the EU or by NATO. In this context, the U.N. is still useful as a (re)builder of state sovereign capacity, although it will be of European variety, one that emphasizes individual rights.

Although postinternationalists share the liberal emphasis on the U.N. as a facilitator of cooperation among states, their perspective on the organization is somewhat different. As they see it, the U.N. has undergone a transformation that corresponds to the changes occurring in the world. For them the evolution of the U.N. and its present conditions bordering on system overload are part of a long-term process of international institutionalization. This process includes the evolution of norms favoring multilateralism, the development of the habit of cooperation, the building of new formal governmental organizations and the expansion of old ones, and the increasing legitimization of nongovernmental organizations as role players within these organizations and institutions—all of which have added to the pace of change that marks U.N. structures and processes.[5] Admittedly, say the postinternationalists, the original purpose of the U.N. was to provide a league of states that would protect states' interests and make up for their deficiencies. But today, sometimes subtly and sometimes quite obviously, the purpose has shifted in the direction of using international institutions to deal not only with the burgeoning transnational and global problems that cannot be managed through cooperation among states alone but also with the problems faced by peoples, by individuals whose needs and wants far exceed what they have. Postinternationalists point to the opening phrase of the U.N. Charter, "We the peoples," as anticipating well the transformation of the micro parameter posited by the turbulence model. And the transformation of this and the other two parameters, a postinternationalist might conclude, is precisely why the veto has not recently been exercised in the Security Council: The evolution of global norms relevant to international cooperation and the pressure of publics for their maintenance has made it increasingly difficult for any of the permanent members to take on the opprobrium that would result from negating the council's will.

As will be seen, the notion of institutionalization at the international level is a key to grasping the role of the U.N. in today's world. This theme is foremost in the postinternationalist interpretation of the U.N.'s new peacekeeping roles and the evolution of the secretary general's position. Indeed, since the U.N. has hosted major conferences of states on the environment, human rights, population, women's rights, and other key issues on the global agenda that have evoked parallel conferences by NGOs in the multi-centric world, the U.N. has emerged as the prime institutional mechanism for bridging the two worlds resulting from the bifurcation of global structures.

State Sovereignty and U.N. Autonomy

At the core of the controversies over the U.N.'s expanding roles is the question of whether it remains the servant of the states that created it in 1945 or, instead, is becoming an autonomous actor with its own authority. Although realists acknowledge that the U.N. has become more central to the course of events than it was in the past, they contend that its expanded activities have been undertaken in response to Articles 7 and 99 of the U.N. Charter and to the wishes of its members as these have been expressed in resolutions adopted by the General Assembly or the Security Council and subsequently implemented by the secretary general or any of the numerous agencies that make up the U.N. system.[6] Accordingly, they argue, states have the capacity in any situation to curb or end the activities of U.N. officials deemed to have exceeded the authority granted them by the Security Council.

Although liberals do not deny that states have ultimate control over the U.N. policies and actions, they emphasize the degree to which this control is not exercised and the large extent to which the U.N. is a site where cooperation among states occurs. Liberals conceive of this cooperation as stemming from the nature of people and their pressure for the fashioning of institutions that foster international cooperation and militate against a resort to coercion. They also regard the cooperation of states in international organizations as both fostered by and resulting from an appreciation that their national interests are served by cooperating on joint projects.

Postinternationalists have still another perspective. They discern in many of the very same cooperative actions some small measure of independent autonomy. They view some of the situations in which the U.N. becomes involved as so complex and urgent that the U.N. officials on the scene must perforce make quick decisions and initiate actions that cannot possibly be monitored by, or referred back to, the Security Council. In turn, such actions are seen as becoming precedents for future responses to a variety of situations. Consequently, it is contended, there are times when U.N. officials have a leeway that, for all practical purposes, is essentially free of supervision and thus amounts to an independent, autonomous authority.

In other words, whereas realists and liberals tend to view U.N. officials and agencies as servants and instruments of states, postinternationalists see them as independent actors. Put more elaborately, whereas realists and liberals interpret U.N. actions as occurring at the convenience of states and thus as always being subject to reversal or cessation by a vote of (or veto in) the Security Council, postinternationalists argue that in subtle but substantial ways the convenience-of-states mentality has given way to a states-are-obliged-to-go-along attitude. They claim the latter attitude can be so pervasive as to result in states not reversing or bringing to a halt U.N. actions even though they continue to retain the formal right to do so.

Whichever of these perspectives one might find most compelling, clearly the question of where authority is located with respect to the U.N. is not a simple either-or matter. States may regard their sovereignty as indivisible, as a set of rights they either have or do not have, but it does not require much reflection to realize that sovereignty is a

variable, that a state's authority may vary from one issue area to another, and that states may pay lip service to their sovereignty even as
they accept unilateral actions by the U.N., nongovernmental organizations, multinational corporations, or other actors central to the course
of events. Realists and liberals may stress that such unilateral actions
are always conditional upon the continual acceptance of states, but at
the same time they appear to recognize that changing circumstances
make it extremely unlikely that any state will, on its own, defy the will
of the international community and insist that, say, the U.N.'s unilateral actions be ended. Such a state might contend that the U.N. has exceeded the authority granted it by the Security Council, or it might
seek the support of other states in calling for a reconvening of the
council, but the norms of international governance no longer encourage it to stand on ceremony, to justify rejection of the U.N.'s action on
the grounds that the sovereignty of states is inviolable.

In focusing on the legal rights of states to exercise their sovereignty,
realists are led to stress the difficulties and failures the U.N. has experienced in taking on a host of new obligations. As they see it, multilateral efforts can, at best, enjoy limited success because the U.N.
lacks the power, the resources, and the decisiveness to cope with conflicts in which the adversaries pit their military forces against each
other. Why? Because U.N. officials derive their authority from agreements reached by states and, since states are ever mindful of their
own interests, such agreements are bound to reflect the contradictory
perspectives of the states that sign them. That is, they are bound to be
watered down by the reluctance of states to set precedents that might
undermine their own sovereignty, by states' unwillingness to commit
their own citizens to battle, and by their need to cope with the constraints of their domestic economies.

Although liberals are also inclined to emphasize the continuing viability of state sovereignty and still view international relations as unfolding at the convenience of states, they acknowledge the existence
of new situations in which states appear to feel obliged to go along
with certain kinds of U.N. actions. This is especially the case in those
situations where humanitarian intervention in the domestic affairs of
tension-ridden states seems warranted. The object of such intrusions
is not to establish world government, which would undo sovereignty,
but rather to protect human rights, a key basis for sound domestic authority and more international peace.

If realists and liberals stress the unchanging dimensions of sovereignty and view the Security Council's intrusions in domestic situations as actions by the powerful hands of the great powers incompletely disguised by velvet gloves, their postinternational counterparts are inclined toward the opposite extreme of the continuum and the notion that sovereignty has changed to the point where its relevance is questionable. They see the readiness of the Security Council to intrude the U.N. into the domestic affairs of member states as a fundamental normative transformation signifying a continuing erosion of the sovereignty principle. Yes, states accept and vote for such intrusions, they argue, but in so doing they accord the secretary general and other U.N. officials considerable leeway to cope with situations, a leeway that amounts to nothing less than an independent autonomy running counter to, and even negating, the principle that states have ultimate authority. Sure, states remain powerful and can get the Security Council to negate or reverse the actions of officials in the field, but the likelihood of this occurring is seen as minimal since the members of the Security Council have a stake in not emasculating the U.N.'s prestige.

The U.N. as an Actor

Given the readiness of realists and liberals to acknowledge that the agenda of world affairs has undergone transformation and the inclination of postinternationalists to concede that states remain powerful, it might be asked whether the three schools of thought are converging on each other and whether, in effect, we are raising a false set of issues, or at least overemphasizing the differences between them. Our answer is no. Whatever the degrees of overlap between the three perspectives, the remaining differences that separate them are considerable and lead to very different interpretations of what drives the course of events. More than mere nuance differentiates the convenience-of-states and states-are-obliged-to-go-along orientations. As will be seen, profoundly different consequences follow from adhering to one or the other approach. Accordingly, to more fully assess these conflicting perspectives, we turn to an examination of several dimensions of the U.N. that have recently become highly salient. The pace and scope of the U.N.'s activities, its peacekeeping efforts, its intrusion into the elections and human rights policies of its members, its work on development and environmental issues, its administrative structures, and its financing have all become the focus of controversies that put in sharp relief how adherents of the three perspectives vary in their perceptions and evaluations of the organization's emergent roles.

Pace and Scope

It is not difficult to demonstrate the large extent to which the U.N.'s activities have expanded since the end of the Cold War. In 1987 the U.N. assigned some 10,000 peacekeepers—mostly troops in blue helmets who were supposed to resort to force only if attacked—to five operations around the world on an annual budget of about $233 million. Over the next seven years the number of troops rose to 72,000 in eighteen different situations at an annual cost of more than $3 billion. Similarly, where the Security Council used to meet once a month, by 1994 its schedule involved meeting every day and often twice a day. In 1993 alone, the Security Council adopted more than 181 resolutions and statements, all of them high-minded in tone (such as a demand for the end of ethnic cleansing in the former Yugoslavia) but few of them enforceable.

Although these new patterns represent a dramatic increase in the U.N.'s role since the end of superpower competition and highlight the need for new modes of cooperation, the extent of the hastened pace and widened scope can be interpreted in several ways depending on whether one is inclined to view history from a realist, a liberal, or a postinternationalist perspective. Some analysts, including realists who worry about the U.N. exceeding its mandate and capabilities, stress that the appointment of an activist, Boutros Boutros-Ghali, as the U.N.'s secretary general in January 1992 contributed to the accelerated involvement of the organization in diverse conflict situations around the world. Knowing of Boutros-Ghali's aspiration to turn the U.N. into "a new instrument in the public opinion, a new instrument for the member states,"[7] such analysts regarded the Security Council as being too quick to follow his lead into new conflict situations. Not so, say liberals and postinternationalists; rather, the pace and scope of the U.N.'s missions accelerated because the processes of fragmentation quickened in a turbulent world no longer readily manageable by direct diplomatic cooperation between states, leaving the U.N. with the opportunity to respond to demands for expanding its activities as new situations evolved to threaten the well-being and stability of people in various parts of the world. Indeed, even Boutros-Ghali was quoted as saying that the structure of world politics, and not personalities, accounts for the broadened scope of the organization's activities:

> Very often people like to compare [secretaries general as less active than me]. I say, "No, let us speak very justly. If I would have been [in office in earlier periods], I would have done exactly the same [as my predecessors did]. And if [they were in the office now, they] would have been compelled, even if [they] did not want to do it, to be more active. So, very often it is the period that creates the man."[8]

Furthermore, whereas realists may ascribe the acceleration of the U.N.'s pace and scope to the onset of multipolarity, those who subscribe to the liberal and turbulence models are likely to interpret the acceleration as deriving from the changing, postinternational structure of world politics. In their view, Boutros-Ghali's immediate predecessor, Javier Perez de Cuellar, left the office at a time when the U.N. had succeeded in helping to bring about an end to violent conflict in a number of diverse situations—Afghanistan, Iran-Iraq, Namibia, Nicaragua, and El Salvador[9]—with the result that "people went from thinking the U.N. could do nothing to thinking it could do everything."[10] These actions supported the momentum that led the Security Council to hasten the pace and expand the scope of the organization's activities.

In short, although states may still view themselves as possessed of the sovereign rights that enable them to slow and narrow, even negate, U.N. activities, the likelihood of their exercising these rights in crucial world situations is more complicated than realism suggests. Yet, as noted below, the structure of world politics is not evolving so quickly as to prevent states from contesting U.N. policies and, in some instances, backing away from them.

Although Boutros-Ghali's activism was one reason he was replaced as secretary general after only one term, his successor, Kofi Annan, was no less ready to intrude the prestige of his office when he felt it was necessary to minimize or reduce conflict. In 1998, for example, he traveled to Baghdad to negotiate with Saddam Hussein over Iraq's harassing U.N. inspection teams searching for weapons of mass destruction, and shortly thereafter he traveled to Libya to negotiate the release of two Libyans to a court in the Netherlands charged with trying them for downing a Pan American airliner in 1988. Although the former mission was not successful, thus seeming to affirm the realist paradigm, the latter mission did succeed, thus supporting the view of the other paradigms of the U.N. as playing a more active role in the course of events.

Peacekeeping, Peacemaking, and Peace Enforcing

Various stages mark the processes whereby peace is established and maintained within and between societies. Violent conflict may be ended through negotiations, or peace may be enforced by preventing adversaries from resuming hostilities while the foundations of a lasting peace are laid. During the Cold War the U.N.'s participation in these processes was highly circumscribed. As was the case in Cyprus or on the Golan Heights, it intervened only when invited by the adversaries to police previously agreed-upon cease-fire lines, thereby giving the politicians time to negotiate a solution. As the political vacuum widened with the end of the Cold War and superpower competition, however, so did the tasks assigned to U.N. peacekeeping forces. Recently the U.N. has been asked, not always by the adversaries, to become involved in what Secretary General Boutros-Ghali called "second-generation operations"[11]—that is, to intervene directly in unfolding situations and to steer them to a desired outcome. The goal may be to help convince an aggressor country to give up its conquered lands (as in the case of Iraq in Kuwait), to manage and oversee elections following the end of bitter conflicts (as in Angola, Cambodia, El Salvador, and South Africa), to deliver food and medicine in war zones (such as Bosnia), to restore order and stability (as in Haiti and Kosovo), or to escort relief convoys and reverse massive social disintegration (as in Somalia and East Timor).

Put differently, participation by intervention has replaced participation by invitation as the basis for U.N. action in many situations. And underlying this shift, a postinternationalist might note, has been a readiness of states to recognize their declining competence and thus to accept U.N. missions that extend beyond the organization's longstanding commitment to impartial peacekeeping and require it, instead, to engage in enforcement actions. Realists, in contrast, would note how U.S. hegemony and great-power agreement contributed to the extension of the U.N.'s roles. As for liberals, they would emphasize that such efforts under the aegis of the U.N. were state-building activities, that strong states make for effective international partners for other states.

The most successful instance of peace enforcement, and one that probably served to encourage many of the other second-generation operations that followed, occurred shortly after the end of the Cold War. In August 1990, Iraq invaded and conquered Kuwait, an action so blatant as to stimulate the United States to mobilize a coalition of thirty-two countries to force Saddam Hussein's Iraqi troops out of Kuwait. At virtually every stage, the United States submitted its proposals to the U.N. Security Council for approval before the U.S.-led coalition took action. For the first time, the Security Council made full use of the collective security provisions of the U.N. Charter (Chapter VII). Early in 1991 the Gulf War was launched, and the U.N.-sponsored coalition defeated the Iraqis in but a few weeks. And the newly discovered capacities of the U.N. did not end with the cessation of hostilities. Confronted with hundreds of thousands of Iraqi Kurds and Shiite Muslim Arabs fleeing Saddam Hussein's brutal repression at the war's end, the horrors of which were captured and repeatedly displayed over global television, the Security Council approved Resolution 688, which condemned the repression and asked the secretary general to investigate the plight of the refugees. The council dismissed Iraq's objection that its handling of the problem was an internal affair and that any U.N. action was "blatant interference," asserting instead that the wave of refugees flowing toward Turkey and Iran threatened "international peace and security." This action was not merely an extension of the peacekeeping obligations that the U.N. took on at the end of the war. Resolution 688 was, rather, an entirely new intrusion into the sovereignty principle.

But the breakthrough into uncharted areas of the sovereignty principle was not clear-cut and unqualified, for Resolution 688 did not back up its statement of concern for the refugees with action to protect them. That came from the United States, which was in large part moved by European pressures and by the television scenes of human suffering to undertake to establish, supply, and protect sanctuary sites for Kurdish refugees in northern Iraq. The United States contended that the building of sanctuaries came under Resolution 688, but Secretary General Javier Perez de Cuellar questioned whether the United States could lawfully intervene on Iraqi soil without a new and explicit authorization by the Security Council. When the United States subsequently sought approval for a U.N. police force to replace its forces in northern Iraq, the secretary general sent an envoy to Baghdad to ask for Iraq's approval of the idea. Iraq rejected the request, claiming it involved an illegal violation of Iraqi sovereignty, and the secretary general reiterated that new Security Council authorization was needed for the U.N. to take over the policing process. The United States did not seek the new authority, apparently fearing that it might be vetoed by the Soviet Union or China—or both. China opposed U.N. intervention without Iraq's consent, thus tacitly affirming the realist paradigm. On the other hand, postinternationalists probed beneath the potential veto and interpreted it as having its roots in the multi-centric world, with the Chinese being fearful that the Tibetans could theoretically appeal for the same sort of U.N. protection and the Soviets having the same fear with respect to the Baltic republics. With respect to Iraq's aspiration to develop nuclear weapons, in contrast, the Security Council continued to govern the course of events and refused to remove economic sanctions until Saddam Hussein allowed U.N. inspectors to monitor its possible nuclear sites and to destroy any materials that could be used to build nuclear weapons.

So in the period extending from late 1990 through early 1991, the tipping of the balance against the sovereignty principle was halting and spasmodic. But it did tip, and the U.N.'s actions were followed not by an outcry in defense of the sovereignty principle but by some criticism of the U.N.'s inaction on the sanctuary issue. More than a few editorials and columnists praised the United States for its compassionate actions and denounced the U.N. for being mired in the sovereignty principle. Humanitarian imperatives, many argued, take precedence over those affirming nonintervention, thus justifying relaxation of the sovereignty principle.[12] And this line of reasoning, along with the success of the coalition in the Gulf War, was surely one source of the U.N.'s subsequent shift to a rash of second-generation operations in Cambodia, Haiti, Bosnia, Somalia, East Timor, and elsewhere.

The U.N.'s involvement in Somalia is perhaps particularly revealing of the difficulties encountered by the second-generation operations. In December 1992, the United States led a twenty-seven–nation coalition of 28,000 troops to protect deliveries of humanitarian aid in a country bordering on starvation as a result of feuding among warlords. Five months later the original goal of providing security so that relief agencies could supply food to starving Somalis was attained as both the famine and the civil war outside the capital, Mogadishu, were brought under control. Hence, the United States withdrew the bulk of its troops and handed over command of the operation to the U.N., which was then given the mandate of turning from peacekeeping to the much more complex task of peacemaking—that is, helping the Somalis reconstruct, rehabilitate, and rebuild their social and political system. But pursuit of this goal was greatly complicated by a continuing armed struggle in Mogadishu between U.N. troops and a recalcitrant warlord, General Mohammad Farah Aidid. In mid-June 1993 General Aidid's forces ambushed and killed twenty-four Pakistani peacekeeping troops, and as a result, the U.N. launched a huge military campaign aimed at destroying Aidid's political and military base. A reward of $25,000 was offered for the general's capture, but this ploy was unsuccessful and the general's supporters went on killing peacekeeping troops.

As the U.N. became more aggressive and escalated the war with Aidid, so did its policies become more controversial. Some argued that negotiations with Aidid were the only way to bring an end to the conflict; others felt that only his capture would bring hostilities to a halt. An Italian general in command of the 2,442-man Italian force in Mogadishu favored negotiations so strongly that, insisting he had to wait for instructions from Rome, he refused to carry out orders from the U.N. commander to wage a more vigorous campaign against Aidid. The Italian general was immediately removed from his post despite a huge outcry from politicians in Rome.

In early August four U.S. soldiers were killed by a remote-controlled bomb set off by Aidid's forces, an action that contributed to a U.S. decision to send a Special Force of commando troops to assist in the search for General Aidid. On October 3, 1993, eighteen of the commandos were killed in a U.N.-led battle with Aidid's forces. There followed a flood of American opinion opposing the U.S. (but not the U.N.) presence in Somalia and a decision by President Clinton to place American troops under U.S. rather than U.N. command and to withdraw them by April 1, 1994. France and Belgium soon an-

nounced that they would also withdraw their troops. The same decision was interpreted by a gang of toughs in Haiti as a sign the United
States lacked the will to carry out its intentions of landing troops and
other advisers to help Haiti's transition to democracy. They were
right: A week later, by creating a commotion at the dock as the first
ship sought to leave its load, they got the White House to order a sus-
pension of the U.S. military effort in Haiti. Viewed from a realist perspective, this sequence of events demonstrates the importance of the
limits states impose on the U.N., whereas liberals and postinternationalists could interpret it as indicating the relevance of domestic
factors and transnational media to throttle the best of plans pursued
by either the U.N. or powerful states.

As a result of these events, which were supplemented by a record
of comparable vacillation and inaction in the former Yugoslavia that
allowed horrendous atrocities to occur in Bosnia, the optimism that
surrounded the U.N. after the Gulf War petered out and yielded two
years later to much skepticism—among publics as well as elites in all
parts of the world—as to the organization's peacekeeping capacities
in the face of many simultaneous challenges that were undermining
the world's post–Cold War order.[13] Some said the U.N. was taking on
more than it could handle, given the limits on its finances and the
availability of trained personnel. Others stressed that the very countries that had come to rely on the U.N. as a peacekeeper were not
ready to put their soldiers' lives at risk in situations that did not
clearly fall within their national interests. The continuing indecision
with respect to the unfolding horrors in the former Yugoslavia served,
along with Somalia and Haiti, as a major source of this conclusion:

> One of the lessons driven home with a vengeance by the Western response
> to the war in Bosnia is that the liberal Western democracies feel themselves
> politically weak. The political cost of fighting war is high in a democracy.
> Peacemaking forces are subject to casualties. Leaders avoid risks unless di-
> rect interests are at stake. . . . But support for collective security still seems to
> be too amorphous, too watery a concept to serve as fuel. So UN members
> steer clear of peacemaking where it is obviously needed. They do so for a
> compelling domestic reason—the fear of body bags. Perhaps they are right
> to do this. Yet until they do otherwise, the UN idea may remain a fig leaf dis-
> guising the reality that in the new order as in the old, the great powers do
> and take what they want, when they want it.[14]

A former U.N. undersecretary in charge of peacekeeping put the same thought in a broader historical context: "After a brief post-cold-war honeymoon, the United Nations is once again suffering from the inability to enforce its decision in critical situations, this time without the excuse of the obstacles created by the Cold War."[15] And the activist Secretary General Boutros Boutros-Ghali concurred with this perspective: "I am firmly committed to the concept of peace enforcement. It is essential if we are to strengthen international peace and security. But there is a new reality: member states are not ready for it. I must accept reality. I also must continue to give you my view."[16] And perhaps the most incisive insight into the problem was provided by the reaction of a U.S. senator, Robert Byrd, to his country's involvement in Somalia: "I do not see in the front of this chamber the U.N. flag. I have never saluted the U.N. flag. I salute Old Glory, the American flag."[17]

In subsequent years the United States, aware of these criticisms and unwilling to risk the further loss of troops in ground warfare, turned to air power and pinpoint bombing in an effort to meet challenges to peace in Bosnia, Yugoslavia, and Iraq. In Bosnia it did so after persuading NATO to sanction the air raids; in Yugoslavia other NATO forces participated in the air raids; and in Iraq the raids were conducted under the U.N.'s 1991 authorization that followed Saddam Hussein's refusal to cooperate with U.N. weapons inspectors.

At first glance, the foregoing account of the U.N.'s peacekeeping missions would appear a vivid vindication of the realist perspective. Adherents of this approach can readily argue that the Gulf War was a quintessential case of how the main actors in the state-centric world cope with disturbances in their established order: Thirty-two states collaborated on behalf of their national interests and in response to the leadership of the world's hegemon to preserve the integrity of one of their kind and restore the status quo ante. Sure, acknowledge the realists, the thirty-two–state coalition proceeded under the auspices of the U.N., and yes, the Security Council did dare to intrude upon Iraq's sovereignty; but in these actions the U.N. simply served as a vehicle of the coordination of states intent upon preventing the spread of nuclear weapons and maintaining the viability of their long-standing system. Indeed, it was a matter of considerable controversy whether the 1998 bombing of Iraq by the United States fell under the U.N.'s original 1991 mandate. Put differently, from a realist point of view, the U.N. is an instrument of the state system and did exactly what it was designed to do, namely, carry out the policies of its members. To quote Boutros-Ghali again, "What is going on in places like Angola, Cambodia, El Salvador, Georgia, Haiti, Somalia, Tajikistan and the former Yugoslavia is nothing less than an effort to preserve the foundations of the state system while beginning to shape a post-cold-war structure of peace and security."[18]

Those who subscribe to liberal and postinternationalist approaches view this realist affirmation as misguided and inaccurate. The liberal is likely to view the history of post–Cold War peacekeeping as a process wherein new cooperative institutions were slowly pieced together. From this perspective the process was admittedly halting and far from completed, but the foundation for new mechanisms of cooperation among (especially Western) states was laid. Likewise, postinternationalists can readily interpret the same sequence of events as still further evidence of the underlying soundness of their approach. First, they would be quick to point out, the realist presumption that states are solitary actors is clearly revealed by these events to be fallacious. The dynamics surrounding the U.N.'s vacillation in Bosnia and its retreat from Somalia and Haiti were driven not by governments pursuing their national interests but by publics unwilling to support peacekeeping operations that involve troop casualties. Even the Gulf War, it might be said, can be interpreted as a state-centric operation only because extensive casualties did not occur on the U.N. side of the battle line. Had there been large numbers of battle deaths, it seems very doubtful indeed whether the coalition would have held together and fought a prolonged war. In sum, the very same skill revolution at the micro level that served to support the multilateralism that led to so many tasks being assigned to the U.N. also operated to foster a retreat from the tasks when their noxious side became predominant.

Furthermore, postinternationalists might well contend that the overloading of the U.N. with peacekeeping tasks is in itself a measure of the extent to which state authority has undergone erosion. Some of this authority, the postinternationalist would say, is being subtly transferred to the U.N., which is not serving as an instrument of states but as an autonomous actor that reflects the needs of the multi-centric world and its more empowered peoples and thus straddles the grand divide of a bifurcated world. The very fact that ambiguity surrounds a number of peacekeeping questions—such as when the U.N. should intrude its blue-helmeted troops into a situation, whose troops will be sent, under whose command, at whose expense, to enforce terms of the peace decided by what authority—suggests the insufficiency of traditional peacekeeping norms enunciated in the 1960s and the emergence of a new world order in which states may not have the final say. Or, perhaps more accurately, although the postinternational model may have no ready-made answers to such questions, certainly it is also the case that realism offers no clear-cut guidelines to help the theorist through this thicket of new questions posed by the onrush of many new peacekeeping roles assigned to the U.N.

For some analysts, the word "multilateralism" fills this analytic gap and offers a modicum of clarity about the new global order by emphasizing that collective action can be taken in a world of weak states and a weak U.N.[19] For realists and many liberals, multilateralism refers to collective actions undertaken by states; for postinternationalists, the term connotes the involvement of publics, the dispersion of authority, and the activity of nongovernmental as well as governmental actors—that is, the presence of the multi-centric as well as the state-centric world. As Boutros-Ghali put it, "Multilateralism is the democracy of international society."[20] But whatever label may be appropriate, it seems clear that a transformation of the world's prime authority structures is under way. Blue-helmeted troops now exercise force on behalf of goals that are better characterized as those of the global community than those of states. Senator Byrd may never have saluted the U.N. flag, but the fact that he felt the need to contrast it with the American flag suggests that it symbolizes the presence of a critical actor on the world stage. Indeed, the fact that the U.N. has acquired enemies (as distinguished from those who bear it no ill will but are simply pessimistic about its peacekeeping capacities)[21]—publics and governments that blame the organization for their problems (as has happened in Somalia and Bosnia)—is perhaps the surest measure of the large extent to which the U.N. has made the transition from holding out an idealistic vision of world order to becoming a major player in the processes whereby some form of order is fashioned in this turbulent era.[22]

Command of Troops

That the changing world scene has given rise to confusion over the question of the U.N.'s authority can be readily seen in the issue of who commands the blue-helmeted troops stationed in numerous situations around the world. The U.N. has a command structure with officers who, although obviously having a particular nationality, are U.N. commanders both in name and in fact. The question is whose command counts when the countries providing the troops give orders that are contrary to those issued by the U.N. commanders? As previously noted, such a clash occurred in Somalia when an Italian general was sent back to Rome because he awaited instructions from the Italian government rather than carrying out the orders of his U.N. commanders on the scene. Less clear-cut is the outcome of the controversy surrounding U.S. policies toward the issue. Early in the Clinton administration, word spread that the president, inclined to support a multilateralist policy and eager to scale back the role of the United States as a global policeman, was prepared to back away from a long-standing policy that required U.S. troops to be under U.S. commanders in combat situations.[23] Ever mindful of the political pitfalls such a shift would encounter in Congress, the projected new policy was to be hedged in a number of ways, including allowing the heads of U.S. military units to disregard orders from U.N. commanders that they considered to be illegal or questionable.[24] But strenuous objections from Secretary General Boutros-Ghali, based on the fact that such a veto could lead other nations to retain the right to ignore U.N. commands, led to the removal of this clause from the draft of a presidential directive on peacekeeping operations.[25] Then, in early October 1993, after eighteen U.S. soldiers were killed in a bungled raid in Mogadishu, President Clinton announced that the United States would send combat reinforcements to Somalia and that these forces would be placed under U.S. rather than U.N. command until the United States finally withdrew from Somalia (which occurred the following April).

Just as was the case when NATO and the Russians moved into Kosovo after the withdrawal of Serb forces in 1999, however, clear-cut lines of authority did not prove easy to work out. The need for close coordination with U.N. forces confounded the drawing of such lines of command. U.S. troops were committed to clearing roadblocks from the streets of Mogadishu and purifying the water for troops in Somalia, for example, and these tasks could only be executed through such extensive contacts with U.N. forces as to blur the chain of authority. Indeed, interviews with military officials both on the scene and in

Washington "portrayed the relationship between United States and United Nations forces as too intertwined to be easily separated. Despite the effort by the Administration to put distance between itself and the United Nations, they said there were reasons that the relationship may grow even closer before the American withdrawal."[26] The United States is the primary state reluctant to put its forces under U.N. command, but its resistance to such an arrangement is not readily implemented.

Yet the United States is not alone in rethinking peacekeeping arrangements. Although deeply committed to involvement in peacekeeping operations, Canada, for example, reevaluated its policies in this regard. Canadian troops experienced severe hardships in Bosnia, thus eroding domestic support for Canada's long-standing tradition of participation in U.N. peacekeeping missions.

In sum, the more the U.N. gets involved in second-generation missions that necessitate it to engage in enforcement activities, the more is its authority likely to get evoked and challenged. The conduct of field operations, whether in military or nonmilitary matters, involves too intricate a set of tasks for state officials to reserve to themselves the final word on issues that urgently require resolution. Whether they want to or not, officials seem bound to cede some authority to those on the scene even if they are wearing blue helmets. Realists might stress that states continue to retain the sovereign prerogative of having the last word, but for all practical purposes such a conclusion runs counter to the actual experience of those who have to relate to the U.N. in the daily crises that mark the course of world affairs.

Election Monitoring

Whereas ambiguity and resistance characterize the U.N.'s involvement in peacekeeping operations, quite the opposite can be said with respect to its newly emergent monitoring role in domestic elections. Along with human rights issues, elections constitute one domestic arena that appears to be increasingly accepting of the idea that the U.N.—as well as numerous transnational nongovernmental organizations—should take on major responsibilities.[27] And here it is also clear that liberalism and postinternationalism fit the evolving pattern more exactly than does the realist approach. No model fully explains the dynamism of the many peacekeeping operations, but in the case of recent elections the focus of liberals on individual rights and all three parameters of the postinternational model contribute to an explanation of why the sovereignty principle has been so extensively breached in the case of that most precious of domestic institutions, the national election. Perhaps the most realists have to offer as an explanation is that the state-centric system has a stake in the domestic stability of its members and thus is ready to authorize its prime intergovernmental organization's participation in their internal affairs. Such an interpretation is undermined, however, by the fact that interventions in domestic elections have not been confined just to the system's prime intergovernmental organization. Upward of 200 transnational organizations, for example, observed and monitored the 1989 Nicaraguan election, a fact that is not easily accounted for by the realist perspective.

But all three parametric transformations of the postinternational model are consistent with the U.N. playing an enhanced role in domestic elections. Consider the macro parameter. There are at least two ways in which its transformation seems likely to have contributed to the emergent pattern. For one, the bifurcation of global structures has weakened the sovereignty, competence, and legitimacy of national governments and made them more ready to accept, if not more dependent upon, collective action by international organizations as a means of coping with the world's trouble spots. Second, initially spurred by a series of U.N.-sponsored covenants on human rights in the 1960s and subsequently promoted mainly by actors in the multi-centric world, the spread of norms protective of human rights on a global scale has fostered a climate of world opinion that serves to legitimate and encourage U.N. participation in the domestic elections of members whose democratic institutions are not firmly in place.

The transformation of the macro-micro parameter has also boosted the U.N.'s role as an election monitor. States that are still governed by highly authoritarian regimes are being put on the defensive in this era marked by a trend toward democratic procedures, and many other states are facing the possibility of a crisis of their authority structures because of the trend toward performance criteria of legitimacy. Thus, during elections, the U.N.'s monitoring teams enter, as it were, an authority vacuum in which their activities stand out as having been sanctioned by the international community as well as the government holding the election. The U.N.'s insistence that it be involved in all stages of the electoral process and that its presence be approved by all major political groups adds further to its authority. Needless to say, the U.N. monitoring teams are also subjected to performance criteria and thus must maintain an impeccable reputation for impartiality in the conduct of their responsibilities if they are to retain their legitimacy. Since all the incentives are conducive to helping the U.N. teams maintain an even-handed approach in carrying out their monitoring tasks, the teams are unlikely to act in such a way as to undermine the expanding authority that attaches to their presence as arbiters of fairness. Indeed, given a record of irreproachable conduct and steadfast unwillingness to approve fraudulent or otherwise flawed elections, the U.N.'s authority in this regard will probably remain untarnished even in those instances when controversy accompanies the election outcome or when the losing regime prevents a freely elected government from taking the reins of power, for then the opprobrium will fall on those individuals or factions who thwart the democratic process.

In short, although the ultimate outcome of elections in developing countries may negate the efforts of outside monitoring teams, the U.N. cannot fail but add to its electoral authority if it adheres to the strict standards of equity it has set for itself as an outside observer of the domestic politics of its members.[28] It has going for it the "politics of shame," which, in effect, attaches blame to those who thwart democratic values rather than to those who seek to implement them.

Turning to the micro parameter, one is led to wonder whether the enlarged analytic skills of citizens will increase their responsiveness to the presence of the U.N. monitoring teams and, if so, whether new habits of compliance will evolve that incrementally add to the organization's authority vis-à-vis that of its member states. Put more generally, is the skill revolution, supplemented by a growing record of successful international involvement in domestic elections, likely to reinforce the global norms that allow for external intervention in the internal affairs of countries? Other things being equal—that is, in the absence of direct confrontations between the monitoring teams and state authorities at polling sites—the question can readily be answered in the affirmative. Citizens will not need to ponder transferring any loyalties or habits of compliance to the U.N., but their expanded analytic skills are likely to enable them to assess for themselves the consequences of international observers being present during the campaign and on election day. Leaving aside those who do not want their authoritarian regime toppled, most citizens seem bound to appreciate that the monitoring teams are present because the teams' sponsors used the politics of shame to persuade the regime to accept them and that they subsequently made it possible for the election to be conducted fairly. Accordingly, it seems probable that the more the analytic skills of citizens undergo expansion, the more likely citizens are to modify any skepticism they may have about the U.N. as an actor in world politics—or, at the very least, the more likely they are to accord salience to the U.N. and move it toward the center of their perceptual range.

These derivations from the turbulence model are supported by recent events. Viewed in the context of the transformative changes that have slowly but steadily accelerated since the end of World War II,[29] the U.N.'s incremental evolution toward readiness to participate in domestic elections, and the recent surge in acceptance of the external monitoring process, is hardly surprising. More accurately, it is not difficult to explain why the first U.N.-monitored election, in Korea in 1952, "failed to create momentum for further election monitoring"[30] and why thirty-eight years then ensued before the organization monitored another election in an independent nation. The initial monitoring situation was a consequence of circumstances that attended the Korean War; indeed, it was the only time in the history of the U.N. that it observed an election without the host country's official permission. In so doing it ignored members of the Korean National Assembly who protested that the country's sovereignty was being violated, but such reasoning soon became worldwide as the Cold War deepened and fostered intensified claims of national sovereignty. Consequently, in the ensuing decades the U.N. declined a number of requests from member states to monitor their elections.[31] Indeed, the sovereignty principle was still intact late in the 1980s when the U.N. secretary general denied a Nicaraguan request for monitoring on the grounds that there was no "precedent whatsoever for carrying out such supervision in an independent country."[32]

During the same period, however, in subtle and incremental ways U.N. organs did move toward a resolution of the clash between the sovereignty principle and the idea of monitoring elections in troubled situations. Not only did they acquire expertise and lay the groundwork for a new precedent by observing or supervising thirty plebiscites and elections in non-self-governing territories between

1956 and 1990, but the issue surfaced in their debates with increasing frequency as time passed, spurred by the global authority crisis that underlay the worldwide proliferation of democratic movements and generated pressures on governments to hold elections. These pressures led governments to look abroad for monitoring teams that, in turn, would add to their domestic legitimacy by sanctioning election outcomes.[33] Wide cracks in the armor of national sovereignty began to appear in 1989, when the U.N. broke its unblemished "hands-off" record by sending an election team to Nicaragua. In taking this action, the U.N. maintained deference toward the sovereignty concept by using wording that allowed and encouraged such missions "in well-defined circumstances . . . primarily in situations with a clear international dimension."[34] Involvement in the Nicaraguan election was viewed as justifiable because it helped to protect the international peace of the region and had come about not only as a consequence of a Sandinista request but also in response to the Esquipulas II initiative of Central American presidents. Then, with the Observer Mission to Verify the Electoral Process in Haiti in October 1990, the U.N. undertook a precedent-setting involvement in a situation without a clear threat to the maintenance of international peace.[35] By 1992 the U.N. had "provided technical assistance for elections in Albania, the Congo, El Salvador, Ethiopia, Guinea, Guyana, Liberia, Madagascar, Mali, Rwanda and Togo, and . . . Angola [and had assisted] in preparations for referendums planned for Eritrea and Western Sahara."[36]

Again, the shift in U.N. policies coincided with a change in the identity and orientations of the secretary general: In 1988 Javier Perez de Cuellar commented that the U.N. "does not send observers to elections . . . [or] take part in political elections," whereas at the end of 1991 his successor-elect, Boutros Boutros-Ghali, was reported to expect "the United Nations to take a wider role in encouraging democracy by helping to organize and monitor elections in developing countries."[37] It would be a mistake, however, to view this shift as resulting simply from the idiosyncratic perspectives of different leaders. Such an interpretation overlooks the parametric transformations outlined above and the way in which they surged forward with the end of the Cold War. The new secretary general could not have made election verification a top priority if the world and its organizations, polities, and peoples had not come to appreciate the limits of the sovereignty principle and the virtues of collective intervention on behalf of an emerging right of political participation. If the impulse to support fair elections ever was subject to the idiosyncratic preferences of a particular secretary general, it is no longer; today it has become embedded as a requirement of the office if the pending electoral situation can be defined as having an "international dimension." And even then, given a bifurcated, ever more interdependent world, the definition of "international dimension" will steadily broaden, and thus the presence of U.N. teams in critical elections will occur with increasing frequency. Indeed, the U.N.'s role in the Cambodian election of May 1993 was deemed "a remarkable success," given that nearly 90 percent of the country's more than 4.7 million eligible voters turned out over six days of polling in the face of repeated threats of violence on the part of the Khmer Rouge guerrilla organization.[38] No less of a success marked the activities of the 1,800 civilian observers sent by the U.N. to help monitor South Africa's first open elections in April 1994.

Human Rights

The same rationale underlying U.N. involvement in domestic elections—that protection of peoples' rights is not subject to national boundaries—has also become increasingly central to the organization's readiness to intrude upon the sovereignty of states with respect to the rights of women, children, indigenous peoples, and minorities as well as the free expression of speech and assembly away from the ballot box. As with election monitoring, the U.N.'s movement in the human rights field came to a halt for a long period during the Cold War. To be sure, its Human Rights Commission and NGOs kept such issues alive during this period, but it was not until the end of superpower hostilities that momentum began to grow. Despite the Universal Declaration of Human Rights that the U.N. adopted in 1948, nothing substantial was done to implement its principles until 1991. In the intervening years, the Western democracies, espousing the universality of human rights, had sponsored resolutions condemning violations of human rights in certain developing countries, but these had been blocked by China and other Asian states on the grounds that such rights existed only as a function of a country's history, level of economic development, and cultural and religious traditions.

For example, intensive debate focused on Myanmar, formerly
Burma, where military rulers had refused to hand over power to a de-
mocratically elected parliament and had placed Daw Aung San Sou
Kyi, the opposition leader and (subsequently) winner of the Nobel
Peace Prize, under house arrest. At first Myanmar's Asian neighbors
blocked passage of U.N. critical resolutions in the hope that they
could promote a change of policies in Myanmar through other means,
but by 1991 the other Asian countries tacitly acknowledged failure to
budge the military rulers, and from that year onward the General Assembly adopted a series of increasingly harsh rebukes of Myanmar. In
1993 the General Assembly adopted a resolution unanimously and
went so far as to ask the secretary general to intervene with the Myanmar government. At the same time, the assembly's Third Committee
adopted critical human rights resolutions on Iraq, Iran, Cuba, the
Sudan, and Yugoslavia.[39]

Resolutions of the General Assembly were not the only sign that the
U.N.'s concern with human rights was accelerating. In June 1993, the
U.N.-sponsored World Conference on Human Rights concluded with
a call for the organization to play a larger role in denouncing abuses.
Although the conference had no legislative authority, it broke new
ground by extolling an extended definition of human rights to include those of children, minorities, indigenous people, and (with a
particularly strong emphasis) women. It is noteworthy from a postinternational perspective that much of the success of the conference was
attributed to extensive lobbying activities undertaken by nongovernmental organizations in the human rights field.[40]

A further sign that the sovereignty principle is undergoing transformation occurred at the end of 1993 when the General Assembly resolved one of its most long-standing contentious issues and agreed to
the proposal establishing a U.N. high commissioner for human rights
who would have the capacity to intervene wherever basic freedoms
were being suppressed. The new post had first been proposed by
Uruguay in 1952 and was subsequently pressed hard by the United
States, but it could not win a majority, much less a unanimous vote,
for forty-one years, or—as postinternationalists would put it—until
the basic parameters of world affairs underwent transformations that
heightened global sensitivities to the fundamental rights of individuals. For realists the new post was hardly a development worthy of
note, but liberals saw it as yet further evidence of the continuing

trend toward democratic states and their world of cooperation. Under the agreement the high commissioner is charged with "promoting and protecting the effective enjoyment by all of all civil, cultural, economic, political and social rights." The position's duties include "preventing the continuation of human rights violations throughout the world," and the commissioner is authorized to "dialogue with all the governments in the implementation of his/her mandate with a view to securing respect for human rights." Yet, to some extent the sovereignty principle retained its vitality in the human rights field despite the creation of the new post: The power to force governments accused of abuses to change their ways was not accorded the new high commissioner, although proponents of the agreement noted that the official could try to shame the abusers by publicizing violations and reporting them to the General Assembly or to the fifty-three–nation Human Rights Commission in Geneva.[41]

There are other indicators that emergent global norms pertaining to human rights have not fully replaced those that affirm the sovereignty principle. In the votes rebuking Iraq for its human rights violations, for example, the number of countries abstaining rose from twenty-six in 1992 to forty-one in 1993, a difference that suggests a broadening sympathy with Iraq's plight vis-à-vis the U.N. sanctions. Similarly, although the governments represented at the World Conference on Human Rights yielded to some of the pressures exerted by NGOs, they resisted the anger of the NGOs and refused to allow them to participate in the deliberations that shaped the final declaration. Perhaps even more telling, when the U.N. Correspondents Association invited a leading Chinese dissident, Shen Tong, to speak and hold a news conference at U.N. headquarters in New York, the secretary general ordered the press room to be locked, posted guards outside the door, and prevented the news conference from being held in the U.N. because the Chinese government had protested the invitation. "In view of its apparent purpose as an act of political opposition to a member state of the United Nations," the secretary general said, "it would not be appropriate for this event to take place on the premises of the Secretariat." Accordingly, although the press room had been the scene of many presentations by Afghan, Iranian, Iraqi, Guatemalan, El Salvadoran, Irish, and Kashmiri dissidents despite the opposition of their governments, Shen's news conference was held on the First Avenue sidewalk, just outside the U.N. visitors' entrance.[42]

Although those who adhere to a realist approach might well be heartened by the secretary general's firmness about the press conference and by the other indicators that sovereignty considerations are still operative in world politics, they may also want to consider the fact that the secretary general apparently felt that in some situations he was free to resolve conflicts over the sovereignty principle on his own without recourse to the Security Council or the General Assembly for policy guidance.[43] The question arises because if this decisional freedom is framed in the context of other observations made by that secretary general about the limits of state action—for example, "The time of absolute and exclusive sovereignty . . . has passed; its theory was never matched by reality"[44]—his refusal to permit the press conference can be interpreted as a temporary expedient on an issue of transitory importance.

As in everything else during a transformative period, in short, the trend line depicting the U.N.'s evolution is anything but smooth. On the one hand, in some respects the realist perspective is alive and well in the conduct of U.N. affairs, and changes in the interpretation of the sovereignty principle are halting and marked by a two-steps-forward-one-step-back kind of rhythm. On the other hand, the central tendency in these turbulent times appears to favor collective intervention into the domestic affairs of countries when democratic and humanitarian values are under assault.[45] The predominance of the new interventionary norms may not always lead to humanitarian values prevailing over nationalistic ones—as indicated by the failure of externally observed elections to establish freely elected and enduring governments in Panama and Haiti, not to mention the U.N.'s failed efforts to prevent ethnic cleansing in Bosnia —but the evolution of the norms, erratic and circuitous as it may be, seems bound to continue as the complex bifurcation of world affairs becomes ever more ingrained. Indeed, although it occurred under NATO rather than U.N. auspices, the 1999 intrusion in Kosovo substantially solidified the norm's trajectory. Another indicator of this trajectory was subsequently evident in remarks made by Secretary General Annan on the day when world pressures led to the landing of U.N. peacekeeping forces in East Timor. Eager to provide verbal support for the intervention, Annan enunciated his belief that states could no longer hide behind sovereignty when they violate the rights of their citizens:

Nothing in the [U.N.] Charter precludes a recognition that there are rights beyond borders. . . . This developing norm in favor of intervention to protect civilians from wholesale slaughter will no doubt continue to pose profound challenges to the international community. In response to this turbulent era of crises and interventions, there are those who have suggested that the Charter itself—with its roots in the aftermath of global interstate war—is ill-suited to guide us in a world of ethnic wars and intrastate violence. I believe they are wrong.[46]

Development and Environment Issues

If realists stress the continuing importance of the state-centric world's mechanisms for handling issues of war and peace, postinternational-ists and some liberals counter with the cruciality of the multi-centric world to development and environment issues. It is in the latter realms, after all, that NGOs are especially active and effective. They tend to define the issues and to mobilize publics eager for new environmental and developmental departures. Although that may be the case, realists respond, the influence of the NGOs is possible only because the priorities of the state-centric world allow for the central presence of multi-centric actors in the development and environment arenas. Such matters are simply less important to states and thus they tolerate significant U.N. activities in these areas.

Whatever roles actors in the two worlds may play with respect to the U.N.'s activities in the fields of economic development and environmental protection, these activities are of considerable importance even though they rarely capture headlines comparable to those that accompany the U.N.'s work in the peacekeeping, domestic elections, and human rights areas. Indeed, in terms of long-run impact, the former activities may be even more significant. Time and space do not permit here an intensive analysis of the U.N.'s diverse programs in the realms of economics, health, population, and related fields, but suffice it to say that the organization has an extensive worldwide network that carries forward the research and assistance required by these programs. It is a network with offices in a majority of the developing countries and is managed by the U.N.'s Development Programme, its Population Fund, its Children's Fund, its International Drug Control Programme, its World Food Program, and many other agencies that are part of the U.N. system. And it is also a network that generates problem-solving ideas that often propose radically new approaches and subsequently generate widespread interest and culminate in global conferences and recommendations that arrest the attention of officials and publics around the world. Thus has the world been apprised of long-term problems associated with the environment, climate change, biological diversity, sustainable development, and a host of other situations that have come to occupy high places on the global agenda.

The U.N. as an Administrative Organization

Like any large-scale organization, over the years the U.N. has been plagued by internal problems that have fostered numerous recommendations and efforts designed to bring about structural reforms—changes that would render the organization less subject to bureaucratic inefficiency and corruption and, accordingly, more capable of adapting to the changing nature of world politics. But the reform process has moved slowly, not only because large bureaucracies tend to be pervaded with inertia, but also because each proposed change has political ramifications that tend to evoke opposition from member states that fear the change will curtail their access to or influence in the policymaking process. Criticism of the management or budgetary practices of one or another subagency of the Secretariat, for example, was long considered an attack on the countries from which the subagency heads came, with the result that often inefficient managers and practices were kept in place longer than would be the case in a less politicized organization. This problem was especially prominent during the U.N.'s early years, when officials occupied their positions through the recommendations of their governments well before the emergence of a tradition in which international civil servants regard themselves as impartial and not beholden to their country of origin. With the Cold War receding into the past, however, and with the U.N. now led by still another generation of administrators, the values of a truly international civil service have begun to win more adherents, thus making it easier for, say, the secretary general to merge subagencies, eliminate bureaucratic layers deemed to be unnecessary, clarify the chains of responsibility, remove aides regarded as inefficient, and otherwise streamline the Secretariat.[47]

It seems likely that history will judge the U.N. trend line of administrative efficiency as being in an upswing in the present era. Nevertheless, the advocates of the three paradigms would interpret such a pattern in very different ways. Whereas liberals would probably contend that the emergence of an international civil service tradition and the secretary general's increased capacity to reshuffle responsibilities, bureaus, and personnel reflect the growing pains any emergent institution would undergo, postinternationalists would likely interpret the same developments as indicative of the declining competence and sovereignty of states. Member states need the services of the U.N. more than ever, the postinternationalists might argue, and thus they will become more and more unlikely to intervene in the streamlining process and more and more prepared to accept its consequences. Nonsense, the realist might reply—the administrative trend line is consistent with the natural evolution of any large organization that manages to persist through time and has little to do with the capabilities or rights of states. After all, it is states—and, most notably, the United States—that are failing to keep up with their financial commitments to the U.N., and there is not much the secretary general can do about it other than continuously press them to meet their obligations. Recall, too, such incidents as the secretary general's cancellation of a press conference at the request of China or his refusal to move against Iraq's treatment of the Kurds without renewed authorization from the Security Council. Surely, the realist might conclude, these are not examples of states yielding the center of the international stage. To such affirmations of realism the postinternationalist might respond by quoting a complaint of a leading realist whose objection is precisely that a former secretary general exercised increasing degrees of independent authority: "Although the U.N. Charter vests all executive power in the Security Council, so far the governments of member states have passively accepted Boutros-Ghali's reinterpretation of his role and theirs. The member states have adopted the secretary general's priorities and programs as if he were the chief executive in a presidential system and the Security Council were a rubber-stamp legislature."[48] That subsequently he was not voted a second term as secretary general and was replaced by Kofi Annan suggests that the passive acceptance of Boutros-Ghali's role interpretation eventually gave way to an active rejection of it.

Enlarged Security Council

Whatever progress may have occurred with respect to improving the quality and quantity of the work performed by the Secretariat, it is the Security Council and its adaptation to the changing nature of world affairs that many observers regard as the first priority on the list of organizational reforms deemed urgent. The core of one argument, advanced most vigorously by the United States, is that membership in the Security Council needs to be altered to reflect the ways in which the distribution of power in the world today is different from what it was when the U.N. was founded in 1945. The issue is a delicate one and, accordingly, hotly contested. Some argue that Germany and Japan should replace France and Great Britain as permanent members of the Security Council—thus gaining the right to veto any action by voting in the negative—in order to bring the council into closer alignment with the present distribution of power. Others insist that such a proposal would go nowhere because France or Britain would veto it and that therefore the number of permanent members should be increased to include Germany and Japan. Still others contend that major countries from the developing world should also be given permanent membership to more accurately represent present-day realities. And although most countries want to preserve the veto and add to the ranks of the Security Council, some of the smaller ones want to abolish permanent seats and vetoes altogether.

At present, the most likely compromise, if one is to occur, would involve maintaining the veto and expanding the ranks of the permanent members of the council by adding those countries that have become major actors on either the world stage or within a particular region. Most experts would agree that Germany and Japan qualify as major actors and that the major regional powers include India, Brazil, and Nigeria. Such an arrangement, moreover, would help to ameliorate the U.N.'s dire financial straits by virtue of the fact that Germany and Japan have enjoyed economic prosperity and could thus be asked to shoulder substantial increases in their financial contribution to the organization if they were to assume permanent council membership.

The matter is further complicated by the expectation that new permanent members should significantly increase their security contributions to the U.N.'s peacekeeping operations. This expectation is controversial because both Germany and Japan are constitutionally prevented from sending troops into combat abroad and because, for some, the idea of remilitarizing these countries is threatening. Others insist that the two countries be required to make the necessary constitutional revisions to ensure full military participation, whereas still others, fearful that, owing to domestic opposition, such a requirement could never get adopted in one or both countries,[49] are willing to settle for an arrangement in which Germany and Japan would participate by contributing medical and logistical support to future peacekeeping missions.

In any event, whatever changes may be made in the structure of the Security Council and the obligations of its permanent members, the proposals to alter it and thereby make the U.N. more adaptive would appear to rest on the realist premise that the U.N. is a state organization run by and for states. However, to propose rendering the organization more adaptive to a changing world is possibly to acknowledge that sovereignty has eroded somewhat and that some sovereignty-free actors have become at least as important as many states. Those who are inclined to take a postinternational approach would focus on the adaptation idea as consistent with their worldviews and in the case of liberals, as reflective of the continuing trend toward the development of institutions suitable to a changing world.

Such differences of perspective on the restructuring of the U.N. has proven to be divisive. In the United States, upon the invitation of President Bush and congressional leaders to assess what changes should be recommended, the sixteen-member Commission on Improving the Usefulness of the United Nations took two years to reach a divided set of recommendations. The majority argued that the end of the Cold War created "a unique chance for a U.S.-led United Nations to fashion common responses to mankind's common problems," whereas a minority of six contended it was "far from clear whether the United Nations is ready for the post-Cold War world and urged the U.S. to defend its interests alone where necessary."[50]

Financing Problems

Because many member states fall behind in their financial obligations to the U.N., it is regularly in dire financial straits, especially now as the organization takes on more and more missions. In late 1993, in fact, the U.N. was deemed to be on the brink of bankruptcy. In September it would have been unable to meet its payroll had the Japanese not made a $194 million peacekeeping payment. So dire was the situation that heads of state and foreign ministers were asked to finish their speeches by 6:00 P.M. so that the building could be closed and overtime costs avoided. Similarly, each delegation was limited to just two copies of official documents—one in English and one in French—and had to purchase translations in any other language.[51]

The ironies and contradictions are staggering: The member states have committed the U.N. to extensive peacekeeping missions in the absence of any other means of addressing festering situations in Bosnia, Somalia, and elsewhere—thereby greatly increasing peacekeeping costs—but then have fallen behind in their payments, largely because they feel the U.N. is not up to the tasks they assign it. Only eighteen countries met the payment deadline on January 31, 1993,[52] but the United States is the most conspicuous culprit: During the 1990s it fell behind by more than $1 billion in its obligations to the U.N., or half the debt the organization was owed. Equally important, although the Clinton administration has been especially vigorous in championing multilateralism through the U.N., the United States has not exercised the leadership in the various situations that could ensure the success of the peacekeeping missions. Thus, it is little wonder that the last three secretary generals, faced with a large and continuing gap between the U.N.'s peacekeeping commitments and the resources to carry them out, recur continuously to the financial problem. "Money, money, money," one is quoted as reiterating, "that is the prerequisite for the United Nations playing the role it could play after the Cold War."[53]

Part of the explanation for the vast numbers of member states that fall behind in their payments, of course, lies in the financial difficulties that are plaguing many of them. There are limits to this explanation, however, since the same states spend considerable sums for their own national defense. The United States, for example, spends $2,016 on defense for every dollar it contributes to peacekeeping,[54] and "on average, the nations of the world invest only $1.40 in peacekeeping for every $1,000 they devote to their own armed forces."[55] No, the explanation must go deeper, and for all three types of theorists a more fundamental analysis is readily available. Realists can easily argue that, of course, multilateralism cannot work. States are too committed to their own narrow interests to be ready to pay for operations far removed from their immediate concerns. Liberals can readily assert that under present-day conditions state-society relations in most countries are too fragile to allow for adherence to their international obligations. Similarly, postinternationalists need only stress the authority crises that have overtaken most states and their subsequent inability to suffer battlefield casualties, which in turn serves as a disincentive to pay their share of the peacekeeping operations. The reasoning follows different paths, but the several schools of thought come to the same negative conclusion with respect to the U.N.'s ability to generate the resources it needs to adequately shoulder its responsibilities.

The Secretary General

Earlier it was suggested that the dynamics presently at work in world politics are too powerful to be significantly shaped by the individual occupying the role of U.N. secretary general, that different persons in the job would make different decisions but that the variability in this regard would not be very great. It does not contradict this insight to also assert that the demands on the secretary general are enormous and the holder of the post has become a critical actor on the world scene. To be sure, other top officials of the U.N. play key roles, but they are not in the public limelight and thus their actions do not have the same extensive consequences as do those of the organization's head. The U.N. secretary general is perhaps the only official on the global scene whose activities and responsibilities are deeply embedded in both the state-centric and multi-centric worlds. Realists would likely claim that the secretary general's role is confined to the former world and that servicing its need for preventive diplomacy and for a respected intermediary who can ameliorate conflicts takes priority, whereas liberals and postinternationalists would doubtless stress the secretary general's role in refugee, human rights, development, environment, and elections problems. All three schools of thought, however, uncover an essential truth about the centrality of the position. Consider, for example, the secretary general's activities in the state-centric world: Not only does the official have to manage a gigantic bureaucracy and preside over a vast system of agencies, but there is also the time-consuming task of negotiating with the states that make up the U.N.'s membership. Boutros-Ghali succinctly described this latter task in the course of explaining the difficulties he encountered in launching peacekeeping operations authorized by the Security Council:

> As a good pragmatist, I must work as well as I can within the current reality that our only power is persuasion. In each case I must begin from Square One. I must telephone the president of a country and say, "Mr. President, please can't you help me? Can you send me some troops? Can you send me two planes? Can you advance the dates on which we will get this help?"
>
> Then I must phone his minister of defense to work out the details. It can take five or six weeks. Then countries change their minds. That has happened in Bosnia and in Somalia. They change the dates on which their help will be available. They promise free transportation and then come back and say we must pay some kind of low-cost price.
>
> Three months, four months go by. Eventually we are able to overcome these difficulties. But rather than doing it in two weeks, we are doing it in months. In the meantime, a lot of people die. This is the price.[56]

This picture of the secretary general's lack of authority with respect to enlarging peacekeeping operations does not obtain, however, with respect to his or her authority over the forces already assigned to the U.N. and the policies they follow in the field. In the case of Boutros-Ghali, for example, he prevailed each time a conflict arose between his strategies and those of the U.N.'s battlefield commanders. This factor has already been noted with respect to the operations in Somalia, but subsequently the same pattern surfaced in Bosnia. The French general Jean Cot, who commanded 26,000 peacekeeping troops in the former Yugoslavia, complained publicly that the troops were dangerously exposed because the Security Council failed to match its words with actions—that is, with air strikes that would combat snipers and artillery fire. General Cot said he had twice asked the secretary general for authority to call for air strikes but had been rebuffed. Thus, he said, the peacekeeping forces were like "a goat tethered to a fence." Boutros-Ghali was said to respond to this remark with "outrage and anger," and he insisted to top French officials that General Cot be removed from the post.[57] Shortly thereafter, the *New York Times* reported, "The French Defense Ministry said today that it would recall

Gen. Jean Cot . . . at the request of Secretary General Boutros Boutros-Ghali."[58]

The liberal and postinternationalist would remind us that focusing just on the secretary general's role in peacekeeping operations runs the risk of downplaying his or her role in other than military situations. Boutros-Ghali's successor, Kofi Annan, has forcefully stressed this more encompassing aspect of the position:

> The end of the cold war transformed the . . . promise of the role of the Secretary General. It allowed him to place the United Nations at the service of the universal values of the charter, without the constraints of ideology or particular interests. In my two years as Secretary General, I have sought to pursue this role in two distinct ways.
>
> First, I have sought to speak out in favor of universal human rights and in defense of victims of aggression or abuse, wherever they may be. For Americans, the Presidency has been seen as a bully pulpit, at least since the days of Theodore Roosevelt. I have sought to make the office of secretary General a pulpit, too. . . . From New York to Teheran to Harare and to Shanghai, I have sought, without attacking specific regimes or individuals, to use it as a vehicle for promoting the values of tolerance, democracy, human rights and good governance that I believe are universal.
>
> Second, I have used my office as a bridge between two or more parties wherever I believed an opportunity for the peaceful resolution of disputes existed. To do so, I have embarked on many missions, confronting not only the doubts of others but my own as well. . . . But I have persisted because I must deal with the world not as I would wish it to be, but as it is.[59]

Conclusion

What does the foregoing analysis of the U.N. tell us about the present state of the organization and its future? What does it tell us about the prospects for cooperation on a global scale that would make the world a better, more hospitable place in which to live, with fewer conflicts and a more equitable future? Is it possible that twenty years from now the global community, through the U.N., will still have difficulty addressing head-on atrocities and the breakdown of community and continued squalor that presently mark life in all too many parts of the world? What light does the discussion shed on which theoretical perspective is best suited to generating appropriate answers to these large questions? Is the U.N. likely to continue to be essentially an institution and instrument of the state-centric world? Or does the trend line suggest that has it begun to acquire an autonomy of its own that locates its authority astride the bifurcation that separates the state-centric and multi-centric worlds?

Readers will have to answer these questions for themselves. And, clearly, it will not be easy to do so. The evidence is mixed, causation is extremely difficult to sort out, the world is in turmoil, nothing is static, and the U.N. may well be in a period of dynamic transformation. Yet, although no one ever said the world was an orderly place, that does not mean it is unfathomable. If readers are to come to terms with the global disorder and locate points in the process where some leverage can be exercised on behalf of desirable change, they have no choice but to ponder the questions and use one or another theoretical perspective to develop responses to them. If neither the realist nor the liberal nor the postinternationalist perspective seems to provide satisfactory answers, then readers must self-consciously develop an alternative approach that provides a modicum of coherence to their grasp of an incoherent world.

8

The Politics of the Antarctic

The continent of Antarctica (see Figure 8.1) belongs to no nation, although a number of states have made claims on sections of it. This unusual state of affairs was created by the 1959 Antarctic Treaty, which came into full force in 1961 and is often referred to as the Antarctic Treaty System (ATS). Australia, Argentina, Belgium, Japan, Norway, South Africa, France, Chile, Great Britain, the Soviet Union, New Zealand, and the United States negotiated the original treaty, and since then forty-one nations have signed it, thereby showing approval of the treaty's aims and committing themselves to its execution. For the first thirty years of the agreement, the treaty could only be revised through unanimous agreement of the voting members. After thirty years, any voting member could call a conference to review the treaty.

The treaty has five unusual features:

1. It was the first arms control agreement of the Cold War—it stipulated that neither military forces nor nuclear weapons could be placed in the Antarctic (although armed services personnel and equipment could be used to move scientists there).
2. The agreement set aside territorial claims for the duration of the treaty; claims over territorial waters were left unaffected. Thus, it did not solve the territorial question, it just put it on hold.
3. It set aside the continent as a preserve for science.
4. It permitted researchers to visit any area at any time.
5. It established procedures for coordinating research and solving any new problems that might arise.

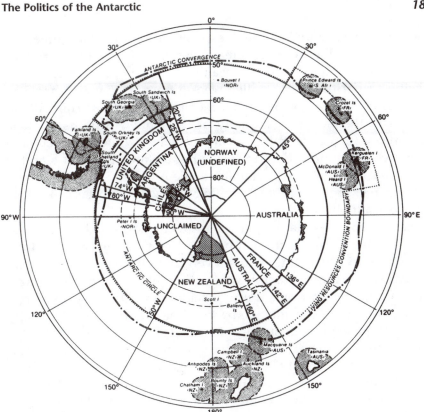

 200 Nautical Mile Zones

Ice Shelves

© Christopher C. Joyner
Woods Hole Oceanographic Institution, 1987

FIGURE 8.1   Map of Antarctica

Source: David B. Newsom, ed., *The Diplomatic Record, 1989–1990* (Boulder: West-view Press, 1991), p. 157.

States that have signed the treaty do not automatically get to make decisions about the management of the Antarctic. Voting on Antarctic issues is confined to the Antarctic Treaty Consultative Parties (ATCPs). Originally, to become a consultative party, a state had to demonstrate that it was capable of conducting substantial scientific research in the Antarctic through expeditions or the establishment of stations. Due to the rigorous climate, this was no small matter; thus, the agreement tended to favor wealthier states with fairly extensive scientific capacities over smaller, weaker ones. This voting arrangement, over the years, came under increasing attack by Third World nations in the General Assembly of the United Nations. In 1990 Greenpeace further complicated the scene by "wintering over" and doing research. Since Greenpeace is not a state, it cannot sign the treaty or vote on matters pertaining to the Antarctic. It did, however, strengthen its argument that it should be allowed to observe meetings of the consultative parties.

The original consultative parties, for their part, sought to address the criticisms of elitism leveled by Third World states by admitting new states to full voting status, even though these countries are barely involved in research.[1] New voting members include Brazil, China, India, South Korea, Peru, Ecuador, and Uruguay, making a total of twenty-six consultative parties. The group has only recently begun to invite nonstate organizations to its meetings.

As the treaty anticipated, scientific work produced information and raised new issues about the continent and the waters around it. Two issues, living resources and mineral resources, are of particular interest because they led to new international agreements. The living resources question is largely covered by the Convention on Antarctic Seals and the 1980 Convention on the Conservation of Antarctic Marine Living Resources (CCAMLR).[2]

Minerals were to be covered by the Convention on the Regulation of Antarctic Mineral Resource Activities (CRAMRA), but this convention has never come into force. In 1991, the Antarctic Environmental Protocol was adopted as an addition to the fundamental Antarctic Treaty. The protocol sets up a new body, the Committee for Environmental Protection, commits the parties to protect the region, and calls for environmental impact assessments of most activities in the Antarctic. These agreements, along with other international treaties that touch on matters related to Antarctic resources (e.g., whaling, Law of the Sea), now form the legal core for the management of Antarctica.

CCAMLR is a weaker agreement in some respects than the one that had been proposed on mining. Like the mining agreement, it is directed to the conservation and use of an important resource.

CCAMLR arose, however, after fin fish in the region were already threatened in some areas. So, it had to respond to existing practices. CCAMLR does have an ecosystem perspective, which is undergoing further development in the ATS as a whole. Yet this has not stopped the overfishing.

In CCAMLR, fishing is permitted with a government license until forbidden. In CRAMRA, mining would have been forbidden unless permitted. The difference may account for the difficulties the Antarctic Treaty states have had recently in managing fishing in the Southern Ocean. The parties recently had the first-ever ministerial meeting of CCAMLR to begin the process of strengthening protection of fish in the Southern Ocean.[3]

Another commercial interest, tourism, has grown in importance as an issue. Tour operators, like environmental organizations before them, have gained observer status for some activities in the region. So far, however, the tour operators seem interested in strong conservation for the region and are, therefore, not far from the interests of the ATCPs. If the ATCPs go entirely for preservation of the region and set strict limits on visiting, then the support from the tourism business may wane.

Despite recent developments, the end of the Cold War seems to have decreased interest in supporting Antarctic science. Funding has been cut by almost all nations. The bulk of what remains is funding for applied research—for example, research on appropriate fishing limits in the light of ecosystem dynamics. The funding cuts are, in many ways, surprising, given the growing importance of the continent as an "early warning" indicator of climate change.

The increasing evidence of warming may eventually force further changes in the management of Antarctica, as states attempt to build early warning systems for vulnerable areas of the world. Bill Frasier, chief scientist at Palmer Station, summarized the changes he had observed in Antarctica: "When I was a graduate student, we were told that climate change occurs but we'd never see the effects in our lifetime. . . . But in the last 20 years I've seen tremendous changes. I've seen islands pop out from under glaciers; I've seen species changing places and landscape ecology altered."[4] The *Evening Post* of Wellington, New Zealand, explained the importance of the global climate change work in Antarctica this way: "Scientists doing sums about global warming . . . are hoping to be able to determine the speed with

which the Antarctic icecaps melt. That will help future residents of
Wellington's harbourside suburbs to determine when it's time to
move, as they most assuredly will—sooner, as it turns out, than original projections."[5] Pressures to improve the basic and applied science
relevant to climate change may increase state funding of research and
prompt new institutions to manage the science.

In this chapter we pose four questions about the political management of the Antarctic. First, why did the Antarctic Treaty come into
being in the first place? Second, why was the minerals convention
(CRAMRA) negotiated? Third, why did CRAMRA fail to go into effect? And fourth, what predictions can we make about the likely future of the Antarctic Treaty System?

Responses to these questions are offered from the realist, liberal,
and postinternationalist perspectives. As can be seen in Table 8.1,
which presents an overview of the responses elicited by each of the
four questions, the three theories tell very different stories about the
origins and workings of the ATS.

The Realist Interpretation

Question 1: Why was the Antarctic Treaty negotiated and put into effect?

*Realist Response 1:   Mutual fears of a widening nuclear arms race—
in an area that had not experienced U.S.-Soviet rivalry—led the two
powers to cooperate.*   The highest concern of states is the preservation of sovereignty, followed by the maintenance of security from military threats. The mid-1950s was perhaps the most intense period of
the Cold War as relations between the USSR and the United States
were bitter and characterized by high levels of distrust. Both nations
"fought" the Cold War through arms racing—getting more and better
weapons—and through gaining allies.

The arms race had been limited to internal acquisition of weapons,
the placement of nuclear-capable bombers in Eastern Europe by the
Soviets, and the establishment of a string of U.S. bases along Soviet
and Warsaw Pact borders. Despite this show of strength and willingness to "go nuclear" if necessary, neither side actually wanted a nuclear war. Thus, a mutual concern over the danger of nuclear war constrained both nations.

During World War II, Britain and Germany had used some of the sub-Antarctic islands for their submarines and had lost some shipping from these operations. Norway had asserted its territorial claim in 1939 to forestall a claim by Nazi Germany.[6] With this history, it took little imagination for both the United States and the Soviet Union to see that Antarctica could become yet another spot where the Cold War might be contested. No nuclear weapons were deployed in the Antarctic, nor were any planned (indeed, until the mid-1950s the Soviets had expressed little interest in the region). If the Antarctic remained a contested area, however, those plans could change. The two states were faced, in essence, with a prisoner's dilemma situation. For the Soviets, the best security outcome would be for it, but not the United States, to place military systems on the continent. The reverse was true for the United States. If each acted as though it expected the other to do nothing, they would both end up with the second worst outcome: both nations with military systems in the area. A second-best option was also available: Keep the arms race out of the region entirely.

Even leaving aside the threat of nuclear deployments, the potential for direct conflict remained. If the United States decided to assert territorial claims or to counteract a Soviet move in the region, the Soviets would encounter trouble. The U.S. Navy and its airlift capacities would serve the United States well as it built and supplied military operations in the Antarctic.

Soviet capacity to project power and build expensive bases in the Antarctic was less than that possessed by the United States. It could be done, of course, but such a project would stretch Soviet capacity and divert its still small navy and airlift forces from the main threat in Europe posed by the North Atlantic Treaty Organization (NATO). At the same time, although the United States did not discount Soviet power, it recognized that sending U.S. forces to Antarctica would divert resources from Europe and the Pacific, where deterring the Soviet threat was essential.

Realist Response 2:   All states with active territorial claims in the Antarctic followed the hegemonic leadership of the United States. Sovereignty is such a crucial aspect of international relations that the answer to why the treaty was negotiated must also explain why those states with territorial claims were willing to set them aside. The

TABLE 8.1   Theoretical Overview of the Antarctic Treaty

Question 1: Why Was the Antarctic Treaty Negotiated and Put into Effect?

Realism	*Postinternationalism*	*Liberalism*
Mutual fears of a widening nuclear arms race—in an area that had not experienced U.S.-Soviet rivalry—led the two powers to cooperate.	A research structure designed by the scientific community provided a convenient framework for states to use in resolving disputes.	States prefer to cooperate.
All states with active territorial claims in the Antarctic followed the hegemonic leadership of the United States.	The normative (value) priorities of the scientific community helped states escape the dictates of sovereignty.	Some of the claimant and nonclaimant states shared a security community with each other.
The strong bipolarity of the international system made it easy to put the treaty in place.		
The United States structured the problem so that states were not likely to be penalized for cooperation.		

Question 2: Why Was the Minerals Agreement Negotiated?

Realism	*Postinternationalism*	*Liberalism*
Mineral exploitation could destroy the entire security regime of the ATS.	Activities by the scientists (SFAs) put minerals on the agendas of states (SBAs).	Continued negotiations on a range of topics within the ATS allowed states to learn the necessity of setting up a nonliving resources regime before exploitation began.
	The "delegation of rule" to the scientific community would be threatened if negotiations occurred outside the ATS.	

(continues)

TABLE 8.1 *(continued)*

Question 3: Why Did CRAMRA Fail to Go into Effect?

Realism	Postinternationalism	Liberalism
Conflicts over different state interests were likely to surface if CRAMRA went into operation; this outcome might have threatened the security regime.	The ability of the ATCPs to enact the agreement had been weakened by authority crises between states and within ATCP states.	Environmental protection became a higher principle than resource conservation within the ATS.

Question 4: What Is the Likely Future of the Antarctic Treaty System?

Realism	Postinternationalism	Liberalism
No change is likely.	The centralizing tendencies in global politics will lead to the subordination of Antarctic governance to multi-centric actors and more encompassing environmental rules.	More institutionalization of the regime will take place as states resolve gaps that have appeared between different regimes for resources and the environment. States may use bans in a widening set of circumstances.

United States wanted to maintain allied unity and prevent the Soviets from exploiting any dissension between the allies, and the allies were also unwilling to have Soviet interference. Therefore, the United States was willing and able to exercise its power and leadership toward those states with claims.

The United States announced that it recognized no claims in the Antarctic and reserved the right to make its own—which continues to be U.S. policy in the 1990s. This approach created a "level" field for the allies; no nation's claim was singled out as better or worse than any other. At the same time, since great powers set the tone for the development and operation of international law, the U.S. stance cast all claims into doubt. Uncertainty and ambiguity now dominated the calculations of Britain, Argentina, and the other states with territorial ambitions. Any attempt by a claimant state to assert strongly its territorial claim might have evoked either a countervailing territorial claim by the United States or U.S. actions designed to show the imperfections of the other nation's territorial claim.

If the United States had asserted its own territorial claim, the legal situation would have become impossibly muddled. Moreover, the allies could easily see that if the United States made a territorial claim, so would the Soviet Union. The conflict this scenario would engender could cost all claimants their existing stakes in the Antarctic or even draw them into a military conflict with the Soviet Union.

If the United States took actions to show that another nation's claim was invalid, the results were not likely to turn out any better for the claimants. The claimant states in the Antarctic might find U.S. personnel acting in a claimed zone as though there were no legal claim; indeed, actions by U.S. personnel in Antarctica prior to the treaty were designed with precisely this attitude. At the very least, such behavior would weaken the international legal claims of the claimant states. At worst, it could lead to direct confrontation between the United States and its allies.

Although the United States strongly preferred not to have any direct conflict with its allies, the outcome would not have been in doubt: U.S. power would prevail. Argentina and Chile, for instance, would not be able to overpower the United States in the area; indeed, not even Britain could hope to win such a contest of wills and capabilities. And, as noted in the previous section, the allies would have little inclination to switch sides to the Soviet-led bloc (for example, Chile and the Soviet Union did not even have diplomatic relations in the 1950s).

Thus, the allies found it acceptable to follow the leadership offered by the United States once it was provided. Since the United States tried to act impartially toward all nations with territorial claims in the region, never actually threatening these states with force but instead engaging in continuous, sensitive diplomacy, it gained a measure of legitimacy. In sum, it exercised hegemonic and not coercive leadership, even taking up and expanding an idea Chilean diplomats had suggested: setting aside claims for a period of time.

Realist Response 3: The strong bipolarity of the international system made it easy to put the treaty in place.   The evidence of U.S. leadership among states with territorial claims underscores the strong bipolarity of the international system at the time. This structure clarified matters for the Soviets and disciplined U.S. options. Essentially, the United States and the Soviet Union had, in addition to conducting an arms race, divided the world into two camps. The United States had its allies, who would generally follow the U.S. lead. So did the Soviets. The bipolarity colored the two superpowers' consideration of the mixed sovereignty questions of the region.

Seven states—Chile, Argentina, Britain, France, Norway, New Zealand, and Australia—had made definite territorial claims to parts of the Antarctic. The claims of Chile, Argentina, and Britain overlapped. Other areas of the continent were claimed by no nation or were in a hazy situation where nations reserved the right to assert territorial claims. Neither the United States nor the Soviet Union had (or have) asserted claims, but both could do so under the legal doctrine of discovery.[7]

From the Soviet perspective, the nations that had long-standing claims in the Antarctic were solid U.S. allies. Even without asserting a direct claim, the United States might well have been able to convince its allies to provide bases to U.S. forces. Certainly, the ring of U.S. bases around the Soviet Union and elsewhere indicated that the Americans viewed this option as an efficacious method of expanding and projecting U.S. power.

Things did not look so sanguine from the U.S. perspective. The overlapping claims, especially between Argentina and Great Britain, could weaken the allies' resolve. Conflict between Argentina and Britain could provoke an unwanted war in the Western hemisphere, thereby necessitating a choice between the long-standing relationship with Britain and the newer, but still valuable, relationships with members of the Organization of American States (OAS) such as Argentina. (This possibility, of course, became reality in 1982 with the Falklands War.)[8]

Two official statements illustrate the concern of U.S. policymakers. The Policy Planning Staff in the State Department circulated a paper in June 1948 that commented,

[That allies had conflicting claims] is a source of embarrassment to the U.S. because of our close relations to Great Britain and our commitments in the Western Hemisphere. This embarrassment is susceptible of exploitation by the USSR to the further disadvantage of the U.S. Our national interest requires that a settlement of this dispute be reached which will be acceptable to the three countries involved.[9]

A few years later, a National Security Council memorandum argued for the following:

Orderly progress toward a solution of the territorial problem of Antarctica, which would ensure control by the U.S. and friendly parties, . . . freedom of exploration and scientific research for the U.S. and friendly parties . . . and access by the U.S. and friendly parties to natural resources discovered in Antarctica.[10]

Still, the clarity of the division of allies (and the Soviets had no allies with important Antarctic interests) made it easier for the Soviets to assess the dangers it faced. For reasons discussed in the next section, there was little likelihood that U.S. allies could be detached and induced to support Soviet claims. Had the division been murkier, the Soviets might have tried to woo, say, the Argentinians to their side. To avoid being left out in the cold or facing the combined strength of the United States and all other claimant states, a negotiated outcome was in order. The United States, rightly or wrongly, placed a high value on the threat to bloc coherence. Although for different reasons, the United States thus had reason to negotiate on this count as well.

Clearly, cogent power politics arguments for demilitarizing the Antarctic could be made on all sides. The sovereignty question gave the United States leverage over its allies, and the combined threat of the arms race and new assertions of territorial claims pressed the United States and the USSR into accommodation.

Realist Response 4: The United States structured the problem so that states were not likely to be penalized for cooperation. Still another reason realists might offer for the successful completion of the Antarctic Treaty is that the United States created a context in which states could risk cooperation. It cut the sovereignty Gordian knot by an artful device: No state's claims could be asserted, but neither could a state's claims be denied for the duration of the treaty. A similar idea had been proposed in the 1940s by Chile, which further legitimated the suggestion among states with an interest in the Antarctic. Moreover, the nations had agreed to let scientific exploration occur without concern about territorial claims during the International Geophysical Year (1957–1958).

At the same time, all the parties pledged not to put any nuclear or military forces in the area. Thus, states with claims did not actually have to forgo them, and because military forces were banned, their cooperation would not likely prove foolish. The United States and the Soviet Union also benefited from the combination: Both could threaten each other with the prospect of a sovereignty claim if the other failed to live up to its disarmament obligations. No state came out worse off than it had been going into the negotiations, and the Soviet Union and the United States came out better off than they had been prior to the treaty. British diplomat John Heap said of the 1959 treaty that although science was the beneficiary, no one "should . . . believe that such altruism was in the minds of the negotiators; it was not. The parties gained little from it but what they all, variously, stood to lose without it made the exercise worthwhile."[11]

One other element of the treaty bolstered the confidence that the obligations undertaken would be observed. Article VII, the inspection provision, said that the parties could freely travel anywhere in the Antarctic and could visit the installations of any nation. Thus, the monitoring problem of the treaty was solved. If the United States, the Soviet Union, Chile, or any other party cheated, everyone else would soon notice.

So it was that this treaty came into force at the height of the Cold War. The security of the United States and the Soviet Union were in potential jeopardy if the arms race were to extend to the Antarctic. Lack of clarity over sovereignty claims provided each nation with a lever of influence over the other and proved a means of disciplining the claimant allies of the United States. These factors were finessed in the treaty through its "setting aside" of claims and disarmament rules.

Question 2: Why was the minerals agreement negotiated?

Realist Response 1:   Mineral exploitation could destroy the entire security regime of the ATS.   Detailed negotiations for what would be called the Convention on the Regulation of Antarctic Mineral Resource Activities (CRAMRA) began in Buenos Aires in 1981 at the eleventh consultative meeting. Negotiations continued until 1988, when a treaty was agreed upon by the ATCPs, then numbering twenty, at Wellington, New Zealand. The ATCPs stipulated that for the treaty to go into effect, at least sixteen of the original twenty states would have to ratify it. That number would have to include all the claimant states, the United States and the USSR, and at least three developing countries.[12] None of the nations, however, formally ratified the agreement, and as we shall see in the next section, it seems unlikely that the treaty will ever go into effect. On May 1, 1990, many of the signatory parties decided to forgo any exploration (even though the regime permitted it) for fifty years; in summer 1991, all parties agreed to the Antarctic Environmental Protocol, which imposes a fifty-year ban on mining.

New Zealand was the first to raise the issue of a need for a regime for nonliving resources. Its reason for doing so was not that exploitation was about to begin. On the contrary, the logistics and exploration costs, not to mention remoteness from markets, made (and still make) exploitation entirely prohibitive. Instead, New Zealand was concerned about the ATS as a whole. "In the worst case," commented Christopher Beeby, who would chair the discussions, "the result could be a breakdown of the treaty, the loss of the disarmament regime that it contains, and more generally, of the stabilizing effect that it has had on the entire area south of 60 S latitude."[13]

Unlike the case of exploiting living resources, the prospect of using mineral and other nonliving resources could have a direct impact on the entire ATS:

Mineral resources (with the notable exception of floating icebergs) cannot move through national zones: they are fixed in place. These resources are thus inherently more capable of being exploited by a single national entity if uncontested jurisdiction over them can be established. Hence, the claims issue is more difficult to avoid for fixed mineral resources than it is for the living resources of the Southern Ocean.[14]

Rather than face renewed conflict on the question of sovereignty, the parties sought to solve the problem before it became one. They negotiated under the same formula as the Antarctic Treaty itself: No sovereignty could be gained or lost through the agreement. In effect, the negotiations were made subservient to the major rules of the game that had so successfully reduced international conflict.

The centrality of the ATS itself was underscored by the fact that the parties did not choose some other context in which to negotiate the minerals regime. The consultative parties chose to keep the minerals question directly under the authority of the ATS. This was not the only option available to the players. As will be seen, they could have chosen the approach in the Convention on the Conservation of Antarctic Marine Living Resources (CCAMLR) or used the U.N. Law of the Sea.

CCAMLR covered animals that came and went into different claimed areas and into areas of the Southern Ocean that were not covered by the ATS at all.[15] Because of the nature of the marine resources, claimant/nonclaimant status was relatively unimportant (although it is instructive that in the CCAMLR negotiations, Chile, the only claimant and fishing state, defended its claim and not its fishing interests). Moreover, because the Southern Ocean is considered the high seas and could be fished by anyone, nations outside the ATS had a legal right to join the negotiations. Some fishing states did. These considerations did not hold in the minerals problem. Minerals stay in one place and could be in a claimant state's territory, thus posing a direct threat to the ATS. As a result, it was easy to exclude non-ATCPs from talks on minerals.

Another potential approach might have been to apply the Law of the Sea (LOS) convention. That document set out boundaries and established a procedure for mining resources not generally thought to be under any one nation's control. This was a most unlikely strategy, however, for the minerals agreement. First, the United States and a number of European allies had just refused to sign the LOS agreement precisely because it gave credence to the idea that areas deemed "the common heritage of mankind" should be controlled internationally and that wealth generated from such areas ought to be shared with poorer nations. Second, even though claimant states might have wanted new international economic rules, they did not want to give up the potential of asserting territorial claims sometime in the future. The Law of the Sea convention was not an option.[16]

Question 3: Why did CRAMRA fail to go into effect?

Realist Response 1: Conflicts over different state interests were likely to surface if CRAMRA went into operation; this outcome might have threatened the ATS security regime.   The evidence for this response lies primarily in the discord generated by the negotiations themselves. As negotiations for CRAMRA went on, disturbing divergent interests among states were revealed. Nonclaimant and claimant states wanted to ensure that the balance of power on regulatory committees in CRAMRA did not favor interests opposed to theirs. Nonclaimants said that "regulation would have to be undertaken by the parties to the regime, acting collectively and without distinctions of any kind, through [the regime's] institutions."[17] Claimants, in general, sought a primary regulatory role.

The states opted to use consensus rather than majoritarian voting. Unlike the consensus procedure in CCAMLR, however, consensus in the context of the mining agreement would have been very difficult to achieve. CCAMLR did not have regulatory committees; the proposed mining agreement did have them. Each committee would have representatives from claimant states and from states that wanted to start mining; the United States and the USSR were guaranteed seats. In itself, this arrangement was not a bad idea, since all interested parties had a say. The critical difference between CCAMLR and CRAMRA consensus lay in this: Under CCAMLR, fishing was permitted until forbidden; in CRAMRA, mining was forbidden until permitted.[18] This stipulation would create a delay in mining because consensus to start something is harder to come by than consensus to stop an activity.[19]

In this setting, states concerned about the environment could stop the exploiting states and exploiting states could brake any further development of environmental rules. Such delays would aggravate existing tensions. Those more interested in preserving the continent for scientific or environmental reasons might decide, for example, that the ATS rule of setting aside, yet preserving, territorial claims was unworkable. Similarly, claimant states, desirous of economic gain from their "territory," might decide that the ATS was holding them back.

Question 4: What is the likely future of the Antarctic Treaty System?

Realist Response 1:   No change is likely.   The interests of states are well protected by the ATS; therefore, no change is likely in the future. States, like people and organizations, are often creatures of habit.[20]

They will persist in maintaining things that work even though there may be leaks and inefficiencies. The ATS protects important security interests of the different states, and so it is satisfactory. In some respects, one can even view the fifty-year ban on mining as an example of this conservatism. Rather than solve a problem and engender more points for conflicts, states chose to "let sleeping dogs lie."

This expectation, however, should be checked against the reasoning used to explain the creation of ATS itself. If the fundamental reasons for the ATS have changed, then business as usual may not continue.

Important changes in world politics have occurred. The end of the Cold War substantially reduced the prospect of extending the arms race to Antarctica. Thus, the United States and Russia are likely to have far less strategic interest in Antarctic matters than in the past. Yet, if the United States were to put Antarctica far down on its strategic, economic, or even environmental agenda, other parties might press their interests more strongly; thus, the prospects for military confrontation by the claimant states still lurk in the background. The Cold War may have ended, but U.S. interests in a stable political environment and in good relations with Britain and the nations of South America still remain. It thus seems quite doubtful that the United States will lose interest in the southern polar region. And since it is the only nation currently capable of sustained military action on a global scale, it is reasonable to anticipate that the United States can maintain the Antarctic Treaty System if it prefers to do so.

A potential source of uncertainty and conflict lies in disputes over economic resources. In fisheries issues, conflict over economic issues could raise the prospect of states defending the resources in their waters, as New Zealand did in the summer of 1998 by sending a naval frigate and Orion aircraft into "their" waters in search of illegal fishing, although officials said this did nothing to affect New Zealand's claim of sovereignty.[21] Were sovereignty claims somehow strengthened by the use of military power, even in the name of the ATS, it is remotely possible that the system could break down.

The uncertainty in the power structure of the international system surely will influence the political calculations of the claimant and nonclaimant states. Even in the event of economic conflict, however, a claimant state would still face pressures from nonclaimants. The United States could still assert a territorial claim if any of the claimant states sought to change the agreement significantly. Moreover, there is no other power with which to ally for support against such U.S. action. Last, other states, already somewhat dissatisfied with the way the ATCPs manage the Antarctic, might become even more vocal and active if claimant states did anything to assert sovereignty over their territorial claims.

The problem of claimants versus nonclaimants brings us to the willingness of other states to follow U.S. hegemonic leadership. In today's international environment, even the former states of the Soviet Union are willing to take leadership cues from the United States. It is true that the Southern Cone states of South America are more powerful than they were in the 1950s, but all of them face daunting economic conditions (which could militate against their taking cues from the United States). They remain, however unhappily, dependent in large measure on U.S. markets and capital. This dependence may reduce the legitimacy of the United States as a leader, but there is a countervailing tendency as well. The United States also serves as a shield against those states outside of the ATS that would somehow internationalize the region. Follow the leader still seems the best course.

In sum, the important changes in the international environment are not so great as to obviate the original reasons for the Antarctic Treaty. The power of the United States still holds. The conditions of irreconcilable differences if national preferences are pressed still remain. States remain better off with the treaty than without it.

The Postinternationalist View

Postinternational theory leads to different kinds of evidence and answers relevant to the questions we just examined from a realist perspective. The turbulence that now engulfs world politics had barely begun when the Antarctic Treaty went into effect. The decision to negotiate this agreement, however, does provide evidence of the early rumblings of turbulent change. The fraying of the agreement over time further illustrates how turbulent world politics has become. To be sure, the state-centric world, with its concerns about sovereignty and security, dominated in the first years, but over time its importance has declined. Instead, the multi-centric world of sovereignty-free actors (SFAs), including the scientific community, has come to share center stage with the sovereignty-bound actors (SBAs). The scientific community recognized early the danger of nuclear war and the need to build cooperative relationships. Thus the pressure for a continent for science, free of security problems and borderless, came not from states but from the sovereignty-free scientific community. In a sense, the scientists who promoted the Antarctic Treaty were precursors to the widening array of competent groups and thoughtful individuals who now are active in the Antarctic and other political arenas.

Question 1: Why was the Antarctic Treaty negotiated and put into effect?

Postinternational Response 1: A research structure designed by the scientific community provided a convenient framework for states to use in resolving disputes.   The idea behind the International Geophysical Year (IGY) of 1957–1958 was to advance understanding of the physical world.[22] Scientific organizations around the world designed projects to investigate a host of geophysical phenomena. On the nongovernmental side in the United States, the prestigious National Academy of Sciences[23] and its operational arm, the National Research Board, organized university work. The National Science Foundation (NSF), a government agency, funded many IGY efforts and was the lead government agency for the U.S. contribution to the project. The Soviet Academy of Sciences coordinated Soviet activities, as did national academies of science in other nations. These national activities, as well as the results of the IGY, were further coordinated by the International Council of Scientific Unions (ICSU), a specialized agency of the United Nations.

Given its centrality to atmospheric and ocean phenomena, the Antarctic received much attention during the IGY. Very little was known about the region; hence, for the duration of the IGY, nations interested in the region were allowed to set up scientific stations in the area without worrying about territorial claims. Eventually, more than forty stations were put into operation. They were run by scientists from the aforementioned twelve nations that would ultimately sign the Antarctic Treaty. Since it was very costly to do research in the Antarctic, the scientists created the Scientific Committee on Antarctic Research (SCAR) to coordinate the Antarctic work. SCAR shared information with the Scientific Committee on Oceanic Research (SCOR), which had links to the ICSU.[24]

IGY research emphasized how very little was known about Antarctica and underscored how much could be learned about the Earth from stations located on the continent. Thus, scientists from the twelve nations who had done research in Antarctica during the IGY went home and started pushing the idea of making the Antarctic a "continent for science." The grip of the scientific community on subsequent political choices shows in the role SCAR played in shaping the formal Antarctic Treaty. First, the countries invited to participate in the negotiations were selected from those that had been represented in SCAR during the IGY. Second, when Poland asked for a seat at the negotiating table, SCAR handled the problem. Poland was told it would be welcome once it had undertaken year-round research.[25] That meant it could join, but it also meant that its application came too late to participate in the treaty negotiations. A situation that could have caused a political conflict between the United States and the Soviet Union was resolved fairly and amicably through the scientific community. Indeed, the rule on year-round research as the basis on which consultative status is determined ended up in the treaty and technically remains in effect to this day.

Domestic science agencies also continued to dominate Antarctic discussions. A good example comes from the United States, where, in 1959, as states were discussing the possibility of an Antarctic Treaty, a dispute arose over who should coordinate U.S. Antarctic research. On one hand, the Department of Defense (DOD) thought it should be the lead government agency, arguing that science was "but one of this country's interests in Antarctica." The department's argument was supported by members of the House Armed Services Committee, who claimed that putting the research under the NSF would "emphasize science 'at the expense of the political, economic, and military considerations.'" The suggestion that the DOD should be the lead government agency "produced dismay among a number of civilian scientists" as well as the State Department. To counteract this trend, the scientific community worked to ensure NSF's dominance. The National Academy of Sciences formed the University Committee on Polar Research to get more scholars involved in Antarctic research. This committee claimed it was uninterested in politics, but *New York Times* science writer Walter Sullivan thought otherwise, saying, "Its formation is, in effect, an emphasis on the scientific approach" to the management of the continent.[26] In sum, the Antarctic Treaty shows the imprint of IGY activity. SCAR became a permanent mechanism for coordinating scientific research; the national academies of science remain active; in the United States, the NSF won out over the DOD and continues to be the lead U.S. government agency for work on the region; and the stations stayed in place. Last, the treaty contains provisions for linking SCAR to SCOR and ultimately to ICSU.

States had been hung up on how to resolve territorial claims without engendering military conflict. Moreover, they needed low-conflict mechanisms for coordinating Antarctic management problems. The decision by states (caused at least partially by domestic and international scientific pressure) to set aside claims so that research could ensue opened the door to the scientists. Their research coordination devices were appropriate not only for their own work but also for the world of states. One scholar put it this way: "Antarctic science is the key to international credibility both for a nation within the Antarctic Treaty System and for the Antarctic Treaty System within the broader international community of nations."[27]

The postinternational model notes that states often yield jurisdiction to SFAs when "governments are paralyzed by prior commitments and SFAs may be able to break the stalemate and when the initiatives of SFAs do not intrude upon prior commitments and may yield desirable results."[28] Living with the IGY status quo would reduce state paralysis, and using the coordination devices of the scientists hardly intruded on the perquisites of states.

A mirror of the states' interests in the scientific solution shows up in the ways the scientific community benefited from collaboration with the SBAs. Here the postinternational model says that SFAs work with SBAs to defend the worthiness of their activities and values and when they can intrude themselves into a situation where their values and competence can affect the course of events.[29] What could better secure the worthiness of the scientific project than a state commitment to their scientific organizations and values? Without a doubt, the most relevant use of Antarctica at the time was for research; thus, the scientists could readily "intrude" themselves into SBA activities without generating SBA resistance.

Postinternational Response 2: The normative (value) priorities of the scientific community helped states escape the dictates of sovereignty. Organization was not the only factor that accorded a prominent role to science. The global scientific community valued free communication and unfettered research. In its own affairs, consensus decisionmaking was the norm. Many scientists believed they had a special, positive role to play in reducing the dangers of nuclear war in the midst of Cold War distrust and had started to seek ways to reduce the threat. The community was able to bring these values to bear in the governance of Antarctica.

Many of the same scientists who had applied their talents to the war effort during World War II were now trying to find avenues to arms control and disarmament. Demilitarizing the Antarctic and banning nuclear weapons from the continent fit in nicely with this normative priority in the scientific community.

Two efforts illustrate the value the community put on preventing nuclear war: Pugwash conferences and the *Bulletin of Atomic Scientists*. In 1957, the first of the International Conferences on Science and World Affairs brought scientists from the United States, the Soviet Union, and other nations to Pugwash, Nova Scotia. The meetings, now called the Pugwash conferences, continue to this day. The idea came from an appeal by Bertrand Russell and Albert Einstein in 1955 to discuss, as objectively as possible, problems science might address. The initial conferences paved "the way for serious negotiation on controlling nuclear armaments, ending the cold war, solving the Vietnam question, and on opening talks on European Security and Cooperation."[30] Each participating nation has a national Pugwash committee that tries to influence its government and international organizations. The *Bulletin of Atomic Scientists* (created before Pugwash), which flowed from the post–World War II "scientists' movement," focused on the danger of atomic (nuclear) warfare.[31]

The scientific community had yet another concern. It viewed the emphasis on secrecy as one of the most disconcerting aspects of the Cold War. Science advances by building on the efforts of others; if important results of work are muzzled in the name of national security, the scientific enterprise itself can be jeopardized. If knowledge gleaned from Antarctic research were classified, many fields of basic science would be hampered. Thus, it was clearly in the interests of the community to advocate freedom of information.

This value accounts for the freedom-of-movement and exchange-of-information clauses found in the treaty. Members of the scientific community were able to locate their interests in the stream of world events and press for outcomes consonant with those interests and values. That the values could also be cast in terms comprehensible to states was all to the good. Both multi-centric and state-centric actors could advance their values and interests.

The character of scientific decisionmaking also lent itself to the political needs of states. As we have seen, typically scientists use committee structures to achieve consensus. They consider the available data, assess the unknowns, reach conclusions about the evidence, and make decisions about what to do next. When everyone agrees on the next step, the decision is "made." Consensus decisionmaking is also used by states—but for rather different reasons. Consensus ensures a state against decisions that would impair its interests. Any state can stop a decision, or force important changes, by simply not agreeing. This approach allows every state to retain its cloak of sovereignty; it can also slow decisions down dramatically and thus perpetuate the status quo.

Until recently, most decisions about Antarctica were so scientifically based that the science version of consensus dominated; that is, decisions were generally quiet and only nominally contentious. Only as issues have become more politicized owing to the minerals agreement has the disjuncture between the two meanings of consensus grown.

The result of this confluence of multi-centric and state-centric interests was a novel form of governance: Sovereignty exists only at the periphery, held in abeyance, so to speak. Freedom to speak and travel freely, and freedom from the fear of war and nuclearization, exist at levels not experienced anywhere else on the globe. The scientists rule Antarctica, although states may believe they retain ultimate control over the rulers. Over time, however, this unusual form of "separation of powers" between scientific rule in an international politico-legal context would yield unanticipated, complex political problems for actors in both the state-centric and multi-centric worlds.

Question 2: Why was the minerals agreement negotiated?

Postinternational Response 1: Activities by the scientists (SFAs) put minerals on the agendas of states (SBAs). The need for CRAMRA would not have arisen at all had it not been for the efforts of scientists. Years of coordinated scientific research produced excellent evidence of mineral wealth on the continent itself and in offshore areas. The character of this information, however, created considerable uncertainty about the economic value of the resources. Thus, scientists "caused" the problem for states by producing highly uncertain information about the actual scale and scope of minerals.

The presence of minerals had been mere speculation at the outset of the treaty. The speculation gained a measure of reality as fossil evidence built up indicating that the climate of Antarctica had once been quite warm. Scientists were interested in how this effect had come about. Had the Earth possessed a much warmer climate all over the globe? Or, as the theory of plate tectonics claimed, had the Antarctic once been located somewhere else?

The answer came in December 1967 when a New Zealand geologist, Peter J. Barrett, found a fragment of what would be identified as a Labyrinthodont in the Trans Antarctic Mountains. The Labyrinthodont fossil looked virtually the same as similar ones found in Africa and Australia; it was unlikely that the Labyrinthodonts "arose independently here and there. It is much more likely that they arose in one center and then spread out."[32] That likelihood would argue for the plate tectonic theory—Antarctica had once been elsewhere. This possibility was further enhanced by another characteristic of the fossil animal: It only lived in freshwater areas. It could not have swum over an ocean of saltwater to reach Antarctica.

With this information and field samples, geologists could reasonably claim that the Antarctic had once been connected to the landmasses that now form Africa, Australia, Madagascar, and South America. If these regions contained minerals, then surely the Antarctic did too. Since the fossil evidence showed a lush, tropical, wet climate, the chances were good that oil and natural gas reserves lay offshore and perhaps also buried under the ice.

Thus, it was the everyday operation of science in Antarctica that raised the prospect of mining. But the information science had provided was not the kind that would normally be collected prior to making a mining decision. According to one author, Bernard P. Herber, "Science has generally given the sort of information that formal prospecting would have provided, but not the more detailed and definitive information which could be provided by formal minerals exploration inclusive of drilling, blasting, and similar procedures."[33]

In the realist discussion of why CRAMRA was negotiated, we set out a subquestion that asked why the ATS was the umbrella for the minerals negotiations. Other options—a new international conference; linkage to other treaties; a stand-alone treaty (like CCAMLR) between interested parties—were available. Postinternational theory suggests a rather different line of reasoning for answering the question, although, as the realist interpretation argued, preservation of the status quo was clearly a value. The difference arose from the nature of the status quo.

Postinternational Response 2:   The "delegation of rule" to the scientific community would be threatened if negotiations occurred outside the ATS.   Gathering information suitable for actual mining decisions would have subverted the rule of "science" in Antarctica by generating information that required different legal rules. According to Herber,

> An important difference exists . . . between mineral deposit information obtained from scientists and that which would have been obtained via formal commercial prospecting and exploration in that the latter information bestows proprietary rights of ownership while the former does not. In fact, such proprietary rights would be technically impossible to establish under the "free exchange of knowledge" requirement of the Antarctic Treaty.[34]

Antarctic scientists feared that their work would be hampered by efforts to assess the economic viability of Antarctic nonliving resources. Two matters concerned them. First, the limited funding for basic science in the area could be diverted to applied research into prospecting and mining engineering under extreme conditions. Second, even limited commercial efforts—never mind actual exploitation—would endanger the environment; disrupt many field efforts; and, indeed, remove the special reasons for setting the continent aside for science. By placing the issue inside the ATS regime, scientists could control much of the information through SCAR and their special relationships at home with the official policy establishment.

Had there been a genuine interest in mining, CRAMRA would not have looked the way it did. It would have been easier to get permission to mine, just as it is relatively easy to fish under the Convention on the Conservation of Antarctic Marine Living Resources. For instance, the special regulatory committees that would have been set up for "certain aspects of the regulation of mining" would have been avoided, as they are in CCAMLR.[35] But by emphasizing the environmental aspects over the economic ones, science could retain its leading role as steward of the continent.

The scientists succeeded in keeping the mining issue well within their sphere of "governance." As in the past, the scientific community benefited from the impasse over sovereignty in the world of states. Any change that would facilitate mining would pose security and sovereignty challenges to the states. CRAMRA would have imposed minimal changes on this status quo. As we shall see, however, the very fact of the negotiations almost radically altered the governance of the region.

Question 3: Why did CRAMRA fail to go into effect?

Postinternational Response 1:   The ability of the ATCPs to enact the agreement had been weakened by authority crises among states and within ATCP states.   Authority crises permeate world politics. Whether expressed at local levels or played out in the United Nations, states can no longer assume their decisions will be followed. This point can readily be seen in two ways through the Antarctica case. First, Third World states pressured for more openness in decisionmaking and even for placing Antarctic activities under direct U.N. auspices. Second, as part of their efforts to stop the exploitation of Antarctica, environmental groups employed two strategies. They allied themselves with states in the General Assembly, and they agitated for changes in policy within the territorial boundaries of the ATCPs. U.N. pressure and environmental group activism combined to reshape what was possible for the states that were to be party to CRAMRA. What looked like a "done deal" in 1988 had unraveled by 1991.

That there had been a change in the ability of the ATCPs to control Antarctic matters can be seen by the initial failures of the U.N. to put the region on the agenda. The General Assembly attempted on a number of occasions to schedule a discussion of the governance of Antarctica.[36] During the International Geophysical Year, India asked that Antarctica be discussed in the General Assembly; the issue was withdrawn, however, after Chile and Argentina vehemently opposed

it. In 1958 the proposal was made again, but by then the treaty negotiations were well on their way, so the proposal failed. In 1974 the
Food and Agriculture Organization considered Antarctic questions
regularly, and it ultimately came to play a role in CCAMLR (in monitoring krill). In 1976 the first major speech about the region was made
in the General Assembly.[37] Soon after the ATCPs began serious negotiations on minerals in 1981, activity in the U.N. on Antarctica increased. But it was not until 1983 that the General Assembly made
Antarctica a regular item of discussion. The questions the General Assembly debated fell into two primary areas: the "property status" of
the region and its development; and second, the perceived elitism of
the ATS.

A number of developing states in the U.N. General Assembly
wanted to designate the Antarctic as the "common heritage of
mankind."[38] This term, first used by Arvid Pardo of Malta in connec-
tion with the Law of the Sea, refers to those areas of the world—the
high seas and outer space, for example—that are not or should not be
considered the property of any single state but rather belong to all of
mankind. This formulation had been strongly resisted (and continues
to be resisted) by the consultative parties. Antarctica, they claim, is
not *res nullius* (the property of nobody), and the U.N. cannot just ignore the past. More important, the common heritage principle implies
development. "Since this purpose," argued Australian diplomats,
"has never been dominant in Antarctica, where the environment is
extremely vulnerable to the activities of man, . . . it would not be appropriate to apply the concept to Antarctica."[39]

The problem of elitism seems mostly to have been a misunder-
standing. Early in the 1983–1984 General Assembly debates, non-ATS
states thought the voting was too secret and the full voting membership rule too elitist. U.N. critics called for open meetings and access to
the treaty, whereas ATS members pointed out that all decisions from
consultative party meetings were made public; surely there was no
need to have open meetings, since this was not common practice in
negotiation. They also noted that any state could accede to the treaty
(as a number of states had done); the rule on voting reflected the fact
that ATCPs bore the costs of Antarctic work and were the ones directly affected by problems in management.

Other SFAs, notably environmental organizations, used the General
Assembly discussions as an entry into Antarctic affairs. Greenpeace

provided information to the United Nations, as did other groups. To make use of the elitism attack, Greenpeace wintered over in Antarctica and conducted its own research, then demanded the right to participate in Antarctic decisionmaking; the ATCPs, however, rejected the proposal.[40]

The efforts of the General Assembly did have an effect, however. The ATCPs opened up their proceedings a bit to counter charges of elitism on the part of developing states, and acceding countries were invited to observe much of CRAMRA's work and make comments about the proceedings. Continued U.N. pressure may also have prompted the ATCPs to admit a number of major Third World countries, notably China and India, to full voting status. Now 80 percent of the world's population is "represented" in Antarctic decisionmaking. The ATCPs have also begun to invite some nongovernmental organizations to observe meetings or to serve on individual delegations of the ATCPs.[41]

The effects of these responses to U.N. pressures proved to be double-edged. On the one hand, the wind was knocked out of the sails of those who said the governance of Antarctica was largely a rich-country affair enhanced by secret proceedings. Once India and China were made voting members, they acted like typical ATCPs. Neither of those states has advocated U.N. control of Antarctica.

On the other hand, the greater availability of information about decisions and problems increased demands for good performance by these self-appointed stewards of Antarctica. Quite simply, everyone knew more about the decisions of the consultative parties, so critics could focus on continuing problems even more effectively. One can already detect a shift in emphasis: The critics are focusing less on the role of states and more on the governance provided by scientists.

Even as these efforts went on, the internal capacity of states to control outcomes was thwarted by environmental activism within their borders and on Antarctica itself. Sheer bad luck may also have hurt the states while helping the environmentalists. For example, an oil spill caused by an Argentine Navy ship off the coast of Antarctica in January 1989 had horrendous ecological results for animal populations—even worse, said some, than oil spills elsewhere.[42]

In December 1988, Greenpeace sent a ship to the Antarctic to protest the construction of a runway at the French Antarctic base, Dumont d'Urville. The runway would have split a penguin rookery in two and forced part of the rookery to cross the runway to get to the ocean.[43] Greenpeace, therefore, claimed the construction was interfering with the habitats of animals, a violation of the Antarctic Treaty. A fight between the construction workers and Greenpeace crew members ensued, and construction stopped. This small incident shows how different the power of SFAs is from that of states. Had a state's warship interfered in such a way, there would have been a major diplomatic crisis, recriminations, perhaps even war. But SFAs do not threaten sovereignty in the same way that states can—even though in this case, the action, as we shall see, certainly stopped states dead in their tracks.

While the "action" at the French base was taking place, Greenpeace was also protesting to the Australian government that the provision of port facilities to the French in Hobart, Tasmania, constituted complicity with France's illegal acts. Accompanying the protest in the Antarctic was an effort to persuade Australia not to agree to CRAMRA.

Greenpeace was not the only active environmental force. Jacques Cousteau lobbied the French government. According to the *New York Times*, he "persuaded the French Government to back out of the agreement," and his efforts were rewarded when, in September 1989, the prime ministers of France and Australia made a joint announcement stating that any mining in Antarctica was unacceptable. Said the August 18 communiqué, "Mining in Antarctica is not compatible with protection for the fragile Antarctic environment."[44] Having succeeded with France and Australia, Cousteau then turned his efforts to other countries.

The withdrawal of France and Australia, two of the key signers of CRAMRA, meant that the whole agreement was now in doubt. The two countries had proposed a long moratorium on any mining. As a result, the floodgates of activism were opened in states not yet convinced that CRAMRA was a bad agreement. This result can clearly be seen in what happened next in the United States, where the process of coalition building became unstable.

U.S. Antarctic policy emerges from consultations within and among government agencies and nongovernmental groups. The Antarctic Policy Group (APG) represents intragovernmental bargaining, whereas the nongovernmental organizations express their views through the Antarctic Public Advisory Committee (APAC).

One description of how the United States reached its negotiating stand for CRAMRA reported, "The negotiating position of the U.S. on Antarctic mineral issues was derived from a set of instructions drawn up by an interagency task force, the Antarctic Policy Group (APG)."[45] The process began with intra-Department of State bargaining between the Bureau of Ocean and International Environmental and Scientific Affairs and the Economic Bureau. That draft document went to the APG proper, which has representatives from the "Departments of State, Interior (especially the U.S. Geological Survey), Energy, Defense and Commerce (the National Oceanic and Atmospheric Administration), as well as the Marine Mammals Commission, the Environmental Protection Agency, the National Science Foundation, and the Arms Control and Disarmament Agency."[46] The APG was then advised by nongovernmental entities via the Antarctic Public Advisory Committee,

> a group drawn from public international organization, industry, and academic community. The APAC meets two or three times each year with the APG and various congressional staff to discuss Antarctic issues and U.S. policies. . . . The Antarctic mineral delegation consisted of a public interest representative from the International Institute for Environment and Development, an industry representative from the American Petroleum Institute, and a private technical advisor from the academic community, as well as APG members.[47]

Very probably, the separate elements in this melange of interests had failed to reach genuine consensus on the U.S. position. When the French and the Australians withdrew their support for CRAMRA, U.S. environmental groups opposed to the minerals agreement stepped up their actions, making an end run around the Antarctic advisory process to reach the U.S. Congress. These groups, especially Greenpeace, the Antarctic and Southern Oceans Coalition, and the National Wildlife Federation, wanted no mining in the region. Their preferred option was to create a world park and to emphasize environmental protection.[48] Greenpeace wanted the U.N. to take over the management of Antarctica. These preferences made their way into Congress. Some proposed bills would have had the Secretary of the Interior prepare plans for a world park; others asked for amendment of the Antarctic Conservation Act of 1978 that would have required environmental impact statements for any U.S. activity. In the end, on October 26, 1990, the House and Senate agreed on wording for HR 3977. This bill prohibited "U.S. citizens from engaging in mineral resource activities in Antarctica" and called "on the Secretary of State to negotiate a new agreement banning mineral development."[49]

Following the congressional action, the State Department notified other Antarctic parties that the United States, too, would have to discuss CRAMRA again. In Madrid in 1991, the United States eventually agreed to a fifty-year moratorium on mining activities.[50] The moratorium succeeded in delaying the park (although de facto it created one) while addressing the interest group and legislative pressures at home.

The end runs around the Antarctic negotiators that produced the ban did satisfy the environmental activists. As one report put it, "Environmental groups were delighted with the results of the Madrid meeting. Greenpeace, speaking in quite moderate tones, said the compromise has been hard for the states to make, but was a good one. The World Wildlife Fund 'said . . . that if the draft protocol was endorsed by the Antarctic Treaty nations it would be a major step toward setting up a world park in Antarctica.'"[51]

The United States at first refused to approve the moratorium proposal. But in early July 1991, the Bush administration reversed its earlier position and agreed to sign provided that a three-fourths agreement of states would replace unanimity as the prerequisite for allowing mining to start. That stipulation was approved, and in October 1991 the moratorium went into effect. What prompted the Bush reversal? Some claimed that it was pressure from Congress, environmentalists, and foreign governments: Both realms of world politics squeezed the president's administration, and he gave in.[52]

The difficulty the consultative parties had in controlling outcomes was thus closely associated with changes in legitimacy afforded them to manage the Antarctic. Gillian Triggs put it this way: "The law-making agenda changes, it seems, not because of carefully articulated government policy and interstate consensus, but because of public opinion which has formed and developed at a transnational level, irrespective of perceived national priorities and interests."[53] This fundamental change, one stemming from alterations in the basic parameters of world politics, may play out in surprising ways in the future.

Question 4: What is the likely future of the Antarctic Treaty System?

Postinternational Response 1:   The centralizing tendencies in global politics will lead to the subordination of Antarctic governance to multi-centric actors and more encompassing environmental rules. Although decentralizing authority crises have shaped current debates over the future of Antarctica, two factors augur for centralization. First, environmental issues encompass large, integrated systems. Or, more correctly, environmental issues form a network of overlapping systems that tend toward the creation of a single system. Second, the existing structures of worldwide scientific communication are likely to grow stronger and denser as environmental research progresses. This could mean that the management of such communications will have to dovetail with global environmental agreements.

Antarctica, already the beneficiary of scientific organization and values, is likely to be folded in with other scientific structures because of its critical role in governing the global climate. It would be unwise to engage in any activity that might alter Antarctica's climate because of the possible cascading effects it might have on the larger climate. Preserving Antarctica would also ensure that scientists could continue to follow their excellent bio- and eco-indicators for pollution and climate change.

Agreements on recent atmospheric problems (ozone depletion agreements are the most notable, but global warming agreements look probable as well) often curtail industrial activities even as they increase the role of scientific research, monitoring, and assessment. Thus, it is unlikely that Antarctica will be opened to minerals development or even offshore drilling. Stricter rules on scientific activities and tourism will likely emerge (and, indeed, at the same time the parties announced the official moratorium, they also set out stricter rules on uses). If this future unfolds, it probably means that the world park idea will not quite take hold—at least in the sense that visitors to Yosemite or Banff might imagine. Parks often get overused and overdeveloped to the detriment of their ecosystems. Antarctica's ecosystem is so fragile that very little visiting could be permitted beyond strictly controlled scientific stays.

Whether the current formal treaty system of voting continues or the U.N. takes over depends on the outcome of a future conflict between economic development and environmental issues.⁵⁴ The idea that some areas may be a common heritage of mankind, the reader may recall, has a development basis. Developing countries do not want the industrialized world to gain all the product and profits from using areas previously inaccessible and unowned, such as the seabed floor. In the U.N. Law of the Sea negotiations, arrangements were made to share any wealth from seabed minerals development. (The United States refused to ratify the convention until 1994, when changes were made in these provisions.) One way of criticizing this seabed arrangement is that it pays too little attention to the environment. Preserving the environment is not at all like redistributing the wealth.⁵⁵

In an effort to preserve the Antarctic status quo, consultative states might simply continue to argue that the General Assembly of the U.N. could not possibly be a steward for the environment, since its interest would largely be in developing the area. Similar arguments might be used to delay almost any U.N. initiative to manage a global resource. The cost of such a tactic, however, would be more and more use of the values and structures of the scientific community.⁵⁶ Under that scenario, we might find increased centralization of environmental issues in the multi-centric half of the world political system. States would, in effect, extend the rule that science governs from Antarctica to other areas.

How would this scenario come about? Developing states that attempted to use the General Assembly to redress global inequities could find themselves without plausible allies. They would probably be deserted by their erstwhile environmental allies: When the moratorium was announced, the environmentalists applauded and dropped the U.N. management rhetoric. Recent disputes over illegal fishing show an evolving relationship between states and environmental organizations. Greenpeace intercepted an illegal fishing ship registered in Belize and chased it away. New Zealand's foreign minister applauded Greenpeace's actions, just as Greenpeace lauded New Zealand's use of its navy to patrol for illegal fishing.⁵⁷

The only possible allies for developing states from the multi-centric world would be the firms from the industrial world that fund and pursue illegal fishing—and the customers in Europe and the United States who happily pay twelve dollars a pound to gobble up the charmingly (but incorrectly) named "Chilean sea bass" delivered by both legal and illegal fishers. Pressure from economic interests, especially if connected to developing country interest in development, could reverse the trend of centralization and incorporation into a larger environmental framework within the multi-centric world.

The struggle between environmental protection and economic use of the Antarctic influences states of all kinds. Environmentalists in developing countries sometimes undermine existing internal power relations (a pattern that is not necessarily bad, since the links among sustainable development, human rights, and the environment may foster a rise in standards of living). Between industrial and developing states, environmentalism—until recently an industrial, middle-class phenomenon—ends up providing issues on which industrial states can maintain their power advantages over developing countries. Thus, rather like the Bush administration at the time of the moratorium, these states may find that environmental arguments are hard to resist at home or abroad and that such arguments are likely to win out against prodevelopment ones. The best option for a developing country is to support management by scientists, not by the U.N., because that route would facilitate participation by their own scientific communities.

Very likely, Antarctica will come increasingly under the sway of actors in the multi-centric world. Even though these actors are not hierarchically ordered and possess vast differences in goals and interests, this direction of change suggests more centralized management of Antarctica. The reasons for the centralization lie in two areas: First, as we have noted, the character of the issue warrants increasing integration. Second, the specific history of Antarctica as a continent for science argues for centralization. The scientific community, although hardly of one cloth, is quite well interconnected and informationally hierarchical. That is, reports flow up and down from local researchers to the larger community and, in the case of Antarctic research, from the individual to SCAR and from there throughout the relevant U.N. agencies and national scientific organizations.

Performance criteria, which in a postinternational world are used to give and withdraw legitimacy to those who would govern, fit nicely with science. Research is (for the most part, but not always) peer evaluated; it is open to others. One must be careful here. Scientific advice on difficult sociopolitical questions can degenerate into the "hired gun" phenomenon, where my expert takes on the views of your expert and everyone ends up more confused than when they started. But so far, SCAR has succeeded in directing the scientific work in Antarctica.

SCAR and the consultative parties acting in their political roles did almost drop the legitimacy ball over CRAMRA. But they seem to have learned that a "no regrets" policy of environmental preservation is the safest course. By shielding the continent through careful and environmentally sound research rules, and by linking the region with larger agreements, the scientific community may gain even more control over the area than it now has.

The Liberal Interpretation

Question 1: Why was the Antarctic Treaty negotiated and put into effect?

Liberal Response 1:   States prefer to cooperate when possible.   The ability of the countries to solve Antarctic issues through peaceful means illustrates the basic liberal premise that international anarchy need not mean the presence of general war. Instead, states can create and deepen patterns of cooperation. The ATS, as scholar Davor Vidas explained, provided a basis for "a unique, continuous cooperation among a group of states" through periodic meetings and regular exchanges of information.[58]

Prior to the Antarctic Treaty, the U.N. and international law were the main means by which cooperation was achieved. The U.N. Charter provides a legal framework that calls upon states to solve problems peacefully. It grew over time to encompass the many activities of states, including the coordination of some scientific research. The International Geophysical Year (IGY) brought scientists from all around the world together to research complex problems of the Earth, its atmosphere, and outer space. The IGY was partially coordinated through the U.N., and the work on the Antarctic was no exception. Together, the duty to seek peaceful means of resolving disputes and the success of the information gathering by scientists during the IGY helped create an international setting where communications were improved enough that peace became more likely than war in the Antarctic.

International law, the fundamental means by which states improve communications, bridged the gap between the United States and the Soviet Union. Some of the most fundamental elements of international law concern the acquisition of territory. Generally, a country has to show effective, continuous (and, if possible, uncontested) control of a territory to claim it. In distant, inhospitable regions of the world, however, international law sets a much lower standard. States could claim land by discovery, but in these regions countries had to do little to show effective and continuous occupation. This feature of international law was the wedge with which both the Soviet Union and the United States could influence each other and the claimant states. Although neither had made a territorial claim, both could do so under the doctrine of discovery as modified for remote regions. Thus, troubled peace became far less troubled through the capacity of international law to clarify the rights and obligations of states.

Liberal Response 2: Some of the claimant and nonclaimant states shared a security community with each other. To this basic international institutional setting for enhanced international cooperation, liberals might also add the importance of a security community between the United States and some of the claimant states, for example, Britain. Intensely peaceful relations between these nations further encouraged cooperation over conflict in the Antarctic. In addition, the United States at the time sought to promote better relations with countries in the Western hemisphere in the hope of promoting democracy and extending peaceful relations to this area.

Question 2: Why was the minerals agreement negotiated?

Liberal Response 1: Continued negotiations on a range of topics within the ATS allowed states to learn the necessity of setting up a nonliving resources regime before exploitation began. Once nations set up an institutional arrangement, it insulates that set of concerns from flare-ups of other arguments between countries. Disputes between ATCP states from one area of international relations did not readily spread to the Antarctic, but cooperation did. The Antarctic agreements, for example, did not fall apart simply because Britain and Argentina fought a hot war over the Falkland/Malvinas Islands.

In addition to insulating against problems from one area affecting another, institutions promote more institutions by facilitating learning. States in the Antarctic had already noted the imperfections of the living resources regime. It was weaker because other traditions in the management of fisheries influenced how the ATCPs could only address living resources. States could regulate the nonliving resources questions within the ATS without encountering the living resources impediments to management. In addition, the ATCPs could see that the exploitation of minerals could set back the patterns of cooperation that had taken hold in the regime.

Question 3: Why did CRAMRA fail to go into effect?

Liberal Response 1:   Environmental protection became a higher principle than resource conservation within the ATS.   CRAMRA failed because of a growing international and domestic consensus that environment was more important than resource conservation and use. Let us begin with the domestic element. It is important to understand that CRAMRA failed only in the sense that it is "politically inert" at the moment due to changes in domestic politics; it is still open to signature.[59] Green political parties in Australia and in France had the power at home to change national policies through democratic processes. Although not as powerful politically in the United States as in other industrial democracies, environmentalists there also had some success influencing U.S. policy. The changed preferences of governments, especially among the democracies, were turned into new policy for the Antarctic.

Even before the domestic political changes came about, the ATCPs had been building consensus on the principle of environmental protection. CCAMLR had a protection provision.[60] CRAMRA also contained strong protection language. In fact, many of the normative aspects of CRAMRA tied to environmental protection found their way into the 1991 Antarctic Environmental Protocol adopted at Madrid.[61] The failure of CRAMRA was hardly complete. Indeed, it may mark the clear transition from an emphasis on resource conservation to one of environmental protection.

The transition from conservation to protection principles is by no means easy to make, because protection influences and limits not only scientific research in the region but also long-held ideas that states can exploit nature's resources. Few international agreements between states have environmental protection as a central goal; usually environmental treaties are directed at the effective conservation of a resource or ecosystem.

Scientific work, although not synonymous with environmental protection, was the key product and activity of the ATS. The work of scientists is used by the governments of the consultative parties in the making of national and international Antarctic policy. As issues that demand scientific input make their way onto state agendas, management changes. For example, the relatively pristine nature of the region had prompted research on animals and then on whole systems of animals and plants. Thus, ecosystem research, led by a quasi-governmental organization, the Scientific Committee on Antarctic Research, appeared early in the region. From ecosystems it was not a long stretch to the adoption by states of the precautionary principle—still imperfect in the region—that exploitation should not be allowed unless those who want to exploit the region can show it will do no harm. Normally, the reverse is true in environmental policy. As with the general principle of protection, the use of the precautionary principle appeared in CCAMLR, then CRAMRA, and finally the Antarctic Environmental Protocol. The precautionary principle is now embedded in the ATS.

In addition to the changing ideas about the environment found in the institutional arrangements of the ATS, the system responded to demands for more participation and openness by including more states and inviting international governmental organizations such as the Food and Agriculture Organization to observe CCAMLR meetings. With CRAMRA's provisions mostly set aside and increased concern with the environment, observer status was extended to some environmental organizations. Most recently, and as a consequence of the primacy of protection, nongovernmental tourism organizations have also found their ways into official meetings. The increased openness produced a widening legitimacy among states and nonstate actors alike for the ATS.

The openness, coupled with the protection principle, even prompted states to change their views on the ATS. "The fears of Consultative Parties—claimants in particular—that the establishment of permanent institutions [new science boards and secretariats for the CCAMLR and the ATS proper] within the ATS might disturb the balance of positions on the sovereignty issue, have gradually become secondary to the actual implementation needs of the new ATS regimes."[62]

In sum, CRAMRA is unlikely to come into force, and thus it can be said to have failed. But even in failure, it contributed positively to the continued institutional development of the ATS.

Question 4: What is the likely future of the Antarctic Treaty System?

Liberal Response 1:   More institutionalization of the regime will take place as states resolve gaps that have appeared between differ-ent regimes for resources and the environment.   Some forty years from now, when the mining ban technically comes to an end, the ATS may well have a single set of regimes, rather than the four related, but overlapping, ones now in place under the original Antarctic Treaty: CCAMLR, failed CRAMRA, Antarctic Environmental Protocol, and an as-yet-unclear one for tourism. States will negotiate the coordina-tion of the regimes and be in firm control of their operation. The set-aside of sovereignty will continue to energize decisionmaking in the region, primarily by encouraging states to ban resource extraction and use activities that could threaten the sovereignty modus vivendi of the ATS. The growing use of ecosystem scientific work, environ-mental protection, and the precautionary principle will create guide-lines usable in every area of concern in the Antarctic.

The use of ecosystem science, protection, and the precautionary principle may well be paralleled in other state-made regimes for man-aging the world's many threatened ecosystems. If so, then the ATS as a whole will be strengthened legally in the world of international law and in the domestic laws of countries around the world. Already, the emphasis on environmental protection and ecosystem science has caused Chile to change its laws to reflect the international commit-ments it has made in Antarctica.

The success of states in managing the Antarctic bodes well for their continued dominance in the region. By co-opting NGOs and by at-tending to the interests of states, whether ATS members or not, the consultative parties have defused further internationalization of the region. Thus, it is likely that Antarctic affairs will not come under the U.N.'s sway or that of environmental organizations but will remain firmly in the hands of states. States have, in sum, withstood the pres-sure put on them to turn the area into either a U.N.-controlled world

222 The Politics of the Antarctic

park or a U.N.-supervised "common heritage of mankind" system of resource conservation and use.

Even the current crisis over illegal fishing may prove a boon to the development of stronger rules for the region by consultative parties. The U.N. cannot possibly monitor or enforce fishing regulations. States can. In fact, states are enforcing the rules, as when New Zealand sent a naval cruiser into the waters off the land it claimed. Enforcement will not erode the system by bringing sovereignty claims back into active play for two reasons. First, New Zealand and others have taken to calling the poachers "pirates." In international law, any state has jurisdiction over the capture of pirates on the high seas. ATCPs have also strengthened their resolve to prosecute their own nationals for illegal fishing. Second, New Zealand's laws prohibit any nationals from fishing illegally, even if they are on a ship bearing a flag of convenience. Neither approach—pirates or control of nationals—poses a threat to the ATS and its unusual arrangements to cope with sovereignty.

Liberal Response 2: States may use bans on activities in a widening set of circumstances. It may prove useful in the future for states to ban fishing and other commercial activities rather than attempt to regulate numbers. Bans are easier to monitor and enforce than fishing limits. Bans are also cheaper, because they do not require the complex and extensive applied scientific monitoring and study of ecosystems needed to set safe harvesting limits. Bans would also serve to enhance the continent-for-science objective of the ATS by returning science to basic rather than applied research. All in all, bans on fishing, on mining, perhaps even on tourism would preserve the region, reduce interstate conflicts, and be easy to monitor.

Conclusion

In this chapter we sought to show how a reasonable interpretation of the Antarctic Treaty, its history, and its future is readily provided by realism, postinternationalism, and liberalism. The question of which of the interpretations is the more sound and incisive can only be answered by readers based on their explanatory preferences. Readers could decide that the relative simplicity (parsimony) of the realist view is preferable to the more complex and "thick" view offered by postinternationalism. Alternatively, they may decide that at least for this case, the complexity of the postinternational perspective offers the analyst a stronger grip over relevant variables. Or, readers may be intrigued by the contrasts between liberals and realists over the nature of interstate relations. The point of these differences is not that one of the theories is more correct than the others, but rather that the coherence and suitability of an explanation depend on one's concerns and theoretical sensibilities.

9
Toward Thinking Theory Thoroughly

There are surely many urgent problems on the global agenda that could usefully be probed in case analyses such as those presented in the previous three chapters. These include severe environmental challenges, the reconstruction of Kosovo, tensions between China and Taiwan, efforts to make peace in the Middle East, the evolution of the European Union, the end of apartheid in South Africa, the twists and turns of U.S.-Japanese relations, and so on through a seemingly endless list of situations. But for two reasons we have chosen neither to proliferate our case analyses nor even to offer a representative sample of present-day crises. One reason is the conviction that political situations rapidly become obsolete and that thus the cases would quickly become exercises in historical documentation. The other, more important reason for stopping here is that our purpose has not been to provide an overview of world politics today. Rather, we have sought to elaborate one main point: that whatever may be the problem of concern, and whenever it may have emerged on the global agenda, it cannot be adequately grasped unless one is self-conscious about the theory one employs to perceive, describe, and assess it.

We have sought to demonstrate this main point by outlining three theoretical perspectives (in Chapters 2 to 4) and then comparing them (Chapter 5) before applying them to empirical cases (in Chapters 6, 7, and 8). So far so good, the reader might conclude, but how I do use this form of inquiry? You have persuaded me that I ought to be self-conscious about the theories I employ, but you have provided no clues whatever about how I might be my own theorist. Can you suggest some guidelines I might follow now that you have got me hooked on the virtues of theory?

The question is a fair one. We are delighted that our main point may seem reasonable and worthy of pursuit. So we accept the obligation to enumerate some simple—yet powerful—rules of thumb for proceeding from a passive observer of world politics to that of an active theorist.

But first it should be noted that to some extent the inclination to perceive and assess the course of events as expressive of larger forces may not be a talent that is easily learned: It may also be a cast of mind, a personality trait, or a philosophical perspective that some acquire early in life. To the degree that this is so, of course, our rules of thumb are not likely to be of much help. One can be introduced to the nature of theories, taught the various purposes theories can serve, exposed to the controversies over the relative worth of different theories, and instructed on the steps required for the construction of viable theories. And, to solidify these lessons, one can then be given the task of formulating concrete hypotheses and tying them together into a theoretical framework. Learning the skills underlying the design of theories is not, however, the equivalent of learning how to think theoretically. To move beyond the dos and don'ts of theoretical design, one has to acquire not a set of skills but rather a set of predispositions, a cluster of habits, a way of thinking, a mental lifestyle—or whatever may be the appropriate label for that level of intellectual existence that governs the use of skills and the application of values. It is this more fundamental dimension of the life of the mind that may not be readily teachable or learnable, a caveat that needs emphasis because the ensuing nine rules of thumb amount to nothing less than a pronouncement on how to think theoretically.

Nine Preconditions for Creative Theorizing

The task of disciplining ourselves to think theoretically consists, first, of identifying the cognitive inclinations and perceptual impulses from which creative theory springs and, second, of forming intellectual habits that assure the prevalence of these inclinations and impulses whenever we turn to theory-building endeavors. The central question examined here is as follows: What are the mental qualities that best enable one to "think theory," and how can their acquisition be best assured? Nine such qualities seem especially conducive to the development of good theorists. Each of the nine seems equally important and there is some overlap among them. Accordingly, the sequence of their elaboration here should not be interpreted as implying a rank ordering.

Rule 1: To think theoretically one has to avoid treating the task as that of formulating an appropriate definition of theory.

Let us start with the proposition that the task of thinking theoretically is not one of developing a clear-cut definition. On balance, it is probably preferable to have a precise conception of the nature of theory rather than a vague one, but definitional exactness is not the only criterion of thinking theoretically and it may not even be a necessary requirement for such thought. It is easy to imagine a young student thinking theoretically about international phenomena well before his or her first course on the subject turns to the question of what constitutes theory and the various uses to which it can be put. Indeed, we have had the good fortune of encountering a few students who were, so to speak, born theoreticians. From their very first comments in class, it was clear that they thought theoretically even though they had never had any methodological training or exposure to the history of international relations.

Most of us are not so lucky. We have to be trained to think theoretically and then have to engage in the activity continuously in order to achieve and sustain a genuinely theoretical perspective. Hence, the fact that a few among us can maintain such a perspective without training and practice is a useful reminder that definitional clarity is not a prerequisite to creative theorizing.

The reminder is important because many of us tend to exaggerate the importance of exact definitions. To be clear about the nature of theory is not to guarantee the formulation of meaningful theory. Such clarity can be misleading. It can provide a false sense of security, a misguided confidence that once one is equipped with a clear-cut definition, one needs only to organize one's empirical materials in the proper way. It is our impression that much of the writing in the field derives from this premise that good definitions automatically yield good theories, as if the definitions somehow relieve the observer of the need to apply imagination and maintain philosophical discipline.

To be sure, much of the writing in the field also suffers from loose and ambiguous conceptions of theory, from a confusion between theory and method. Such research would, obviously, be more valuable if it proceeded from a tighter and clearer notion of what the theoretical enterprise entails. So, to repeat, we are not arguing against definitional clarity. On the contrary, we believe it is highly appropriate to help students achieve such clarity by introducing them to the vast array of articles and books now available on the dynamics, boundaries, uses, and abuses of theory in the international relations field. But we are arguing for more than definitional clarity. In digesting the literature on theory and building a more elaborate conception of what it involves, one has to avoid leaning too heavily on definitions for guidance. Also needed is a cast of mind, a mental set that builds on definitions and encourages creative theorizing.

Rule 2: To think theoretically one has to be clear as to whether one aspires to empirical theory or value theory.

Progress in the study of international affairs depends on advances in both empirical and value theory. But the two are not the same. They may overlap; they can focus on the same problem; and values always underlie the selection of the problems to which empirical theories are addressed. Yet they differ in one overriding way: Empirical theory deals essentially with the "is" of international phenomena, with things as they are if and when they are subjected to observation, whereas value theory deals essentially with the "ought" of international phenomena, with things as they should be if and when they could be subjected to manipulation. This distinction underlies, in turn, entirely different modes of reasoning, a different rhetoric, and different types of evidence.

The habit of making the necessary analytic, rhetorical, and evidential distinctions between empirical and value theory can be difficult to develop. Indeed, such a habit can be weak and elusive for any of us who have strong value commitments and a deep concern for certain moral questions. The more intense are our values, the more are we tempted to allow our empirical inquiries to be guided by our beliefs rather than by our concern for observation. For this reason, becoming habituated to the is-ought distinction is extremely difficult. One can understand the distinction intellectually and even explain and defend it when pressed, but practicing it is another matter. Empirical analysis can easily slip into moral judgment without one being aware of it, as if one somehow fears that one's values and goals will be undermined if one allows oneself to focus on observable phenomena. Such a result, of course, need not be the case. On the contrary, moral values and policy goals can be well served, even best served, by putting them aside and proceeding detachedly long enough to enlarge empirical understanding of the obstacles that hinder realization of the values and progress toward the goals.

This is the one line of reasoning on behalf of thinking theoretically that the most value-committed citizens find persuasive. If empirical theory is posited as a tool of moral theory, fledgling theorists can approach it instrumentally and see virtue in habituating themselves to distinguishing between the two. It takes a while, however, before the perceived virtues of habituation are translated into actual habits, and, in fact, some people never manage to make the transition, hard as they may try. Impatient with the need for change, convinced that time is too scarce to afford the slow pace of empirical inquiry, many simply give up and dismiss the is-ought distinction as one of those picayune obsessions to which some academics fall prey.

It is our impression that impatience with empirical theorizing is likely to be especially intense among students of international relations from developing countries. An intense consciousness of the long-standing injustices built into developed-developing country relationships and perhaps a frustration over the premises of social science in developed countries have encouraged resistance to detached empirical theorizing on the part of theorists in developing countries. Their resistance gives analysts in developed countries pause: Is the insistence on habituating oneself to the is-ought distinction yet another instance of false superiority, of projection onto the developing world practices that have worked in industrial societies? It could be. We are keenly aware of the biases that may underlie our intellectual endeavors and thus we are not prepared to brush aside the idea that the is-ought distinction may be inappropriate to theorizing in much of the world. Still, the habit remains and resists being broken. The relevance of the distinction strikes us as global, as independent of any national biases, as necessary to thinking theoretically wherever and whenever enlarged comprehension is sought. Empirical theory is not superior to moral theory; it is simply preferable for certain purposes, and one of these is the end of deepening our grasp of why international processes unfold as they do.

Aware that our own expertise, such as it may be, lies in the realm of empirical theory, the ensuing discussion makes no pretense of being relevant to thinking theoretically in a moral context. All the precepts that follow are concerned only with those mental qualities that may render us more thoroughgoing in our empirical theorizing.

Rule 3: To think theoretically one must be able to assume that human affairs are founded on an underlying order.

A prime task of empirical theory is to explain why international phenomena are structured as they are or behave as they do. To perform this task one must assume that each and every international phenomenon is theoretically explicable, that deeper understanding of its dynamics could be achieved if appropriate instruments for measuring it were available. To assume that everything is potentially explicable is to presume that nothing happens by chance, capriciously, at random—that for every effect there must be a cause. That is, there must be an underlying order out of which international relations springs. If this were not the case, if events could occur for no reason, there would be little point in theorizing. If some events are inherently inexplicable, efforts to build creative theory are bound to fall short to the extent that they embrace phenomena that may occur at random. Indeed, in the absence of the assumption of an underlying order, attempts to fashion theory are futile, pointless exercises, a waste of time that could be better spent writing poetry, playing tennis, or tending the garden.

This is not to say that thought only acquires the status of theory when it purports to account for every event. As indicated below, theory is also founded on the laws of probability; hence, it only purports to account for central tendencies. But this claim is unwarranted if an assumption of underlying order is not made—that is, to think theoretically one must presume that there is a cause for every effect even though one does not seek to explain every effect.

Some people have a difficult time becoming habituated to the assumption of an underlying order. They see this premise as a denial of their own freedom. To presume there is a cause for everything, they reason, is to deprive people of free will, perhaps even to relieve them of responsibility for their actions. The assumption of an underlying order does not necessarily have such implications, however. One's freedom of choice is not lessened by the fact that the choices made are not random and instead derive from some source. Yet, fearful about compromising their own integrity, many people cannot accept this subtlety and insist on the premise that people have the capacity to cut themselves off from all prior experience and to act as they please for no reason whatsoever. To support their resistance to the assumption of an underlying order, they will often cite instances of international history when the unexpected occurred or when a highly deviant, impetuous, and irrational action was undertaken, as if somehow irrationality and impetuosity are capricious and do not stem from any sources.

Besides patiently reassuring those who may be dubious that there are no insidious threats in the assumption of an underlying order, one can lessen, even perhaps break, resistance to the idea by pointing out how the assumption offers hope for greater understanding and deeper comprehension. To presume that there is a cause for every effect is to assume that everything is potentially knowable, that inquiry can pay off, that one is not necessarily destined to go down an intellectual path that dead ends, leads nowhere. The assumption of an underlying order, in other words, is pervaded with hope. We do not make the assumption just so we can be hopeful, but making it does have that consequence. Assuming that the affairs of people are patterned and that the patterns are susceptible to being uncovered enables us to view ourselves as fully in charge of our own investigations, limited only by our imaginations and the resources at our disposal. It allows us to approach the chaos we perceive in the world around us as a challenge, as an orderliness that has yet to be identified and traced, and permits us to dare to think theory thoroughly.

Rule 4: To think theoretically one must be predisposed to ask about every event, every situation, or every observed phenomenon, "Of what is it an instance?"

Of all the habits one must develop to think theoretically, perhaps none is more central than the inclination to ask this question at every opportunity. It must be a constant refrain, a melody that haunts every lurch forward in the process of moving from observations to conclusions. For to see every event as an instance of a more encompassing class of phenomena is to sustain the search for patterns and to avoid treating any phenomenon as inherently unique. To think theoretically is to be at home with abstractions, to generalize, to discern the underlying order that links otherwise discrete incidents, and such a mode of thinking cannot be achieved and maintained unless every observed phenomenon is approached as merely one instance of a recurring sequence.

Again, many may have a hard time building up this habit. They may be inclined to probe for the special meaning of an event, to explore it for what sets it apart from all other events, rather than to treat it as an instance of a larger pattern. They may, for example, want to understand the collapse of the Soviet Union, rather than collapsing systems as a social process, and to the extent that this is their preference, to that extent they resist building up the impulse to always reach for more general theoretical insights. Indeed, all too many people simply do not know where to begin when asked to indicate of what pattern some event they regard as important is an instance. Their faces turn blank and their tongues turn silent. They are paralyzed. They do not know what it means to treat the event as merely an instance of something, as just part of a larger category. And so they stumble, mumble, or otherwise resist thinking in those elementary terms out of which theorizing springs.

Our response here is twofold. First, we stress the pleasure, the sheer joy, to be had from taking steps up the ladder of abstraction. Fitting pieces into larger wholes offers, we believe, a special sense of satisfaction, a feeling of accomplishment not unlike that which accompanies solving a puzzle or a mystery. Indeed, theory building can readily be viewed as puzzle solving, as uncovering the dynamics embedded deep in the interstices of human relationships, and there are few among us who are not intrigued by the challenge of solving puzzles.

If one's curiosity does not succeed in getting one to ask habitually, "Of what is this an instance?" (and often it is not a sufficient incentive), one can revert to a second line of reasoning. The implications of stumbling and mumbling are unmistakable: To be paralyzed by the question "Of what is this an instance?" is to not know what one is interested in, to be lacking questions that generate and guide one's inquiry, to be confused by the phenomenon one claims to be worthy of investigation. If there is an underlying order, no phenomenon exists in isolation, unique only unto itself, and thus there is always an answer to the of-what-is-this-an-instance question, whether we know it or not. Accordingly, the task is not one of figuring out an answer presently unknown to us; it is rather that of explicating an answer that we have already acquired but that has yet to surface.

We are arguing, in other words, that one does not get interested in an international phenomenon for no reason, that the interest stems from a concern about a more encompassing set of phenomena, and that there is therefore no need to be paralyzed by the question if one presses oneself to move up the ladder of abstraction. Once shamed into acknowledging that their concerns are not confined to the lowest rung on the ladder, most people are willing to begin to venture forth and approach the phenomena they observe as mere instances of something else. It is said that if a child is given a hammer, everything becomes a nail. We suggest that if a student evolves a theoretical orientation, everything becomes an instance.

Rule 5: To think theoretically one must be ready to appreciate and accept the need to sacrifice detailed descriptions for broad observations.

One cannot begin to mount the rungs of the ladder of abstraction if one is unable to forgo the detailed account, the elaborated event, the specific minutiae. As indicated, the theoretical enterprise is committed to the teasing out of central tendencies, to encompassing ever greater numbers of phenomena, to moving up the ladder of abstraction as parsimoniously as possible. Thus, theory involves generalizing rather than particularizing and requires relinquishing, subordinating, or not demonstrating much of one's impulse to expound everything one knows. It means, in effect, that one must discipline oneself to accept simple explanations over complex ones.

These are not easy tasks. Most of us find comfort in detail. The more details we know, the more we are likely to feel we have mastered our subject. To forgo much of the detail is to opt for uncertainties, to expose ourselves to the criticisms of those who would pick away at our generalizations with exceptions. The temptations to fall back on details are thus considerable and much concentration on the upper rungs of the ladder of abstraction is required if the temptations are to be resisted.

Happily, this step is less of a problem for beginners than it is for more mature theorists who are introduced late to the theoretical enterprise. The former have yet to acquire extensive familiarity with details and are therefore not likely to feel threatened by the loss of their knowledge base. They want to focus on the unique, to be sure, but at least it is possible to expose them to the case of theorizing before they find security in endless minutiae. Exactly how more mature analysts accustomed to the comforts of detail can be persuaded to be theoretically venturesome is, we confess, a problem for which we have yet to find anything resembling a solution.

Rule 6: To think theoretically one must be tolerant of ambiguity, concerned about probabilities, and distrustful of absolutes.

To be concerned about central tendencies, one needs to be accepting of exceptions, deviations, anomalies, and other phenomena that, taken by themselves, run counter to the anticipated or prevailing pattern. Anomalies ought not be ignored, and often explorations of them can lead to valuable, path-breaking insights, but neither can anomalies be allowed to undermine one's focus on central tendencies. Empirical theories deal only with probabilities and not with absolutes, with how most phenomena are likely to respond to a stimulus and not with how each and every phenomenon responds. Theorists simply do not aspire to account for every phenomenon. They know there will be anomalies and exceptions; indeed, they are suspicious on those unlikely occasions when no exceptions are manifest. Their goal, however, is to build theories in which the central tendencies encompass the highest possible degree of probability, with certainties and absolutes being left for ideologues and zealots to expound.

Although they engage in such thinking continuously in their daily lives, some people tend to be resistant to the necessity of thinking probabilistically when they turn to theorizing. More accurately, they tend to be reluctant to ignore ambiguity, to be restless with anything less than perfect certainty, as if any exception to anticipated central tendencies constitutes a negation of their reasoning. This low tolerance of ambiguity is difficult to contest. Some people, fearful of uncertainty, can get fixated on the exception, and it is very hard at that point to recapture an interest in central tendencies. The very rhetoric of their everyday language—that things are "completely" the case or that an observation is "absolutely" accurate—reinforces their intolerance of ambiguity. In this mood only the "whole truth" seems valid, and central tendencies appear as partial rather than legitimate forms of knowledge.

We confess to perplexity over how to handle this obstacle to theorizing. In the past we have tried elaborating on the many ways in which probabilistic thinking underlies daily life. We have tried drawing analogies between the physicist and the political scientist, pointing out that the former does not aspire to account for the behavior of every atom any more than the latter aspires to account for every voter. We have tried stressing the noxious values that derive from a concern with absolutes. Neither alone nor in combination, however, do such techniques seem to have any effect. Whatever its sources, for some people intolerance of ambiguity is apparently too deep-seated to yield to reasoning or persuasion. So, reluctantly, we have concluded that those with a low tolerance of ambiguity and a high need for certainty are unlikely to ever think theory thoroughly.

Rule 7: To think theoretically one must be playful about international phenomena.

At the core of the theorizing process is a creative imagination. The underlying order of world affairs is too obscure and too complex to yield to pedestrian, constricted, or conventional minds. Only deep penetration into a problem, discerning relationships that are not self-evident and might even be the opposite of what seems readily apparent, can produce incisive and creative theory. Thus, to think theoretically one must allow one's mind to run freely, to be playful, to toy around with what might seem absurd, to posit seemingly unrealistic circumstances and speculate about what would follow if they were ever to come to pass. Stated differently, one must develop the habit of playing and enjoying the game of "as if"—that is, specifying unlikely conditions and analyzing them as if they prevailed.

Put in still another way, good theory ought never be embarrassed by surprises, by unanticipated events that have major consequences for the system on which the theory focuses. A Hitler-Stalin pact, a

Nixon resignation, a Sadat peace initiative, or a Cold War's end should not catch the creative theorist unawares, because part of his or her creativity involves imagining the unimaginable. One imagines the unimaginable by allowing one's variables to vary across the entire range of a continuum even if some of its extreme points seem so unlikely as to be absurd. To push one's thinking beyond the previously imagined extremes of a continuum is to play the game of "as if," and it involves a playfulness of mind that mitigates against surprises as well as facilitates incisive theorizing.

How one develops playfulness is, of course, another matter. In some important sense it is an intellectual quality that cannot simply be adopted. One acquires—or perhaps inherits—creativity early in life and no amount of subsequent training can greatly enhance the imaginative powers of those with tunnel vision and inhibited mentalities. And yet, encouraging playfulness can bring out previously untapped talents in some people. Many have become so used to letting others do their thinking for them that their creative impulses have never been legitimated and, accordingly, they have never even heard of the "as if" game. So no harm can be done by pressing others (not to mention ourselves) to be playful and flexible in their thinking, and just conceivably such an emphasis may produce some unexpected results.

Rule 8: To think theoretically one must be genuinely puzzled by international phenomena.

Creative use of the imagination requires humility toward international phenomena. One must be as concerned about asking the right questions about the order underlying world affairs as one is about finding the right answers. To focus only on answers is to be sure about the questions one wants to probe, and this certainty imposes unnecessary limits on one's capacity to discern and integrate the deeper structures of global politics. If, however, one is genuinely puzzled by why events unfold as they do, one is committed to always asking why they occur in one way rather than another and, in so doing, pressing one's theoretical impulses as far as possible.

Genuine puzzles are not simply open-ended questions; they involve, rather, perplexity over specific and patterned outcomes. To be genuinely puzzled about the declining capacity of governments to

govern effectively, for example, one does not ask, "Why do governments do what they do?" Rather, one asks, for example, "Why are
most governments unable to control inflation?" or "Why do they alter
their alliance commitments under specified conditions?" Genuine
puzzles, in other words, are not idle, ill-framed, or impetuous specu-
lations. They encompass specified dependent variables for which adequate explanations are lacking. We do not see how one can begin to
think theoretically if one does not discern recurrent outcomes that
evoke one's curiosity and puzzlement. Some analysts may believe
they are starting down the road to theory when they start asking
what the outcomes are, but such a line of inquiry leads only to dead
ends, or worse, to endless mazes, because one never knows when one
has come upon a relevant outcome. Genuine puzzles can lead us
down creative paths, however, because they discipline us to focus on
particular patterns.

One cannot instruct others in how to be puzzled. The ability is very
much a matter of whether curiosity has been repressed or allowed to
flourish at an early age. It is possible, however, to persist with the
simple question, "What genuinely puzzles you about international affairs?" Repetition of the question may prove to be sufficiently challenging to facilitate a maximum expression of curiosity, whatever potential along these lines a person may possess.

**Rule 9: To think theoretically one must be constantly ready to be
proven wrong.**

Perhaps nothing inhibits the ability to be intellectually puzzled and
playful more than the fear of being embarrassed by the inaccuracies
of one's theorizing. Many of us have fragile egos that are so sensitive
to error as to lead us to a preference for sticking close to conventional
wisdom rather than risking speculation that may be erroneous. It is as
if our stature as thoughtful persons depends upon the soundness of
our observations.

Fragile egos are not readily bolstered, and some may never be capable of venturing forth. However, there is one line of reasoning that
some may find sufficiently persuasive to lessen their fears of appear-
ing ridiculous. It involves the notion that comprehension of international phenomena can be substantially advanced even if theories
about them prove to be woefully wrong. Such progress can occur in

two ways. First, falsified theory has the virtue of indicating avenues of inquiry that no longer need be traversed. Doubtless, egos are best served by theoretical breakthroughs, but if one presumes that knowledge is at least partly developed through a process of elimination, there is satisfaction to be gained from having narrowed the range of inquiry through theory that subsequently proves fallacious.

Second, unsound theory can facilitate progress by provoking others into demonstrating its falsity and attempting to show how and why it went astray. Indeed, if we assume that the erroneous theory focuses on significant matters, we may conclude that, often, the more outrageous the theory is, the more it is likely to provoke further investigation. Thus, even if one cannot negotiate a theoretical breakthrough on one's own, one can serve one's ego by the possibility that one's errors may sustain the knowledge-building process. This idea is surely what one astute analyst had in mind when he observed, "It is important to err importantly."[1]

Conclusion: Bringing It All Together

Plainly, there is no easy way to evolve the habit of thinking theoretically. Indeed, if the foregoing nine precepts are well founded, it can be readily argued that theorizing is the hardest of intellectual tasks. Clearing away the confusion of day-to-day events and teasing out their underlying patterns is not merely a matter of applying one's mental skills. Sustained, disciplined, and uninhibited work is required, and even then theory can be elusive, puzzles difficult to identify, details hard to ignore, and probabilities tough to estimate. And the lures and practices of nontheoretical thinking are always present, tempting us to forgo the insecurities and ambiguities of high levels of abstraction in favor of the comfortable precision available at low levels.

Yet the payoffs for not yielding to the temptations and persisting to think theoretically are considerable. There is an exhilaration, an exquisiteness, to be enjoyed in the theoretical enterprise that virtually defies description. Stimulated by the rarefied atmosphere, energized by the freedom to roam uninhibitedly across diverse realms of human experience, one gets giddy at high levels of abstraction. It is that special kind of giddiness that comes from the feeling that one is employing all the resources and talents at one's command, moving beyond anything one has done before. And if one should be so fortunate as actually to achieve a theoretical breakthrough, then the exhilaration, the excitement, and the sense of accomplishment can approach the thrill of discovery that Darwin, Einstein, Freud, and the other great explorers of underlying order must have experienced at their moments of breakthrough.

For all the difficulties it entails, then, thinking theoretically is, on balance, worth the effort. And so, therefore, is the effort to do so thoroughly. The habits of theoretical thinking are not easy to develop, but we can testify to the enormous pleasures that come with success in this regard. And in encouraging others to think theoretically, we hope that we, too, will refine and enlarge our own capacities for comprehending the underlying order that sustains and alters the human condition.

Notes

Chapter 1

1. Although philosophers of science often draw technical distinctions among theories, paradigms, and models, in subsequent chapters we shall use the terms interchangeably.

Chapter 2

1. For a useful table illustrating changes and continuity in realist thought, see the appendix to Ashley J. Tellis, "Reconstructing Political Realism: The Long March to Scientific Theory," pp. 3–100, in Benjamin Frankel, ed., *The Roots of Realism* (London: Frank Cass, 1996).

2. Thucydides, *The Peloponnesian War*, trans. Rex Warner (New York: Penguin, 1978), p. 402.

3. Ibid., p. 49.

4. Robert Connor, *Thucydides* (Princeton: Princeton University Press, 1984), p. 3.

5. Hans Morgenthau, *Power Among Nations*, 3rd ed. (New York: Knopf, 1964), p. 4.

6. Ibid.

7. E. H. Carr, *The Twenty Years Crisis* (London: Macmillan, 1946).

8. Some scholars claim neorealism and structural realism are distinct enough to be treated as separate variants. See Barry Buzan, Charles Jones, and Richard Little, eds., *The Logic of Anarchy: Neorealism to Structural Realism* (New York: Columbia University Press, 1993), p. 9.

9. Kenneth N. Waltz, *Theory of International Politics* (Reading, Mass.: Addison-Wesley, 1979), p. 73.

10. Joseph M. Grieco, "Anarchy and the Limits of Cooperation: A Realist Critique of the Newest Liberal Institutionalism," *International Organization*, Vol. 42, No. 3 (Summer 1988), pp. 485–507, reprinted in David A. Baldwin, ed., *Neorealism and Neoliberalism: The Contemporary Debate* (New York: Columbia University Press, 1993), p. 127.

11. Michael W. Doyle, *The Ways of War and Peace* (New York: Norton, 1997), p. 73.

12. Ibid., pp. 52–53.

13. Robert O. Keohane, *After Hegemony: Cooperation and Discord in the World Political Economy* (Princeton: Princeton University Press, 1984), especially pp. 27–29.

14. George Tsebelis, *Nested Games* (Berkeley: University of California Press, 1990), p. 18.

15. Joseph M. Grieco argues that the international environment penalizes states that don't protect themselves. See Grieco, "Anarchy and the Limits of Cooperation," p. 488.

16. Graham Allison, *The Essence of Decision: Explaining the Cuban Missile Crisis* (Boston: Little, Brown, 1971), p. 28. The literature on rational choice as applied to the behavior of states is quite large. To get a taste of the variety, see Robert Axelrod, *The Evolution of Cooperation* (New York: Basic Books, 1984); Robert Gilpin, *War and Change in World Politics* (New York: Cambridge University Press, 1981); Baldwin, *Neorealism and Neoliberalism;* Duncan Snidal, "Relative Gains and the Pattern of International Cooperation," *American Political Science Review,* Vol. 85 (September 1991), pp. 701–726. Snidal offers evidence against the neorealist notion that states pay the most attention to relative gains by noting that relative gains are situational rather than constant.

17. Robert O. Keohane, ed., *Neorealism and Its Critics* (New York: Columbia University Press, 1986), p. 7.

18. Ibid., p. 11.

19. Tsebelis offers a more formal discussion of rationality rules in *Nested Games,* pp. 18–28.

20. Keohane, *After Hegemony,* p. 66; Arnold Horelick and Myron Rush, *Strategic Power and Soviet Foreign Policy* (Chicago: University of Chicago Press, 1965).

21. See Alan James, *Sovereign Statehood* (London: Allen Unwin, 1986), for a discussion of the various meanings of sovereignty.

22. Ibid., p. 39.

23. Oran Young, "Anarchy and Social Choice: Reflections on the International Polity," *World Politics,* Vol. 30 (January 1978), pp. 241–263. However, Young is not a realist; he believes the "international political system exhibits a high degree of heterogeneity with respect to the basic principles of organization of its members" (p. 243).

24. Robert Jervis, "Cooperation Under the Security Dilemma," *World Politics,* Vol. 30 (January 1978), pp. 167–214. Jervis explains how the anarchical structure of the system causes problems for cooperation: "Because there are no institutions or authorities that can make and enforce international laws, the policies of cooperation that will bring mutual rewards if others cooperate may bring disaster if they do not" (p. 167).

25. Stephen M. Meyer, "Verification and Risk in Arms Control," *International Security,* Vol. 8 (Spring 1984), pp. 111–126.

26. See especially Hedley Bull, *The Anarchical Society* (London: Macmillan, 1977). Benjamin Miller also classifies Bull's work in the Realist camp in his "Competing Realist Perspectives on Great Power Crisis Behavior," pp. 309–357, in Benjamin Frankel, ed., *Realism: Restatements and Renewal* (London: Frank Cass, 1996).

27. Ibid., p. 16.

28. Ibid., p. 17.

29. Stephen Kocs, "Explaining the Strategic Behavior of States: International Law as System Structure," *International Studies Quarterly*, Vol. 38 (December 1994), pp. 535–556.

30. Bull, *Anarchical Society*, p. 18.

31. Ibid., p. 19.

32. There are many other approaches to the study of power. See, for instance, David A. Baldwin, *Paradoxes of Power* (London: Basil Blackwell, 1989); Zeev Maoz, "Power, Capabilities, and Paradoxical Outcomes," *World Politics*, Vol. 41 (January 1989), pp. 239–266; Jeffrey Hart, "Three Approaches to the Measurement of Power in International Relations," *International Organization*, Vol. 30 (April 1976), pp. 299–305.

33. For more on the impact of great powers, see Jack S. Levy, "Theories of General War," *World Politics*, Vol. 37 (April 1985), pp. 344–374, especially pp. 366–368.

34. Waltz, *Theory of International Politics*, p. 131.

35. To understand more fully the logic of land versus sea power, see Paul Kennedy, "Mahan Versus Mackinder: Two Interpretations of British Sea Power," in his book, *Strategy and Diplomacy, 1870–1945* (London: Fontana, 1984).

36. Waltz, *Theory of International Politics*, p. 126.

37. Paul Kennedy, *The Rise and Fall of the Great Powers* (New York: Random House, 1987), especially pp. 432, 533–534.

38. See World Trade Organization, "World Trade Growth Accelerated in 1997, Despite Turmoil in Some Asian Financial Markets," 19 March 1998, Appendix Table 1., p. 13 of 24 http://www.wto.org/wto/intltrad/internat.htm Site accessed March 3, 1999.

39. Susan Strange, "The Persistent Myth of Lost Hegemony," *International Organization*, Vol. 41 (Autumn 1987), pp. 551–574.

40. Kenneth N. Waltz, "A Response to My Critics," in Keohane, ed., *Neorealism and Its Critics*, p. 342.

41. Charles Krauthammer, "The Unipolar Moment," *Foreign Affairs*, Vol. 70, No. 1 (1990–1991), pp. 23–33.

42. Samuel P. Huntington, "The Lonely Superpower," *Foreign Affairs*, Vol. 78, No. 2 (March-April 1999), pp. 35–49.

43. Kennedy, *The Rise and Fall of the Great Powers*, p. 535.

44. Some believe that the concept is an "obscurity enshrined" that should be laid to rest, because although everyone uses the term, it has many meanings and therefore is useless as an analytical concept. See Ernst B. Haas, "The Balance of Power: Prescription, Concept or Propaganda?" *World Politics*, Vol. 5 (July 1953), pp. 442–477.

45. Bull, *Anarchical Society*, pp. 106–107.

46. Ibid., p. 11.

47. Ibid., pp. 10–11. For more distinctions between traditional realism and neorealism, see James E. Dougherty and Robert L. Pfaltzgraff, *Contending Theories of International Relations*, 3rd ed. (New York: Harper & Row, 1990), pp. 30–35.

48. As quoted in F. H. Hinsely, *Power and the Pursuit of Peace* (Cambridge: Cambridge University Press, 1963), p. 64.

49. Stephen Walt, "Alliance Formation and the Balance of Power," *International Security,* Vol. 9 (Spring 1985), pp. 3–43.

50. These categories were derived from Edward Vose Gulick, *Europe's Classical Balance of Power* (Ithaca, N.Y.: Cornell University Press, 1955), Chap. 3.

51. Connor, *Thucydides,* p. 123.

52. Tsebelis, *Nested Games,* p. 69. See also Axelrod, *The Evolution of Cooperation,* pp. 10–11, 20.

53. Connor, *Thucydides,* pp. 124–125.

54. Bull, *Anarchical Society,* p. 106.

55. Morgenthau, *Power Among Nations,* p. 163.

56. One might note that the legitimacy of U.S. leadership in the region has declined over time as the United States initiated more actions without widespread international assent.

57. Keohane, *After Hegemony,* p. 46.

58. Walt, "Alliance Formation and the Balance of Power," pp. 18–24. For his extended treatment of the subject, see Stephen Walt, *The Origins of Alliances* (Ithaca, N.Y.: Cornell University Press, 1987).

59. David Forsythe, *The Internationalization of Human Rights* (Lexington, Mass: Lexington Books, 1991), p. 92.

60. Stephen Krasner, "Structural Causes and Regime Consequences: Regimes as Intervening Variables," pp. 1–21, in Stephen Krasner, ed., *International Regimes* (Ithaca, N.Y.: Cornell University Press, 1983), p. 1.

61. Levy, "Theories of General War," p. 345.

62. John Gerard Ruggie, "Continuity and Transformation in the World Polity: Toward a Neorealist Synthesis," pp. 131–157, in Keohane, ed., *Neorealism and Its Critics.*

63. Ibid., p. 141.

64. Christopher Layne, "Kant or Cant: The Myth of the Democratic Peace," *International Security,* Vol. 19 (Fall 1994), pp. 10–11.

Chapter 3

1. Michael W. Doyle, *The Ways of War and Peace* (New York: Norton, 1997), p. 211.

2. Ibid., throughout Chap. 8.

3. There is disagreement currently over whether free markets in capital are a good idea or not. Some liberal scholars argue that a free movement of capital has different effects on the global economy than the movement of goods..

4. Emmanuel Kant proposed this idea. For an extended discussion of the logic, see the chapter on Kant's contribution to liberalism in Doyle, *The Ways of War and Peace,* pp. 251–300.

5. Karl W. Deutsch, S. A. Burrell, R. A. Hann, M. Lee Jr., M. R. Lichterman, R. E. Lindgren, F. L Loewenheim, and R. W. Van Wagenen, *Political Community and the North Atlantic Area, International Organization in the Light of Historical Experience* (Princeton: Princeton University Press, 1957).

6. John R. Oneal and Bruce M. Russett, "The Classical Liberals Were Right: Democracy, Interdependence, and Conflict, 1950–1985," *International Studies Quarterly,* Vol. 41 (1997), pp. 267–294. The discussion of democracy and peace is large and growing, but students might begin with one of these studies: E. Weede, *Never at War: Why Democracies Will Not Fight One Another* (New Haven: Yale University Press, 1997); W. J. Dixon, "Democracy and the Peaceful Settlement of International Conflict," *American Political Science Review,* Vol. 88 (1994), pp. 1–17; David Lake, "Powerful Pacifists: Democratic States and War," *American Political Science Review,* Vol. 86 (1992), pp. 24–37; Joanne Gowa, "Democratic States and International Disputes," *International Organization, V*ol. 49 (1995), pp. 511–522; C. Layne, "Kant or Cant: The Myth of Democratic Peace," *International Security,* Vol. 19 (1994), pp. 5–49; and Doyle, *The Ways of War and Peace.* Robert Axelrod has even carried out computer simulations of the process, but he does not explicitly model the democracy/nondemocracy thesis. See his chapter, "Building New Political Actors," in his *The Complexity of Cooperation: Agent-Based Models of Competition and Collaboration* (Princeton: Princeton University Press, 1997).

7. See Karen A. Mingst and Margaret P. Karns, *The United Nations in the Post–Cold War Era,* (Boulder: Westview, 1995), p. 11.

8. Robert O. Keohane and Joseph S. Nye, *Power and Interdependence* (Boston: Little, Brown, 1977).

9. Ibid., p 20.

10. Ibid., p. 9.

11. Ibid., p. 24.

12. Ibid., p. 25.

13. James N. Rosenau, "Toward the Study of National-International Linkages," pp. 44–63, in James N. Rosenau, ed., *Linkage Politics: Essays on the Convergence of National and International Systems* (New York: Free Press, 1969).

14. Keohane and Nye, *Power and Interdependence,* pp. 30–37.

15. Daniel Deudney and John Ikenberry, *Structural Liberalism: the Nature and Sources of the Postwar Western Political Order,* Working Paper, University of Pennsylvania, May 1996.

16. Those with a more economic outlook on the world might say that this is an opportunity cost. To get all the nice things one gets from cooperation with others, one has to give up some of the nice things one gets from acting alone. Being married and being single both have their delights and drawbacks, but one cannot be both at once.

17. Deudney and Ikenberry, *Structural Liberalism,* p. 6.

18. Ibid., p. 20.

19. Ibid., p. 21.

20. Ibid., p. 25.

21. Ibid., p. 29.

22. Andrew Moravcsik, "Taking Preferences Seriously: A Liberal Theory of International Politics," *International Organization,* Vol. 51 (Autumn 1997), p. 316.

23. Ibid., p. 318.

24. Ibid., p. 320.

25. Alexis de Tocqueville, *Democracy in America,* vol. 2, trans. Henry Reeve (New York: Schocken, 1967), p. 128.

26. For a clear discussion of these issues, see Stephen C. Hackett, *Environmental and Natural Resources Economics* (Armonk, N.Y.: M. E. Sharpe, 1998), especially Chap. 3.

27. Benjamin Barber, "Democracy at Risk: American Culture in a Global Culture," *World Policy Journal* (Summer 1998), pp. 29–48.

28. For a range of perspectives on the nature and sources of the European democratic deficit, see any of the following articles: Kees Van Kersbergen and Bertjan Verbeek, "The Politics of Subsidiarity in the European Union," *Journal of Common Market Studies,* Vol. 32 (June 1994), pp. 215–236; Kevin Featherstone, "Jean Monnet and the 'Democratic Deficit' in the European Union," *Journal of Common Market Studies,* Vol. 32 (June 1994), pp. 149–170; or Juliet Lodge, "Transparency and Democratic Legitimacy," *Journal of Common Market Studies,* Vol. 32 (September 1994), pp. 343–368.

Chapter 4

1. An extensive presentation of this paradigm can be found in James N. Rosenau, *Turbulence in World Politics: A Theory of Change and Continuity* (Princeton: Princeton University Press, 1990). For a series of essays about the paradigm, see Heidi Hobbs, ed., *Pondering Postinternationalism: A Paradigm for the 21st Century?* (Albany: State University of New York Press, 2000).

2. For a discussion of the role anomalies played in the construction of the postinternational model, see Rosenau, *Turbulence in World Politics,* pp. 92–98.

3. John Lukacs, "The Short Century—It's Over," *New York Times,* February 17, 1991, Sec. 4, p. 13.

4. For the historical analysis that underlies this conclusion, see Rosenau, *Turbulence in World Politics,* Chap. 5.

5. Elsewhere one of us has captured the nature of these tensions by combining their contradictory dynamics into a single concept—that of "fragmegration." For an elaboration of fragmegrative dynamics, see James N. Rosenau, *Along the Domestic-Foreign Frontier: Exploring Governance in a Turbulent World* (Cambridge: Cambridge University Press, 1997), Chap. 6.

6. For an extended effort to demonstrate and explain this expanding skill, see James N. Rosenau, "The Relocation of Authority in a Shrinking World: From Tiananmen Square in Beijing to the Soccer Stadium in Soweto via Parliament Square in Budapest and Wencelas Square in Prague," *Comparative Politics,* Vol. 24 (April 1992), pp. 253–272.

7. For an astute discussion of how the combination of mass media and the massive movement of people around the world has so fully unleashed imaginations everywhere that "the imagination is today a staging ground for action, and not only for escape," see Arjun Appadurai, *Modernity at Large: Cultural Dimensions of Globalization* (Minneapolis: University of Minnesota Press, 1996). The quote is from p. 7.

8. It is worth noting that the sovereignty principle began to be undermined when it was redefined during the decolonizing processes of the former European empires after World War II. In using self-determination as the sole criterion for statehood, irrespective of whether a former colony had the consensual foundations and resources to govern, a number of sovereign states were created, recognized, and admitted to the U.N. even though they were unable to develop their economies and manage their internal affairs without external assistance. As a result of these weaknesses, the value of sovereignty seemed less compelling once the struggle for independence was won and the tasks of governance taken on. Rather than being an obvious source of strength, sovereignty thus often seemed to be less a source of independence than an invitation to interdependence. For an extensive discussion of how the sovereignty principle got redefined—how "decolonization amounted to nothing less than an international revolution . . . in which traditional assumptions about the right to sovereign statehood were turned upside down"—in the processes of decolonization, see Robert H. Jackson, *Quasi-States: Sovereignty, International Relations and the Third World* (Cambridge: Cambridge University Press, 1990), Chap. 4. The quotation is from p. 85.

9. For an explanation of why the terms "sovereignty-bound" and "sovereignty-free" seem appropriate as labels to differentiate between state and non-state actors, see Rosenau, *Turbulence in World Politics,* p. 36.

10. For a cogent discussion of one major aspect of the organizational explosion, see Lester M. Salamon, "The Rise of the Nonprofit Sector," *Foreign Affairs,* Vol. 73 (July/August 1994), pp. 109–122.

11. For a number of essays that explore the evolution of new loci of authority in the multi-centric world, see A. Claire Cutler, Virginia Haufler, and Tony Porter, eds., *Private Authority and International Affairs* (Albany: State University of New York Press, 1999).

12. The pace of technological advance shows no sign of slowing down. It is estimated that by the end of the century new generations of supercomputers will be capable of calculating more than a trillion operations each second. See "Transforming the Decade: 10 Critical Technologies," *New York Times,* December 1, 1991, p. 18.

13. On the first night of the Gulf War, CNN's prime-time viewership went from its normal 560,000 to 11.4 million. See Thomas B. Rosenstiel, "CNN: The Channel to the World," *Los Angeles Times,* January 23, 1991, p. A12.

14. An account of *Actuel*'s efforts can be found in *Europe: Magazine of the European Community* (April 1990), pp. 40–41.

15. Erik Eckholm, "A Trial Will Test China's Grip on the Internet," *New York Times,* November 16, 1998, p. A8.

16. For an extensive elaboration of the diverse ways in which the microelectronic revolution has influenced the conduct of public affairs, see Rosenau, *Turbulence in World Politics,* Chap. 13.

17. For discussions along these lines, see James N. Rosenau, "The State in an Era of Cascading Politics: Wavering Concept, Widening Competence, Withering

Colossus, or Weathering Change?" pp. 17–48, in J. A. Caporaso, ed., *The Elusive State* (Newbury Park: Sage Publications, 1989); and Giulio M. Gallarotti, "Legitimacy as a Capital Asset of the State," *Public Choice*, Vol. 63 (1989), pp. 43–61.

18. There is considerable evidence, for example, that the collapse of authority in East Germany in the fall of 1989 was stimulated by the televised scenes of authority being challenged in Tiananmen Square several months earlier. See Tara Sonenshine, "The Revolution Has Been Televised," *Washington Post National Weekly Edition,* October 8–14, 1990, p. 29.

19. An account of the loyalty and membership problems faced by Norway can be found in William E. Schmidt, "Norway Again Debates European Membership, Rekindling Old Hostilities," *New York Times,* May 6, 1991, p. A3.

20. John Darnton, "Vote in Norway Blocks Joining Europe's Union," *New York Times,* November 29, 1994, p. 1.

21. The quotes are taken from Alan Riding, "France Questions Its Identity as It Sinks into 'Le Malaise,'" *New York Times,* December 23, 1990, pp. 1, 7.

22. A stunning measure of the impact of travel, for example, is provided by the fact that in 1997 a total of 220.7 million people (a 4.6 percent increase over the previous year) went abroad by airplane ("Worldwide Air Traffic: Rose in May," *New York Times,* August 20, 1997, p. C2). Nor are the figures for travel within countries any less stunning. Whereas the population of the United States grew 20 percent between 1977 and 1997, for example, the number of miles traveled long distance (journeys of 100 miles or more) increased by 116 percent. The total number of domestic miles traveled on such journeys in 1996 was 827 billion. Cf. Nicholas Timmins, "Long-Distance Travel in U.S. 'Has Doubled,'" *Financial Times,* November 11, 1997, p. 7. Of course, only a tiny proportion of human migration occurs on airplanes. A preponderance of the world's migrants, walk, take trains, or hitch rides on trucks.

23. The conception of developing countries as quasi-states can be found in Jackson, *Quasi-States,* Chaps. 1 and 7.

24. For a useful delineation between positive and negative sovereignty, see Jackson, *Quasi-States,* pp. 26–31.

25. For an extended analysis of the future scenarios inherent in the turbulence model, see Rosenau, *Turbulence in World Politics,* Chap. 16.

Chapter 5

1. *Casenote Legal Brief—International Law* (Beverly Hills, Calif.: Casenote Publishing Co., 1988), p. 25.

2. Margaret E. Keck and Kathryn Sikkink, *Activists Beyond Borders: Advocacy Networks in International Politics* (Ithaca, N.Y.: Cornell University Press, 1998), p. 1.

3. Michael Akehurst, *A Modern Introduction to International Law,* 6th ed. (London: George Allen and Unwin, 1984), p. 14.

4. Kenneth N. Waltz, *Theory of International Politics* (Reading, Mass.: Addison-Wesley, 1979), p. 94.

Chapter 6

1. For a discussion of this distinction, see Charles Perrow, *Complex Organizations*, 3rd ed. (New York: McGraw-Hill, 1986), p. 259.

2. The characterization is borrowed from Charles Tilly, *Big Structures, Large Processes, Huge Comparisons* (New York: Russell Sage Foundation, 1984).

3. See, for example, Graham T. Allison, *Essence of Decision: Explaining the Cuban Missile Crisis* (Boston: Little: Brown, 1971); Coral Bell, *The Conventions of Crisis: A Study in Diplomatic Management* (Oxford: Oxford University Press, 1971); Michael Brecher, ed., *Studies in Crisis Behavior* (New Brunswick, N.J.: Transaction Books, 1978; and Charles F. Hermann, ed., *International Crises: Insights from Behavioral Research* (New York: Free Press, 1972). For a recent exception that gives due attention to systemic variables, see James L. Richardson, *Crisis Diplomacy: The Great Powers Since the Mid-Nineteenth Century* (Cambridge: Cambridge University Press, 1994), especially Chap. 10.

4. As quoted in Stephen M. Meyer, *The Dynamics of Nuclear Proliferation* (Chicago: University of Chicago Press, 1984), p. 47.

5. "India and Pakistan: More Heat Than Light," *The Economist,* June 13, 1998, p. 42.

6. Paul H. Nitze and Sidney D. Drell, "This Treaty Must Be Ratified," *Washington Post,* June 21, 1999, OP-ED section, p. A19.

7. Brahma Chelaney, "India Crosses World's Nuclear Fence in Style," *Jakarta Post,* May 27, 1998.

8. John Ward Anderson and Kamran Khan, "Pakistan Sets Off Nuclear Blasts," *Washington Post,* May 29, 1998, p. A1.

9. As quoted in Jonathan Manthorpe, "Nuclear Tension: Asia Faces Growing Threat as Pakistan Tests Weapons, " *Montreal Gazette,* May 29, 1998, p. A1.

10. "India and Pakistan: More Heat Than Light," p. 42.

11. As quoted in Barry R. Schneider, "Nuclear Proliferation and Counter-Proliferation: Policy Issues and Debates," *Mershon International Studies Review,* Vol. 3 (1994), p. 227.

12. Chelaney, "India Crosses World's Nuclear Fence in Style."

13. Manthorpe, "Nuclear Tension: Asia Faces Growing Threat As Pakistan Tests Weapons," p. A1.

14. "An End to Tit for Tat," *Straits Times* (Singapore), April 17, 1999, Commentary Analysis section, p. 64.

15. Chelaney, "India Crosses World's Nuclear Fence in Style."

16. "India and Pakistan: More Heat Than Light," p. 42.

17. "Why India Loves the Bomb," *The Economist,* May 16, 1999, p. 37.

18. "Pakistan: Sick as a Parrot," *The Economist,* May 23, 1998, p. 38.

19. "India: Over the Moon," *The Economist,* May 23, 1998, p. 38.

20. Ibid., p. 37.

21. Nicholas D. Kristof, "World Ills Are Obvious, the Cures Much Less So," *New York Times,* February 18, 1999, pp. A1, A14.

22. Edward Luce and Philip Coggan, "Worldwide Jitters Spur Stampede to Super-Safe Havens," *Financial Times,* October 6, 1998, p. 13.

23. Bernie Sanders, "Globalization's the Issue," *The Nation*, September 28, 1998, p. 4.

24. Walter Russell Mead, "Rule 1: Don't Panic; Rule 2: Panic First," *Esquire*, October 1998, p. 95.

25. Michael Lewis, "Going-Out-of-Business Sale," *New York Times Magazine*, May 31, 1998, p. 37.

26. Kevin Sullivan, "A Generation's Future Goes Begging," *Washington Post*, September 7, 1998, p. 1.

27. Mary Jordan, "Middle Class Plunging Back to Poverty," *Washington Post*, September 6, 1998, p. 1.

28. Sullivan, "A Generation's Future Goes Begging," p. 1.

29. Jordan, "Middle Class Plunging Back to Poverty," p. 1.

30. Keith B. Richberg, "For Migrant Workers, Path from Boom to Bust Leads Home," *Washington Post*, September 8, 1998, p. 1.

31. Ibid.

32. Jordan, "Middle Class Plunging Back to Poverty," p. 1.

33. Mead, "Rule 1: Don't Panic; Rule 2: Panic First," p. 94.

34. Nicholas Kristof, "Crisis Pushing Asian Capitalism Closer to U.S.-Style Free Market," *New York Times*, January 17, 1998, p. 1.

35. Mark Landler, "Gore, in Malaysia, Says Its Leaders Suppress Freedom," *New York Times*, November 17, 1998, p. A6.

36. David E. Sanger and Mark Landler, "Asian Rebound Derails Reform as Many Suffer," *New York Times*, July 12, 1999, p. 1.

37. Ibid.

38. See, for example, Jeffrey Sachs, "Global Capitalism: Making It Work," *The Economist*, September 12, 1998, pp. 23–25; Roger C. Altman, "The Teetering World Economy Can Be Righted Again," *International Herald Tribune*, September 17, 1998, p. 8; Jeffrey E. Garten, "In This Economic Chaos, a Global Bank Can Help," *International Herald Tribune*, September 23, 1998, p. 8; Henry Kissinger, "Perils of Globalism," *Washington Post*, October 5, 1998, p. A21; and Stephen Fidler, "Ward for Contagious Diseases," *Financial Times*, October 6, 1998, p. 23.

39. Paul Blustein, "22 Nations Plan Rules on Flow of Capital," *Washington Post*, October 6, 1998, p. A1.

40. David E. Sanger, "Economic Leaders Differ in Strategy on Halting Crisis," *New York Times*, October 4, 1998, p. 1; and David E. Sanger, "Meeting of World Finance Leaders Ends with No Grand Strategy but Many Ideas," *New York Times*, October 8, 1998, p. A6.

41. Andrew Maykuth, "World Ignores Angola War Refugees," *Toronto Star*, July 1, 1999.

42. National Public Radio, "African Refugees Are Not Getting the Same Resources as Their Balkan Counterparts Mainly Because of Their Skin Color," *Morning Edition*, June 29, 1999. Transcript.

43. Paul Lewis, "U.N. Issues New Appeal for Rwandan Cease-Fire," *New York Times*, July 15, 1994, p. A10.

44. Raymond Bonner, "Rwandan Refugees Caught 'Between Two Deaths,'" *New York Times*, July 27, 1994, p. 1.

45. Jerry Grey, "Rwandans Face Daunting Task: Reviving Trust," *New York Times*, August 12, 1994, p. A10.

46. Raymond Bonner, "Rwanda's Leaders Vow to Build a Multiparty State for Both Hutu and Tutsi," *New York Times*, September 7, 1994, p. A10.

47. *Annex from the Final Report of the International Commission of Inquiry (Rwanda) to the Security Council of the United Nations* S/1998/1096, November 18, 1998, p. 3 of 27. http://www.rwandemb.org/un1.html. Downloaded July 4, 1999.

48. "Congo Peace Talks Resume Amid Reports of Renewed Fighting," newswire from Deutsche Presse-Agentur, July 2, 1999, p. 1 of 3.

49. *Annex from the Final Report*, pp. 21–22 of 27.

50. "The Descent into Another Balkans War," *The Economist*, June 13, 1998, p. 47.

51. Quotes are from the official U.S. State Department chronology at http://www.state.gov/www/regions/eur/fs_kosovo_timeline.html. Accessed July 4, 1999.

52. This chronology is taken from the official U.S. State Department chronology at http://www.state.gov/www/regions/eur/fs_kosovo_timeline.html. Accessed July 4, 1999.

53. *Annex from the Final Report.*

54. Richard Ned Lebow, *Between Peace and War* (Baltimore: Johns Hopkins University Press, 1983), pp. 1–11.

55. "I.M.F. Admits Errors in Asia but Defends Basic Policies," *New York Times*, January 20, 1999, p. A5.

56. David Malpass, "The G-7's Missed Opportunity," *Wall Street Journal*, February 23, 1999, p. A22.

57. David E. Sanger, "As an Economy Sinks, U.S. Sees Painful Choices," *New York Times*, January 14, 1999, p. A1.

Chapter 7

1. Hans Morgenthau, *Power Among Nations*, 3rd ed. (New York: Alfred A. Knopf, 1964), p. 479.

2. Ibid., 496.

3. Ibid., 495.

4. Inis Claude, *Swords into Plowshares*, 4th ed. (New York: Random House, 1984), p. 17.

5. For a cogent discussion of the U.N. as part of the processes of international institutionalization, see Margaret P. Karns, "The Changing Architecture of World Politics: Multilateralism, Cooperation, and Global Governance," pp. 267–284, in Kenneth W. Thompson, ed., *Community, Diversity and a New World Order: Essays in Honor of Inis L. Claude, Jr.* (Lanham, Md.: University Press of America, 1994).

6. A full diagram of the vast array of specialized agencies, programs, regional commissions, functional commissions, special funds, ad hoc bodies, and offices that make up the U.N. system would include more than fifty distinct units, some thirty of which have executive heads that are subject to periodic election or appointment. For one effort to pull together diagrammatically all the units of the

U.N. system, see Brian Urquhart and Erskine Childers, *A World in Need of Leadership: Tomorrow's United Nations* (Uppsala, Sweden: Dag Hammarskjöld Foundation, 1990), pp. 90–91.

7. Quoted in Brian Hall, "Blue Helmets, Empty Guns," *New York Times Magazine*, January 2, 1994, p. 22.

8. Ibid., p. 23.

9. For another explanation that supplements rather than contradicts this interpretation of the U.N.'s success in these situations, see James N. Rosenau, "Interdependence and the Simultaneity Puzzle: Notes on the Outbreak of Peace," pp. 307–328, in C. W. Kegley, Jr., ed., *The Long Postwar Peace: Contending Explanations and Projections* (New York: HarperCollins Publishers, 1991).

10. Hall, "Blue Helmets, Empty Guns," p. 23.

11. Quoted in Paul Lewis, "Reluctant Warriors: U.N. Member States Retreat from Peacekeeping Roles," *New York Times*, December 12, 1993, p. 22.

12. For instances of this argument being advanced in the United States, see Brian Urquhart, "Sovereignty vs. Suffering," *New York Times*, April 17, 1991, p. A15; Jonathan Mann, "No Sovereignty for Suffering," *New York Times*, April 12, 1991, Sec. 4, p. 17; and editorial, "The U.N. Must Deal with Kurds' Plight," *Los Angeles Times*, April 30, 1991, p. B6.

13. See, for example, B. Drummond Ayres, Jr., "A Common Cry Across the U.S.: 'It's Time to Exit,'" *New York Times*, October 9, 1993, p. 1; Elaine Sciolino, "The U.N.'s Glow Is Gone," *New York Times*, October 9, 1993, p. 1; R. W. Apple, Jr., "Policing a Global Village," *New York Times*, October 13, 1993, p. 1; and Lewis, "Reluctant Warriors," p. 22.

14. Randolph Ryan, "Can the UN Keep Peace?" *Boston Globe*, June 19, 1993.

15. Brian Urquhart, "The UN and International Security After the Cold War," pp. 81–103, in Adam Roberts and Benedict Kingsbury, eds., *United Nations, Divided World: The UN's Role in International Relations* (Oxford: Clarendon Press, 1993).

16. Quoted in Lewis, "Reluctant Warriors," p. 22. Perhaps a good measure of the extent to which the secretary general is torn in opposing directions by the bifurcated world is to be found in the fact that just as here he perceives "a new reality" in the resistance of member states to peacekeeping operations, so did he discern a few months earlier "a new reality . . . that a growing number of member states are concluding that some problems can be addressed most effectively by U.N. efforts" (Boutros Boutros-Ghali, "Don't Make the U.N.'s Job Harder," *New York Times*, August 20, 1993, p. A29).

17. Quoted in Sciolino, "The U.N.'s Glow Is Gone," p. 7.

18. Boutros-Ghali, "Don't Make the U.N.'s Job Harder," p. A29.

19. See, for example, John Gerard Ruggie, ed., *Multilateralism Matters: The Theory and Praxis of an Institutional Form* (New York: Columbia University Press, 1993).

20. Boutros-Ghali, "Don't Make the U.N.'s Job Harder," p. A29.

21. For instance, see Donatella Lorch, "In Another Part of Somalia, Resentment of the U.N.," *New York Times*, September 30, 1993, p. A3.

22. Interestingly, after the enmity of General Aidid led him to refuse a U.N. offer of transportation to peace talks in Ethiopia designed to bring order to Somalia, he was ferried to the talks on a U.S. Army jet on the grounds that his participation in the meeting was crucial to its success. Upon his arrival in Ethiopia, moreover, U.S. military bodyguards escorted Aidid to the talks. The fact this event transpired just two months after the killing of eighteen U.S. soldiers in a battle with Aidid's forces evoked considerable criticism in Washington, but the United States insisted it had little choice in the situation if the talks were to proceed. These circumstances suggest, on the one hand, that Aidid was well ensconced in the realist world (he was interested in who had power), but, on the other hand, that the United States is more likely to engage in cooperative behavior when the U.N. is involved. In effect, the United States was unwilling to use the power that Aidid ascribed to it. See Douglas Jehl, "Clinton Defends Use of U.S. Plane to Take Fugitive Somali to Talks," *New York Times*, December 7, 1993, p. A5.

23. R. W. Apple, Jr., "U.N. and the Pentagon," *New York Times*, February 14, 1993, p. 18.

24. Steven A. Holmes, "Clinton May Let U.S. Troops Serve Under U.N. Chiefs," *New York Times*, August 18, 1993, p. 1.

25. Barton Gellman, "U.S. Reconsiders Putting GIs Under U.N.," *Washington Post*, September 22, 1993, p. 1.

26. Douglas Jehl, "New U.S. Troops in Somalia Are Still Tied to U.N. Operation," *New York Times*, November 15, 1993, p. A11.

27. For an elaboration of the role of transnational organizations and other private actors in the emergent pattern of externally monitored elections, see James N. Rosenau and Michael Fagen, "Domestic Elections as International Events," pp. 29–68, in Carl Kaysen, Robert A. Pastor, and Laura W. Reed, eds., *Collective Responses to Regional Problems: The Case of Latin America and the Caribbean* (Cambridge, Mass.: American Academy of Arts and Sciences, 1994).

28. For a discussion of the self-imposed standards used by the U.N., see David Stoelting, "The Challenge of U.N. Monitored Elections in Independent Nations," *Stanford Journal of International Law*, Vol. 28 (Spring 1992), passim.

29. The turbulence model locates the 1950s as the onset of parametric transformations in world politics. See James N. Rosenau, *Turbulence in World Politics: A Theory of Change and Continuity* (Princeton: Princeton University Press, 1990), pp. 107–112.

30. Stoelting, "The Challenge of U.N. Monitored Elections in Independent Nations," p. 377.

31. Ibid., p. 378.

32. Ibid., p. 378.

33. Samuel P. Huntington, *The Third Wave: Democratization in the Late Twentieth Century* (Norman: University of Oklahoma Press, 1991), pp. 183–185.

34. Stoelting, "The Challenge of U.N. Monitored Elections in Independent Nations," p. 374.

35. Thomas M. Franck, "The Emerging Rights to Democratic Governance," *American Journal of International Law*, Vol. 86 (January 1992), pp. 72–73.

36. Boutros Boutros-Ghali, *Report on the Work of the Organization from the Forty-sixth to the Forty-seventh Session of the General Assembly* (New York: United Nations, 1992), p. 36.

37. Stoelting, "The Challenge of U.N. Monitored Elections in Independent Nations," p. 372.

38. Paul Lewis, "The U.N. Is Showing Promise as Poll Watcher for the World," *New York Times*, May 30, 1993, Sec. 4, p. 5.

39. Paul Lewis, "U.N. Rebukes Myanmar Leaders on Human Rights and Democracy," *New York Times*, December 7, 1993, p. A10.

40. Alan Riding, "Rights Forum Ends in Call for a Greater Role by U.N.," *New York Times*, June 26, 1993, p. 2.

41. Paul Lewis, "U.N. Agrees to Create Human Rights Commissioner," *New York Times*, December 14, 1993, p. A14.

42. Paul Lewis, "U.N. Chief Bars Chinese Dissident's News Briefing," *New York Times*, May 26, 1993, p. A10.

43. For a vigorous complaint that the secretary general "has sought to assume unprecedented powers and functions that the United Nations Charter vests in the Security Council," see Jeanne Kirkpatrick, "Boutros-Ghali's Power Grab," *Washington Post*, February 1, 1993, p. A19. On the same point, also see Richard L. Armitage, "Bend the U.N. to Our Will," *New York Times*, February 15, 1994, p. A19.

44. Boutros Boutros-Ghali, *An Agenda for Peace* (New York: United Nations, 1992), p. 9.

45. For an extensive elaboration of this point, see James N. Rosenau, "Sovereignty in a Turbulent World," pp. 191–227, in Michael Mastanduno and Gene Lyons, eds., *Beyond Westphalia: National Sovereignty and International Intervention* (Baltimore: Johns Hopkins University Press, 1995).

46. Quoted in Barbara Crossette, "U.N. Chief Wants Faster Action to Avoid Slaughter in Civil Wars," *New York Times*, September 21, 1999, p. A1.

47. See, for example, Boutros-Ghali, *Report on the Work of the Organization from the Forty-sixth to the Forty-seventh Session of the General Assembly*, pp. 9–16, and Elaine Sciolino, "U.N. Secretary General Dismisses Top-Ranking Aide from the U.S.," *New York Times*, January 19, 1994, p. A9.

48. Kirkpatrick, "Boutros-Ghali's Power Grab," p. A19. For a more elaborate set of criticisms along this line, see Michael Lind, "Alboutros: The Imperial U.N. Secretary General," *The New Republic*, June 28, 1993, pp. 16–20.

49. There is especially fierce resistance to such a constitutional amendment in Japan, so much, in fact, that a cabinet minister was forced to resign because he declared that Japan's limitations on the use of military force were out of date and should be replaced with an amendment that permitted full Japanese participation in U.N. peacekeeping operations. See David E. Sanger, "Japan Aide Ousted; He'd Criticized Arms Role," *New York Times*, December 3, 1993, p. A6.

50. Paul Lewis, "U.S. Panel Divided in Its Study of Ways to Improve the U.N.," *New York Times*, September 13, 1993, p. A13.

51. Paul Lewis, "United Nations Is Finding Its Plate Increasingly Full but Its Cupboard Is Bare," *New York Times*, September 27, 1993, p. A8.

52. Independent Advisory Group on U.N. Financing, *Financing an Effective United Nations* (New York: Ford Foundation, 1993), pp. 7–8.

53. Ibid.

54. Ibid., p. 32.

55. Ibid., p. 2.

56. Quoted in John M. Goshko, "U.N. Chief: Political Will, Money Needed," *Washington Post,* November 22, 1992, p. A33.

57. Roger Cohen, "Dispute Grows over U.N.'s Troops in Bosnia," *New York Times,* January 20, 1994, p. A20.

58. "France to Recall Commander," *New York Times,* January 19, 1994, p. A3.

59. Kofi A. Annan, "Walking the International Tightrope," *New York Times,* January 19, 1999, p. A19.

Chapter 8

1. Wei-chin Lee, "China and Antarctica: So Far and Yet So Near," *Asian Survey,* Vol. 30 (June 1990), pp. 576–586.

2. Matthew Howard, "The Convention on the Conservation of Antarctic Marine Living Resources: A Five-Year Review," *International and Comparative Law Quarterly,* Vol. 38 (January 1989), pp. 104–149.

3. Jonathan Milne, "Upton Welcomes Toothfish Resolution," *The Dominion* (Wellington, New Zealand), June 10, 1999, p. 10; "Antarctic Ministers See for Themselves, *Evening Post* (Wellington, New Zealand), January 29, 1999, Features section, p. 4.

4. David Helvarg, "Antarctica's Hints of Global Warming," *Sacramento Bee,* March 20, 1999, p. B7. Originally published in the *New York Times.*

5. "Antarctic Ministries See for Themselves," *Evening Post,* January 29, 1999.

6. P. W. Quigg, *A Pole Apart: The Emerging Issue of Antarctica* (New York: New Press, 1983), p. 18.

7. For additional information on how states acquire territory, see Michael Akehurst, *A Modern Introduction to International Law,* 6th ed. (London: George Allen and Unwin, 1984), Chap. 11; and Gerhard von Glahn, *Law Among Nations,* 5th ed. (New York: Macmillan, 1986), Chap. 15. For a summary of the application of this law to the Antarctic, see Steven J. Burton, "New Stresses on the Antarctic Treaty: Toward International Legal Institutions Governing Antarctic Resources," *Virginia Law Review,* Vol. 65 (1979), especially pp. 458–470.

8. Jack Child, *Antarctica and South American Geopolitics: Frozen Lebensraum* (New York: Praeger, 1988), offers a detailed survey of how South American states, notably Chile and Argentina, view Antarctica.

9. Peter J. Beck, *The International Politics of Antarctica* (New York: St. Martin's, 1986), p. 37. In a more recent publication, Beck assesses whether security still matters in Antarctic politics. See Peter J. Beck, "Antarctica as a Zone of Peace: A Strategic Irrelevance? A Historical and Contemporary Survey," pp. 192–224, in R. A. Herr, H. R. Hall, and M. G. Howard, eds., *Antarctica's Future: Continuity or Change?* (Hobart, Tasmania, Australia: Tasmanian Government Printing Office, 1990).

10. Beck, *The International Politics of Antarctica*, p. 41.

11. Quoted in ibid., p. 52.

12. James E. Mielke, "Antarctic Mineral Resource Activities: Regulate or Prohibit?" *CRS Review* (November/December 1990), pp. 22–23.

13. Christopher Beeby, "The Antarctic Treaty System as a Resource Management Mechanism—Nonliving Resources," in Polar Research Board, *Antarctic Treaty System*, proceedings of a workshop held at Beardmore South Field Camp, Antarctica, January 7–13, 1985 (Washington, D.C.: National Academy Press, 1986), p. 271.

14. William Westermeyer and Christopher Joyner, *Negotiating a Minerals Regime for Antarctica*, Pew Case Study #134 (Washington, D.C.: Institute for the Study of Diplomacy, Georgetown University, 1988), p. 6.

15. Howard, "The Convention on the Conservation of Antarctic Marine Living Resources," p. 111. For a number of perspectives on the living resources question, see Francisco Orrego Vicuña, ed., *Antarctic Resources Policy* (Cambridge: Cambridge University Press, 1983).

16. For a discussion of the complex relationship between the Antarctic Treaty and the Law of the Sea, see Christopher Joyner, *Antarctica and the Law of the Sea* (Dordrecht, The Netherlands: Nijhoff, 1992).

17. Beeby, "The Antarctic Treaty System as a Resource Management System," p. 277.

18. For an overview of the institutional choices, see Beeby, "The Antarctic Treaty System as a Resource Management Mechanism," or Westermeyer and Joyner, *Negotiating a Minerals Regime*.

19. Barry Buzan, "Negotiating by Consensus: Developments in Technique at the United Nations Conference on the Law of the Sea," *American Journal of International Law*, Vol. 75 (1981), pp. 324–348.

20. See James N. Rosenau, "Before Cooperation: Hegemons, Regimes, and Habit-Driven Actors in World Politics," *International Organization*, Vol. 40 (Autumn 1986), pp. 849–894.

21. "Permits Offered to Catch Toothfish for Science," *The Dominion*, May 14, 1999, p. 2.

22. For a history of the IGY, see Sydney Chapman, *IGY: Year of Discovery* (Ann Arbor: University of Michigan Press, 1959). A discussion of plans for Antarctic science in the IGY can be found in American Geophysical Union, *Antarctica in the International Geophysical Year* (Washington, D.C.: National Academy of Sciences, 1956).

23. The National Academy of Sciences, although not a government agency, was chartered by Congress. See Philip M. Boffey, *The Brain Trust of America: An Inquiry into the Politics of Science* (New York: McGraw Hill, 1975); or Rexmond C. Cochrane, *The National Academy of Science: The First Hundred Years* (Washington, D.C.: National Academy Press, 1978).

24. For a detailed discussion of SCAR, see James H. Zumberge, "The Antarctic Treaty as a Scientific Mechanism—The Scientific Committee on Antarctic Research and the Antarctic Treaty System," in Polar Research Board, *Antarctic Treaty System*, pp. 153–168.

25. Walter Sullivan, "Poland Requests Role in Antarctica," *New York Times,* April 4, 1959, p. 16.

26. Walter Sullivan, "Academic Talent Sought at Poles," *New York Times,* September 24, 1959, p. 11.

27. Patrick G. Quilty, "Antarctica as a Continent for Science," in Herr et al., eds., *Antarctica's Future,* p. 29.

28. James N. Rosenau, *Turbulence in World Politics: A Theory of Change and Continuity* (Princeton: Princeton University Press, 1990), p. 306.

29. Ibid., p. 308.

30. W. K. Chagula, B. T. Feld, and A. Parthasarathi, eds., *Pugwash on Self-Reliance* (Dar es Salaam, Tanzania: Anakar Publishing House, 1977), p. 2.

31. The scientists' movement is explored in Alice Kimball Smith, *A Peril and a Hope* (Cambridge: MIT Press, 1970). The December 1985 edition (Vol. 41, No. 11) of the *Bulletin of the Atomic Scientists* is devoted to the relationship between the scientists' movement and the *Bulletin.*

32. Isaac Asimov, *The Ends of the Earth* (New York: Weybright and Talley, 1975), p. 341.

33. Bernard P. Herber, "Mining or World Park? A Politico-Economic Analysis of Alternative Land Use Regimes in Antarctica," *Natural Resources Journal,* Vol. 31 (1991), pp. 839–859.

34. Ibid., p. 841.

35. Polar Research Board, *Antarctic Treaty System,* p. 276.

36. In 1947, a "proposal was made in the Trusteeship Council that the polar regions . . . should be placed under the aegis of the UN." This might well have happened had the Arctic not been included with Antarctica. From Philip Quigg, *Antarctica: The Continuing Experiment* (New York: Foreign Policy Association, March/April 1985), p. 37.

37. Ibid., pp. 37–38.

38. This concept is discussed by Bernard P. Herber, "The Common Heritage Principle: Antarctica and the Developing Nations," *The American Journal of Economics and Sociology,* Vol. 50 (October 1991), pp. 391–406.

39. Moritaka Hayashi, "The Antarctica Question in the United Nations," *Cornell International Law Journal,* Vol. 19 (1985), p. 288.

40. For a general discussion of the aims of nongovernmental organizations in Antarctic matters, see Anthony Parsons, *Antarctica: The Next Decade* (Cambridge: Cambridge University Press, 1987), Chap. 3.

41. Christopher C. Joyner, *The Role of Domestic Politics in Making United States Antarctic Policy* (Lysaker, Norway: Fridtjof Nansens Institutt, IARP Publication Series, No. 2, 1992).

42. Malcolm Browne, "France and Australia Kill Pact on Limited Antarctic Mining and Oil Drilling," *New York Times,* September 25, 1989, p. A10.

43. Paul Bogart, "On Thin Ice," *Greenpeace,* Vol. 13, No. 5 (September-October 1988), pp. 7–11.

44. Malcolm Browne, "Pact Would Ban Antarctic Mining," *New York Times,* September 25, 1989, p. A10.

45. Westermeyer and Joyner, *Negotiating a Minerals Regime for Antarctica,* p. 14.

46. Ibid.

47. Ibid. See also Christopher C. Joyner, "The Antarctic Minerals Negotiating Process," *American Journal of International Law,* Vol. 81, No. 4 (October 1987), especially pp. 895–897.

48. This issue is explored in depth in O. Rothwell, *A World Park for Antarctica* (Hobart, Tasmania, Australia: Institute of Antarctic and Southern Ocean Studies, University of Tasmania, 1990).

49. Mielke, "Antarctic Mineral Resource Activities," p. 24.

50. S.K.N. Blay, "New Trends in the Protection of the Antarctic Environment: The 1991 Madrid Protocol," *American Journal of International Law,* Vol. 86 (April 1992), pp. 377–399.

51. "Pact Would Ban Antarctic Mining," *New York Times,* May 1, 1991, p. A9.

52. Malcolm W. Browne, "U.S. Agrees to Protect Minerals in Antarctic," *New York Times,* July 6, 1991, p. 1.

53. Gillian Triggs, "A Comprehensive Environmental Regime for Antarctica: A New Way Forward," in Herr et al., eds., *Antarctica's Future,* pp. 103–118.

54. There need not be a break between economic development and environment. Pollution prevention policies can produce jobs even as they reduce negative impacts on the environment. But this formulation, at least so far, applies in areas already "developed." The concept of sustainable development is not appropriate in the unique circumstances of Antarctica proper, although it may well come to govern fisheries in the Southern Ocean. The environmental rule for Antarctica seems increasingly to boil down to the following: no development, no pollution.

55. There is an exception to this rule. Some countries, such as Costa Rica, say that rich northern countries should pay for any samples of flora and fauna, on the grounds that the raw genetic information has monetary value. The effect of such a rule would both preserve the environment and redistribute the wealth (and probably scientific knowledge as well). This practice would also be a remarkable use of sovereignty. For more on biodiversity in Costa Rica, see John Hamilton, "Cathedrals of the 21st Century," in his *Entangling Alliances* (Cabin John, Md.: Seven Locks Press, 1990). Edward O. Wilson's *The Diversity of Life* (New York: Norton, 1992) provides a sound grounding in the whole subject of biodiversity.

56. Although we have treated the scientific community as though it were a single entity with standards of virtue and reason beyond the reach of most individuals, this is, of course, not the case. Deeper analysis would have to ask when and where controversies within this community are likely to emerge and to what effect. It is quite likely that the still small Antarctic scientific community might well enter into conflict with the larger "atmosphere" or "oceans" communities. Or that the chemical, physical, and biological components within each of these areas might argue over what to do and how to spend available funds. The potential for conflict as different scientific organizations sought to maintain autonomy would, presumably, be quite high. Outside of places like Antarctica, this conflict could prove disastrous for the actual management of environmental problems: Rome could burn while the scientists fiddled. That would provoke lack of compliance by activist environmental groups, which then might provoke action by states.

57. "Fishing Pirates Stone Pursuers, *The Dominion*, March 5, 1999, p. 7; "Mystery Ship Prompts Call," *The Dominion*, March 4, 1999; "Greenpeace Sea Patrol Welcomed," *The Dominion*, January 23, 1999, p. 10.

58. Davor Vidas, "The Antarctic Treaty System in the International Community: An Overview," in Olav Schram Stokke and Davor Vidas, eds., *Governing the Antarctic: The Effectiveness and Legitimacy of the Antarctic Treaty System*, Cambridge: Cambridge University Press, 1996, p. 37; Stokke and Vidas, ed., *Governing the Antarctic*.

59. Christopher C. Joyner, "The Effectiveness of CRAMRA," in Stokke and Vidas, ed., *Governing the Antarctic*, p. 171.

60. Francisco Orrego Vicuña, "The Legitimacy of the Protocol on Environmental Protection to the Antarctic Treaty," in Stokke and Vidas, *Governing the Antarctic*, p. 272.

61. Joyner, "The Legitimacy of CRAMRA," p. 257 makes this point directly. Vicuña does so more indirectly in "The Legitimacy of the Protocol on Environmental Protection to the Antarctic Treaty." Both can be found in Stokke and Vidas, eds., *Governing the Antarctic*.

62. Vidas, "The Antarctic Treaty System in the International Community," p. 58.

Chapter 9

1. Marion J. Levy, "'Does It Matter If He's Naked?' Bawled the Child," in Klaus Knorr and James N. Rosenau, eds., *Contending Approaches to International Relations* (Princeton: Princeton University Press, 1969), p. 93.

Name Index

Akehurst, Michael, 88 (n3), 193 (n7)
Allison Graham T., 15 (n16), 102 (n3)
Altman, Roger C., 118 (n38)
Anderson, John Ward, 107 (n8)
Annan, Kofi A., 182 (n59)
Appadurai, Arjun, 53 (n7)
Apple, R. W., Jr., 160 (n13), 164 (23)
Armitage, Richard L., 173 (n43)
Asimov, Isaac, 206 (n32)
Axelrod, Robert, 15 (n16), 28 (n52), 37 (n6)
Ayres, B. Drummond, Jr., 160 (n13)

Baldwin, David A., 13 (n10), 15 (n16), 19
    (n32)
Barber, Benjamin, 46 (n27)
Beck, Peter J., 194 (nn 9, 10), 195
    (n11)
Beeby, Christopher, 196 (n13), 198
    (nn 17, 18)
Bell, Coral, 102 (n3)
Blay, S.K.N., 213 (n50)
Blustein, Paul, 118 (n39)
Boffey, Philip M., 201 (n23)
Bogart, Paul, 211 (n43)
Bonner, Raymond, 123 (nn 44, 46)
Boutros-Ghali, Boutros, 160 (n13), 161
    (n16), 162 (n18), 163 (n20), 169 (n36),
    173 (n44), 175 (n47)
Brecher, Michael, 102 (n3)
Browne, Malcolm W., 210 (n42), 211 (n44),
    213 (n52)
Bull, Hedley, 18 (nn 26, 27, 28, 30), 19 (n31),
    24 (n45), 25 (nn 46, 47), 28 (n54)
Burrell, S. A., 36 (n5)
Burton, Steven J., 193 (n7)
Buzan, Barry, 198 (n19)

Caporaso, J. A., 68 (n17)
Carr, E. H., 12 (n7)

Chagula, W. K., 204 (n30)
Chapman, Sydney, 201 (n22)
Chelaney, Brahma, 107 (nn 7, 12), 108 (n13),
    109 (n15)
Child, Jack, 193 (n8)
Childers, Erskine, 150 (n6)
Claude, Inis, 146 (n4)
Cochrane, Rexmond C., 201 (n23)
Coggan, Philip, 111 (n22)
Cohen, Roger, 181 (n57)
Connor, Robert, 12 (n4), 28
    (nn 51, 53)
Cordesman, Anthony H., 21(table)
Crossette, Barbara, 174 (n46)
Cutler, A. Claire, 62 (n11)

Darnton, John, 70 (n20)
de Tocqueville, Alexis, 41 (n25)
Deudney, Daniel, 39 (n15), 40 (nn 17, 18, 19,
    20), 41 (n21)
Deutsch, Karl W., 36 (n5)
Dixon, W. J., 37 (n6)
Dougherty, James E., 25 (n47)
Doyle, Michael W., 14 (nn 11, 12), 35 (n1),
    35 (n2), 36 (n4), 37 (n6)
Drell, Sidney D., 107 (n6)

Eckholm, Erik, 64 (n15)

Fagen, Michael, 165 (n27)
Featherstone, Kevin, 46 (n28)
Feld, B. T., 204 (n30)
Fidler, Stephen, 118 (n38)
Forsythe, David, 30 (n59)
Franck, Thomas M., 169 (n35)
Frankel, Benjamin, 11 (n1), 18 (n26)

Gallarotti, Giulio M., 68 (n17)
Garten, Jeffrey, 118 (n38)
Gellman, Barton, 164 (n25)

57. "Fishing Pirates Stone Pursuers, *The Dominion*, March 5, 1999, p. 7; "Mystery Ship Prompts Call," *The Dominion*, March 4, 1999; "Greenpeace Sea Patrol Welcomed," *The Dominion*, January 23, 1999, p. 10.

58. Davor Vidas, "The Antarctic Treaty System in the International Community: An Overview," in Olav Schram Stokke and Davor Vidas, eds., *Governing the Antarctic: The Effectiveness and Legitimacy of the Antarctic Treaty System*, Cambridge: Cambridge University Press, 1996, p. 37; Stokke and Vidas, ed., *Governing the Antarctic*.

59. Christopher C. Joyner, "The Effectiveness of CRAMRA," in Stokke and Vidas, ed., *Governing the Antarctic*, p. 171.

60. Francisco Orrego Vicuña, "The Legitimacy of the Protocol on Environmental Protection to the Antarctic Treaty," in Stokke and Vidas, *Governing the Antarctic*, p. 272.

61. Joyner, "The Legitimacy of CRAMRA," p. 257 makes this point directly. Vicuña does so more indirectly in "The Legitimacy of the Protocol on Environmental Protection to the Antarctic Treaty." Both can be found in Stokke and Vidas, eds., *Governing the Antarctic*.

62. Vidas, "The Antarctic Treaty System in the International Community," p. 58.

Chapter 9

1. Marion J. Levy, "'Does It Matter If He's Naked?' Bawled the Child," in Klaus Knorr and James N. Rosenau, eds., *Contending Approaches to International Relations* (Princeton: Princeton University Press, 1969), p. 93.

Name Index

Subject Index

Absolute gains, 40, 78, 82
Abstraction, in theorizing, 2–7, 10, 231
Access to power, 78, 83
Actors, proliferation of, 61–63
Actuel, 64
Advocacy groups, 87–88
Afghanistan, 155
Africa, 73–74, 120
Africa Watch, 120
Aggregations, 78, 89
Aidid, Mohammad Farah, 159
AIDS, and interdependence, 66–67
Albania, 124–125
Albanians, Kosovar, 37, 119–121, 124–125, 147
Alliances, 25–27, 30, 60, 88–89
American Petroleum Institute, 212
Amnesty International, 88
Anarchical interstate systems, 17–18, 23, 32, 35, 38, 40, 42–43, 52(table), 57, 78–79, 91–92, 131
Angola, 119–120, 156
Annan, Kofi, 124–125, 155–156, 173–174, 182
Anomalies, 6, 48–50, 233
Antarctica, 184–223, 185(map)
Antarctic and Southern Oceans Coalition, 212
Antarctic Conservation Act, 212
Antarctic Environmental Protocol, 186, 196, 219–221
Antarctic Policy Group (AGP), 211–212
Antarctic Public Advisory Committee (APAC), 211–212
Antarctic Treaty, 186, 188–195, 201–205, 217–218
Antarctic Treaty Consultative Parties (ATCPs), 185–187, 196, 200, 208–210, 219–220, 222

Antarctic Treaty System (ATS), 195–197, 203, 207, 220
and elitism, 186, 209–210
features of, 185–186
future of, 198–200, 214–217, 221–222
Argentina, 184, 191–193, 208, 218
Arms control, 17, 184, 204
Arms Control and Disarmament Agency, 212
Arms races, 17, 63, 107, 109, 188, 194–195, 199
Arms trade, 124
Asia, 73–74, 111, 170–171
Asian financial crisis, 103–104, 111–119, 131, 135, 139–140
causes and effects of, 91, 111–115
Athens, 11–13, 28
Aung San Sou Kyi, Daw, 171
Australia, 37, 147, 184, 193, 211, 219
Authoritarianism, 52
Authority, 16, 18, 111, 181
crises of, 54, 62–63, 68, 74–75, 80–81, 85, 128–129, 136–137, 168, 208, 214–217
relocation of, 48–49, 51, 53–57, 61, 65–67, 70–71, 128–129, 214–217
Authority dilemma, 44–45, 78–79, 82
Autonomy, 68, 78, 82

Balance of power, 24–27, 31, 89, 108, 198. *See also* Polarity of systems
Barrett, Peter J., 206
Beeby, Christopher, 196
Belgium, 184
Belgium peacekeeping troops, 159–160
Belgrade, 37, 125
Bharatiya Janata Party (BJP), 105, 109, 111
Bhutto, Benazir, 108–109

Bifurcation of global structures, 57–61, 119, 132, 166
Bipolar systems, 23, 89, 91, 146, 192–193
Bosnia, 37, 139, 146–147, 156, 160, 165, 173, 179, 181
Boundaries, 49, 64, 115, 135
  domestic-foreign, 43, 46, 66–67, 78, 84–85, 87, 103, 119, 126–127, 133–135, 138
  of issues, 103
  and mobility, 72–73
  See also Sovereignty; Territory
Boutrous-Ghali, Boutrous, 154–156, 161–164, 169, 176, 181–182
Brazil, 64, 106, 111–112, 177, 186
Bulletin of Atomic Scientists, 204
Bureau of Ocean and International Environmental and Scientific Affairs, 212
Bush, George Herbert Walker, 29, 178
  Bush administration, 213, 216
Byrd, Robert C., 161, 163

Cable News Network (CNN), 64
Cambodia, 143, 147, 156, 170
Canada, 37–38, 55, 108, 165
  power status of, 19–22
Capital, 65–66, 116
Cascades, 64, 77–78, 109, 136, 138–139
  in Asian financial crisis, 113, 119
  in multi-centric systems, 57–60
  in nuclear proliferation crisis, 110–111
Catholic Church, 16, 55
CCAMLR. *See* Convention on the Conservation of Antarctic Marine Living Resources (CCAMLR)
Centralization. *See* Authority, relocation of
Change, 31–33, 47–50, 78, 91–92, 99–101, 137–140
Chernobyl, 66
Children's rights, 170–171. *See also* Human rights
Chile, 208, 221
  and Antarctica, 184, 192–194
China, People's Republic of, 20–21, 25, 99, 109, 125, 147, 158, 176, 186, 210
  authority crises in, 55, 64, 104
  and human rights, 170, 172
  and nuclear proliferation, 105–108
Citizens. *See* Individuals
City-state system, 12–13

Civil service, international, 175–176
Climate change, 187–188, 214
Clinton, Bill (William Jefferson), 107, 159, 164
  Clinton administration, 164–165, 179
Coalitions, 26, 78, 89, 100
Co-binding, 39–40
Coercive leadership, 29–30
Cold War, 144–145, 149, 156, 168
  and Antarctica, 188, 199
  conditions arising from end of, 48–50, 146
Collectivities, 50–51, 62–63, 78, 81–82, 85, 100
Committee for Environmental Protection (Antarctica), 186
"Common heritage of mankind," 209
Communications media, 45, 64–65, 78(table), 86, 137–138, 157, 160
Compensation, 26, 107–108
Complexity, 47–48, 50–51, 53, 77, 78(table), 79–81, 93
Comprehensive Test Ban Treaty (CTBT), 105–106
Conflict resolution, 39, 41
Congo, Democratic Republic of, 124
Conservation, of resources, 190, 219–221
Convention on Antarctic Seals, 186
Convention on the Conservation of Antarctic Marine Living Resources (CCAMLR), 186–187, 197, 207–208, 219–221
Convention on the Regulation of Antarctic Mineral Resource Activities (CRAMRA), 186–187, 195–196, 205–206 , 217
  failure of, 197–198, 208–214, 219–221
  and mining, 186
Cooperation, 14, 27–31, 34, 36, 38, 41, 43, 48, 108–109, 117, 127, 132, 146–147, 149, 162
  and Antarctica, 194, 217–219
Corporations, international, 111, 118
Costs, mutual, 38–39
Cot, Jean, 181–182
Cousteau, Jacque, 211
CRAMRA. *See* Convention on the Regulation of Antarctic Mineral Resource Activities (CRAMRA)